MONEY AND LIBERATION

MONEY
and
LIBERATION

The Micropolitics of
Alternative Currency Movements

PETER NORTH

University of Minnesota Press
MINNEAPOLIS | LONDON

Parts of chapter 5 were originally published in *Alternative Currencies as a Challenge to Globalisation? A Case Study of Manchester's Alternative Currency Movements* (Aldershot, Hampshire, UK: Ashgate, 2006); reprinted by permission of Ashgate Publishing Company. Parts of chapter 6 originally appeared in "Constructing Civil Society? Green Money in Transition Hungary," *Review of International Political Economy* 13, no. 1 (2006): 28–52; reprinted with the permission of Taylor and Francis, www.tandf.co.uk. Parts of chapter 7 were originally published in "LETS in a Cold Climate: Green Dollars and Neo-Liberal Welfare in New Zealand," *Policy and Politics* 30, no. 4 (October 2002): 483–500; reprinted by permission of *Policy and Politics*.

Published by the University of Minnesota Press
111 Third Avenue South, Suite 290
Minneapolis, MN 55401-2520
http://www.upress.umn.edu

Library of Congress Cataloging-in-Publication Data

North, Peter, 1962–
Money and liberation : the micropolitics of alternative currency movements / Peter North.
p. cm.
Includes bibliographical references and index.
ISBN 978-0-8166-4962-4 (hc : alk. paper)
ISBN 978-0-8166-4963-1 (pb : alk. paper)
1. Money. 2. Monetary policy. 3. Currency question. I. Title.
HG220.A2N67   2007
332.4—dc22   2006038757

Printed in the United States of America on acid-free paper
The University of Minnesota is an equal-opportunity educator and employer.

12 11 10 09 08 07   10 9 8 7 6 5 4 3 2 1

CONTENTS

ACKNOWLEDGMENTS

THERE ARE TOO MANY PEOPLE TO THANK FOR THE PRODUCTION of this book and the research from which it was constructed for me to hope to name them all individually. I would like to thank colleagues at the Universities of Bristol, Sheffield, London South Bank, and Liverpool who have helped and encouraged me and critiqued my work over the years; in particular I would like to call attention to the efforts of Paul Burton, Irene Bruegel, Roger Lee, and Colin Williams.

From the world of local exchange trading schemes (LETS) I would like to thank Nigel Leach, Michael Linton, Liz Shephard, Angus Soutar, and Harry Turner (sadly, no longer with us; he will be missed). They all got me thinking. From Manchester LETS I would like to thank everyone I met with, including (but not limited to) Malcolm Allum, Jo Bend, Linda Bloomfield, John and Wendy Clifford, Marian Daltrop, Inland Driftwood, Bernard Ekbury, Spencer Fitzgibbon, Peter Gay, Gilli Gladman, Siobhan Harpur, Karsten Jungnickel, Bob Kirby, Steven Knight, Kos, Katrina Long, Margaret Mansoor, Alison Milner, John Piprani, Mike Scantlebury, Rose Snow, Storm Steel, and Lyn Woolry, John from Withington Cycles, and Andy, Chris, Fraser, Kai, and Kryshia from LETSGo.

I would particularly like to thank Éva Izsák for involving me in the development of Talentum and Kör in Hungary and then for translating "simple, clear, uncomplicated" Hungarian into English for me. Who could have known what would come from a chance meeting in the House of Commons? The British Council and the Association of Nonprofit Human Services of Hungary financed my early visits. I would like to thank everyone I met in Hungary, and Tamás Almassy, Csilla and Otto Koronka, and Gyorgy Zsomboc from Budapest; Gábor Nagy from Gödöllő; Lázsló Mészáros from Miskolc; Ferenc and Erika Tóth from Szolnok; and Sándor Frank from Tiszalúc were especially helpful.

Helen Dew, Bryan Duxfield, and Maureen Mallinson deserve special mention for inviting me to New Zealand, and I must thank Professor Lydia Wevers and all at the Stout Centre for New Zealand Studies at Victoria University of Wellington for providing a haven for me while I wrote this book. I met too many people in New Zealand to list them individually, but particular note is owed to Lynn Merrifield, Neville Millar, Nicky Pharland, Mike Stonely, and Maxine Wain from Blenheim; Briar, Christoph Hensch, and Amrita Styles from Christchurch; Murray Rogers from Golden Bay; Carolyn Hughes and Eva from Motueka; Linda Cleary and Lindsay Dukes from Nelson; Jim and Noelene McCaughan and friends from Timaru; Hayden McGrail from the Wairarappa; Jan Machin from Wellington; and Davina and Jim and Heide and Vance, good companions.

Ulli Huber was my research associate, translator, and all-around good egg in Argentina. Again there are too many people I met from that country to thank them all, but Heloisa Primavera provided a good introduction to Argentina in 2002, while in 2003 Carlos Perez Lora from Mar-y-Sierras Trueque, Alberto Marini from Mendoza, Ruben Ravera and Horacio Cobas from RGT (Red Global de Trueque, Global Barter Network in English) Bernal, Charly del Valle from RTS (Red de Trueque Solidario) Buenos Aires, and Fernando Sampayo from Zona Oeste offered invaluable thoughts and in general gave me their time.

All I have done in this book is to take the ideas of those mentioned: the ideas remain theirs, not mine.

Finally, I would like to thank Carrie Mullen and Jason Weidemann from the University of Minnesota Press for their support and encouragement for this project, while Nancy Sauro and Marilyn Martin contributed invaluable copyediting.

Introduction

THINKING ECONOMIES OTHERWISE

T HIS IS A BOOK ABOUT GROUPS OF PEOPLE WHO HAVE JOINED
together with the modest agenda of fundamentally challenging
capitalism by creating and using new forms of money. They do this by
creating trading networks that use a currency created and spent by
ordinary people. These trading networks, developed at first by environmentalists, have emerged globally over the past twenty years and
range from local exchange trading schemes or LETS (in the United
Kingdom) and Talentum (in Hungary and Germany) to networks using such currencies as "time dollars" and "hours" (in the United Kingdom and the United States), "green dollars" (in New Zealand, Australia, and Canada), and "grains of salt" (used by a network called SEL in
France). For a review see Dauncey (1988); Douthwaite (1996); Solomon (1996); and Lietaer (2001). To begin trading, members of the network create a form of currency that they agree to accept from each
other, which they back by their "commitment" to earn, at a later date,
credits from someone else. The currency may be in the form of a note,
a check, a scorecard, or just an entry on a computer. Members trade
with other members of the network at markets or by contacting each
other through a directory or a notice board, paying each other with
the currency they have mutually created and give value to. The networks build on barter in that reciprocal exchange between partners
for each trade is not required. For example, one trader can get another to fix his car and can earn the currency by providing others with
child care, gardening, help with decorating, and the like.

Essentially what members of these networks are making is a claim that conventional "money" is simply a discourse, a social construction, a collective agreement to accept a certain form of measurement, store of value, and unit of exchange. Advocates claim that once we accept that money is not a thing "out there," external to us, we can change it: make collective agreements to use other forms of money that might work more effectively than the money issued by states, which have in the past claimed a monopoly on the right to issue money. As we shall see later, this is a claim that is contestable, but that is not the point. What is important is the claim that "better" money can be created, money that values people and work before profitability, stresses liquidity to ensure that needs are met before artificial scarcity occurs to ensure labor discipline and exchange rate or price stability, and, by being limited to a specific geographical area, will encourage the development of localized economies that will be more sustainable (Douthwaite 1996, 1999; North 1999a; Hines 2000). For example, when we say that a drug that exists cannot be provided for a patient who needs it because, while there are available supplies, it is too expensive, we artificially limit our possibilities by elevating a socially enacted discourse of "affordability" into an unsurpassable barrier or structure. "If I can't afford it, I can't have it. Simple." This book examines the effectiveness of this political critique of the nature of money as a strategy for creating more liberated futures.

As we shall see in this book, the creation of alternative forms of money is a political strategy that, while never hegemonic, runs as a thread back to the critiques of "utopian socialists" (Fourier, Owen, Proudhon) at the dawn of capitalism through the Populist uprising in late nineteenth-century America to the "swap," "scrip," and Social Credit movements of the Great Depression. The current wave of monetary contestation emerged out of the green movement in the countercultural 1960s. While many "dropped out," joined communes, and tried to live off the land, others, not wanting such a total withdrawal from society, set up skills-share networks to enable members to share their skills without the use of money (Weston 1992). These were networks of people who were opposed to capitalist exploitation and to technological modern society, wanting to exchange skills within smaller-scale convivial communities without using capitalist money but valuing an hour of each other's labor equally. They used notes denominated not in dollars or pounds but in hours of labor. At the other end of the political spectrum, businesses used commercial barter networks both to save money and to break into new markets, such as the communist countries where currency exchange facilities were as yet undeveloped. These networks were big business and were efficient but served no progressive function. Hoping to marry the efficiency of commercial barter with the liberatory potential of the countercultural exchanges, the progenitor of the current effervescence of alternative money networks, Michael Linton, organized a computerized exchange network using a beautifully simple concept called the LETSystem in Comox Valley, Vancouver Island, Canada, in 1983. The elegant LETSystem worked using a computerized accounts system that would balance currency issued by one trader with that paid into the recipient's account. If I pay you ten green dollars, my account goes down by ten and yours goes up by ten; the balance of the system as a whole is zero. This simplicity and elegance caught the imagination.

Linton's second innovation was to use a unit of currency linked not to the hour but to the Canadian dollar, the green dollar. This had the potential of widening participation in the network considerably, for new members did not have to buy into the philosophy of the equality of labor time in advance to join, an advantage in the 1980s, when New Right ideas were dominant and equality seemed an out-of-date holdover from socialism or the 1960s. Linton's Comox LETSystem eventually grew to about five hundred members. Linton promoted local exchange trading schemes (LETS) around the world, and the idea spread to Australia, where by the mid-1990s there were thought to be 164 systems, and New Zealand, where there were 55 (Jackson 1995). LETS were introduced to the United Kingdom in 1986 (Ekins 1986), and by 1996 there were thought to be some 350 LETS involving some twenty thousand participants (see Lang 1994; Croall 1997). U.K. LETS, German Talentum, and French SEL (with a currency called "grains of salt") differed from the LETSystem in that they used a form of local currency related in some way to a moral valuation of time and used a locally significant name for their currency, such as tales in Canterbury, brights in Brighton, or bobbins in Manchester.

"Hours" are watermarked, often exceptionally high-quality time-denominated currency notes that circulate in Ithaca (New York), Salmon Arm (British Columbia), and up to twenty other cities in

North America (Greco 1994, 2001; Glover 1995; Boyle 1999; Maurer 2003, 2005). Remuneration is calculated both in time spent and by reference to the local average wage, so that, for example, an hour's labor would equal ten hours if the local average wage per hour was ten dollars. Participants get their first hours in return for placing an advertisement in the network's local newspaper, and then earn others through trading. No central record is kept beyond the number of notes printed. Hours cannot be spent until they are earned, although interest-free loans are available. In 1997, the Argentine nongovernmental organization Programa de Autosuficiencia Regional imported the Ithaca Hours model to Argentina, where, as a result of that country's financial collapse in 2001 (Powell 2002; Pearson 2003), which we shall explore in more detail in chapter 8, scrip notes took off at a level that dwarfs their usage everywhere else.

LETS, Talentum, the use of hours, and similar systems are all examples of a contemporary flourishing of alternative forms of money that involve, worldwide, thousands of members outside Argentina, where there are millions. This book explores their liberatory potential and what their emergence, successes, and failures mean for the way we think about economies and money. Are they precursors to a new twenty-first-century economy founded on alternative forms of money, which will give rise to new economic opportunities to provide livelihoods focused on need rather than profit, on supporting communities and human need, and in a way that is in balance with the natural world? Are those participating in them the early adapters foreseeing fundamental changes for the good in the economy, through markets for all, the libertarian capitalism of technojunkies championed by *Wired* magazine (Frank 2002), or are they foreseeing changes for the bad, as climate change and the end of cheap oil foretell the end of carbon-burning industrial capitalism (Roberts 2004)? Alternatively, are they postindustrial utopians (Frankel 1987), Luddite throwbacks to a precapitalist economy that emerges in periods of crisis, attractive only to those who prefer a nostalgic world of small communities meeting basic needs, who hate globalization (Wolf 2004, 194–99)? Or are they both? Are the failures of these systems roadkill on the way to a brighter future, or do they just not work? This book aims to explore these questions in search of answers.

Markets Hegemonic?

The recent rise of alternative currency networks as liberatory forms of politics needs to be seen within a wider political-economic perspective: the elite claim that since 1989 conceptions of economic life organized through markets have won a decisive historical battle with the former de rigueur view of the left, of economic life organized through and directed by the state (McMillan 2002; Wolf 2005). True, in the nineteenth century markets seemed to lead to imperialism, war, racism, colonialism, and great suffering for millions, and in the first half of the twentieth century they led to two world wars and one great depression. The Second World War, the huge economic leaps forward made by the Soviet Union and China, and the long boom achieved by state capitalist Keynesianism in the 1950s and 1960s seemed to herald the triumph of the state over the market, but by the late 1970s the state seemed unable to maintain economic development. It seemed slow, sluggish, and unable to predict, plan for, and meet the myriad demands of consumers in complex late capitalist society. Western economies became mired in stagflation and beset by unrest. The New Right argued that markets gave rise to better allocation systems and, operationalizing this, U.K. Prime Minister Margaret Thatcher and U.S. President Ronald Reagan rolled back state involvement in economies. In 1989, millions in eastern Europe shoved off Soviet domination and embraced markets. The right saw this as a legitimation of capitalism. Fukuyama (1992) announced the End of History: human development would best be served by free markets and liberal democracy.

The "Washington Consensus" seemed hegemonic (Wade 2002). No one would seriously debate it any more than they would discuss whether the Earth was round. Neoliberals argued that if the state recognizes that it is people, not states, who create wealth and removes "superfluous" restrictions and market distortions, market relations will emerge spontaneously given what Adam Smith called the human species' innate tendency to trade. If the "invisible hand" of the market is able to operate unimpeded, the rational actions of millions of self-interested and intelligent economic actors will ensure that goods and services are efficiently allocated, for, in the words of President Bill Clinton's Treasury Secretary Lawrence Summers, "The laws of economics are like the laws of engineering. There is only one set of laws and they work everywhere" (quoted by Wade 2004, 147). However, the reality did not meet the expectations of the theorists (Gore 2000). The poor economic performance of transition economies in the early 1990s, the Russian and East Asian financial crises in the mid-1990s, and the economic collapse in Argentina in 2001–2 now show that the neoliberal agenda was doctrinaire and overly economistic (Stiglitz 2002; Wade 2002, 2003, 2004). Schumpeterian "creative destruction" led not to market nirvana but to a catastrophic drop in economic performance; for example, in 1999 the gross domestic product of Georgia or Moldova was 25 percent of that of 1989 (Gwynne et al. 2003, 134). Wider problems included a collapse of social cohesion, hunger, collapsing services, public health crises, and the emergence of "gangster," "crony," or "wild" capitalisms (Smith and Swain 1998; Freeland 2001; Åslund 2002). Rather than breaking through to prosperity, too many emerging markets got stuck in the transitional phase, in which new economic opportunities had yet to emerge, yet policies to help those at the sharp end were outlawed (Wade 2004, 152). By the end of the twentieth century, the post-1989 euphoria about markets as a panacea was replaced with a more sober understanding of their limits. Yet the rise of market-friendly social democracy in the shape advocated by President Clinton or Prime Minister Tony Blair, by Brazilian President Luiz Inácio Lula da Silva, or even by communist West Bengal (Ramesh 2006) suggested that while markets were imperfect, there was still no alternative to them as allocation mechanisms.

In these circumstances, Polanyi's (1944) critique of markets as, far from being "natural" phenomena, being constructed in a coordinated and purposeful fashion by state action gained a new salience. Polanyi saw the attempt to build a self-regulating market as a utopian project that would lead, if unchecked, to the destruction of the human spirit and of livelihoods in the face of market rationality:

> It is our thesis that the idea of a self adjusting market implied a stark utopia. Such an institution could not exist for any length of time without annihilating the human and natural substance of society: it would have physically destroyed man and transformed his surroundings into a wilderness. Inevitably, society took measures to protect itself, but whatever measures it took impaired the self regulation of the market, disorganised industrial life, and thus endangered society in another way. (Polanyi 1944, 4)

Polanyi looked to the importance of social and cultural processes as well as economic rationality in the construction of markets. He argued that market economies, far from being technical phenomena that work in the same way everywhere, are inevitably regulated by local social and cultural practices that prevent them from acting unchecked in pathological ways, thus protecting society. For example, if the cheapest and most rational way of getting chimneys cleaned was to send small children up them, that was what should happen. If an industry could keep its costs down by simply pumping its waste into the nearby river, that was also what should happen. But this, obviously, would impoverish society, so regulation was required to prevent such outcomes. Consequently, trading on the narrow basis of self-interested rationalism was so far from the "natural" human condition, Polanyi argued, that the state had to actively *impose* markets on society through, for example, enclosure, the monetization of subsistence economies, the "black acts" that vastly increased the number of capital offenses in the United Kingdom, and the prohibition of trade unions (Thompson 1981).

Society needed to be forcibly removed from the economic realm, yet this led to the anarchic barbarism of the early nineteenth century with its dark satanic mills. Markets were not a Smithian utopia where all provided for each other by doing what they did best. Polanyi consequently argued that markets are subsumed in social and cultural relationships, such as trust and confidence, and regulated by custom and law. Without regulation, the market is destructive of human freedom.

> The alleged commodity "labour power" cannot be shoved about, used indiscriminately, or even left unused, without affecting also the human individual who happens to be the bearer of this commodity. In disposing of man's labour power the system would, incidentally, dispose of the physical, psychological and moral entity "man" attached to that tag. Robbed of the protective covering of cultural institutions, human beings would perish from the effects of social exposure; they would die as the victims of acute social dislocation. . . . Finally the market administration of purchasing power would periodically liquidate business enterprise, as shortages and surfeits of money would prove as disastrous to business as floods and droughts in primitive society. (Polanyi 1944, 73)

Building on Polanyi, it is now widely recognized that market relationships are not given, but constructed, perhaps contested:

People are born and socialised into a particular set of social relations which script the norms through which they relate to each other and shape the ways in which they conduct their economic activity. Individuals and groups may merely accept, or alternatively challenge, celebrate or reject the social relations in which they find themselves. Thus social relations are social constructs. They are products of historical relations of social struggle and discourse . . . through which they come to be formed, sustained, challenged and transformed. (Lee 2002, 340)

Within development economics the World Bank's Post–Washington Consensus perspective recognized that Polanyi had to some extent been right. Functioning, efficient capitalist markets would not just happen; they had to be built (Öniş and Şenses 2005). Just as Polanyi had predicted, unregulated capitalism was giving the brand a bad name just when it was beginning to seem hegemonic, especially after the antiglobalization movement erupted in 1999 in Seattle. Free markets introduced through overly rapid deregulation—for example, in the former Soviet Union—performed poorly when compared with the empirical success of state-led export-oriented growth in East Asia and in the social democratic Nordic countries, their experience suggesting that government did have a role in facilitating capitalist development and that sectors of the economy not guided by profits and free markets could contribute to welfare. Rather than embracing state-led development or social democracy, the Post–Washington Consensus view argued that the construction of markets should be facilitated at a pace that took more cognizance of local conditions. "Mediating institutions" such as the rule of law and property rights (de Soto 1989), trust (Fukuyama 1995), or "social capital" (Putnam 1993, 2001) and basic welfare nets should be constructed alongside market reform (Fine 2000). These mediating institutions would connect citizens with each other through democratic cultures that would develop open, transparent governance processes and trust as a de Tocquevilleian guarantor against despotism and enhance the ability of citizens to influence their political future from below (Cohen and Arato 1992; Arato 1999). Welfare services, self-help groups, micro finance, and job brokering and business development agencies would smooth the path of transition to the market for those at the sharp end of economic changes (Kuti 1997). The institutions that would make markets work needed to be constructed. The World Bank's Civil Society perspective therefore assumed that while markets are the best allocation systems and capitalism is the optimum form of economic activity, markets need help to emerge. States should facilitate the development of markets and regulate them to prevent the worst abuses, but their touch should be light.

The antiglobalization left that emerged in the late 1990s as a response to the doctrinaire prescriptions of the Washington Consensus largely did not counterpoise the state to the market. No one argued for five-year plans: rather they argued for "globalisation from below" (Brechter et al. 2000; Notes-from-Nowhere 2003), for community-based, bottom-up citizen action to build a better world, which would be more participatory and democratic in both political and economic spheres (Feffer 2002). They certainly argued that the World Bank and the World Trade Organization should not be able to dictate agendas to southern countries (Houtart and Polet 2001) and argued against the wholesale intrusion of the capitalist market into areas of life previously outside it through privatization (for example, Bolivia's gas and water wars; see Olivaria 2004). Tony Blair's attempts to bring markets into education and health in the United Kingdom are being hotly debated while I write this. But although few radicals now argued for state-led development, the anticapitalist movement's alternative—participatory development—was undertheorized. If not the state, would markets be the allocation systems in alternatives to the Washington Consensus?

Therefore, the left's position, perhaps by default, was that markets had a role. No one wants a future in which the state allocates economic roles and the proletariat selects its goods from state warehouses. Outside social policy,[1] libertarian visions seem to have won out over statist ones. Yet the left has thought little about *progressive* forms of markets. If under neoliberalization marketization always means privatization, does that also mean that markets must always be privatized systems? Can markets be collectively regulated? Are they always capitalist, or could they be more neutral, or even democratic, allocation systems? If markets are constructed in ways not inevitable or following laws of engineering that are the same everywhere, and if local cultural and social practices affect the construction of markets, can different sorts of markets that do aid human liberation be constructed? If states must privatize and construct markets and then regulate them from above, can markets also be constructed and regulated from below, in participatory, democratic, noncapitalist ways that do not entail the extension of capitalist values into more and more areas of life? Is the community-regulated market an alternative to the free market (Thorne 1996)? Can we think about markets in more creative ways? These questions give movements that aimed to create new forms of money a new salience.

Thinking the Capitalist Economy Otherwise

A number of theorists have looked to take these questions further with a deeper enquiry into what *markets* means. Does *markets = capitalism?* How, exactly, are different forms of economic relationships, often subsumed under the catch-all *markets,* constructed, given political, cultural, and social considerations? Is *state* opposed to *market* actually a false dichotomy that obscures more than it reveals, in particular obstructing the myriad ways that politics, culture, society, religion, folk beliefs, and the like construct market relations? Might some market-based relations provide freer, more liberated and interesting livelihoods than others?

   In the mid-1990s some authors explored, not too conclusively, "market socialism" as an alternative to neoliberalism (Le Grand and Estrin 1989; McNally 1992), while others sought to rediscover economic activity based on cooperatives and associations (Hurst 1995). Keith Hart (2001) asked: Which forms of entrepreneurialism, wealth creation, or accumulation strategies or processes were compatible with cooperation and social welfare and which were harmful or destructive of the social fabric? In what circumstances is an entrepreneur creating wealth through market transactions a robber baron to be pilloried, in what cases a pioneer to be admired? How can we reconcile individual accumulation through market transactions with equality, cohesion, and social obligation? When are market transactions simple allocation mechanisms that can seem to work well when contrasted with the sometimes ludicrous decisions of state bureaucracies, such as Prime Minister Robert Muldoon's decision that New Zealanders did not need fresh orange juice as it could not be grown locally? Croatian writer Slavenka Drakulić offered a hilarious account of the inability of state planning to provide makeup and lipsticks that match the complexity of skin tones and fashion decisions:

Once when I was in Warsaw, a friend told me about a spate of red-headed women: suddenly it seemed that half of the women in the city had red hair, a phenomenon that could not pass unnoticed. It might have been a fashion caprice. More likely, it had to do with the failure of the chemical industry to produce or deliver other kinds of dye. Imagine these women confronted by the fact there is no other colour in the store where they buy their dye, and knowing that if there isn't any in one store, it's useless searching the others. There is only one shade of red (I've seen it: it's burgundy red that gives hair a particularly artificial look, like a wig). They have no choice. They either appear untidy, with bleached ends and unbleached roots sticking out, or they can dye their hair whatever colour they can find. So they dye it, hoping that other women won't come to the same conclusion. They don't exactly choose. (Drakulić 1987, 24)

Hart wanted to explore how through markets we can enrich ourselves at no one's expense rather than being rapacious capitalists, how we can generate wealth collectively, ensure that it is distributed fairly, and maintain a strong community through market allocation systems — in other words, whether markets are inevitably capitalist markets (Hart 2001, 102). To understand this we need to unpack the term *market*.

Perhaps the most interesting attempt to unpack the "economic" and uncover a diversity of economic relations within markets is the work of J. K. Gibson-Graham (1996) and the Community Economies Collective (CEC) (2001).[2] Julie Gibson and Kathy Graham, writing as the collective J.K. Gibson-Graham, argued that to claim that because there are large numbers of Christians in the United States that country is a Christian nation occludes the considerable religious diversity in the United States. Similarly, representing a wide variety of economic relations within an all-encompassing metanarrative of "capitalism" occludes the diversity of relations that construct an economy and, in particular, ignores the diversity of existing noncapitalist practices. Gibson-Graham wrote that it is "the way that capitalism has been 'thought' that makes it so difficult for people to imagine its supersession" (Gibson-Graham 1996, 3) and that to move forward we need an idea of the "economic" that is not so subject to closure, more open-ended and diverse. They argued that representations of "capitalism" *construct* a discourse of economic domination that seems overawing, unbeatable, or inevitable, and it is this construction that is the problem, for it does not reflect a more diverse reality. Representations of capitalism thus call into the world a phantom block to progress that impedes our imagination and our ability to envisage alternatives. To move forward, Gibson-Graham suggested a conceptualization of the economy as a "heterospace" of capitalist and noncapitalist economic practices that includes not only production for profit but also mutual aid, household economies, production for need, production for self-consumption, caregiving, maintaining the planet's ecology, loving, or making purchases for political, ideological, or affective (rather than strictly economic) reasons. In particular, they argue that referring to a secular drive for "capital accumulation" within economies is as unsustainable as ascribing a "maternal instinct" to all women. We can no more assume a priori that a capitalist firm wants to make a huge profit to be appropriated by the entrepreneur than we can say that a woman wants to be a mother. We must be aware of the differences among the practices and motivations of economic actors through a theory of economic difference.

Of course, as we shall see later, understanding that there are many ways in which economic life is carried out is not new. The difference is that these alternative economic practices have usually been seen as precapitalist holdovers or doomed utopian experiments that are unable to compete with capitalism as the world historic system, while capitalism is associated with progress and modernity. Capitalism is seen either as a good thing in and of itself (by neoliberals) or as a sublime uprooting of traditional, closed, conservative cultures that is a painful but inevitable and ultimately progressive step on the road to human emancipation once we go *beyond it* to socialism, communism, anarchism, or ecology. Gibson-Graham saw this as teleological and totalizing, rejecting a conceptualization of capitalism as a unified, singular, and total system, with noncapitalist forms existing only in the interstices or within capitalism (Gibson-Graham 1996, 258). Rather, they sought to uncover the diversity of economic practices and saw social change as something that can be implemented through everyday practices.

Critics argued that an attempt, in effect, to "think capitalism away" by seeing economic practices in a different light was making what Castree (1999), following Bhaskar, called the "epistemological fallacy," which conflates knowledge and the world. For Castree, the economy is a concrete, real-world phenomenon based on real commodities, prices, and profitability levels, not a performance or representation. It exists independently of people's ability to call it into reality through practices and has a logic of accumulation that operates outside individual perception. Castree argued that the essential characteristics and logics of capitalism can be theoretically identified, even if they are hard to find in their pure state in the real world, conditioned as they are by other social phenomena. Following a long line of Marxist criticism that we examine in more detail in chapter 2, Castree would thus doubt the extent to which radical political action can develop real-world alternatives that are not disciplined by capitalist rationality. Gibson-Graham countered this through their empirical analyses, which examined actually existing, grounded, concrete economic practices, not just representations (CEC 2001; Cameron and Gibson 2005; Gibson-Graham 2006).

Castree (1999, 145) argued that without any attempt to reconstruct theoretically what alternatives to capitalism might look like, empirical analysis of actually existing economic practices is likely to degenerate into a "flabby pluralism or explanatory 'everythingism'" in which examples of noncapitalist rationality or interesting experiments are uncritically championed. In a similar vein, Samers (2005) argued that Gibson and Graham and others have a tendency to celebrate "alternatives" without investigating the extent to which they genuinely *are* examples of freer, more unconstrained and liberated forms of economic activity for those who engage in them. Are they better than capitalism, or are they coping mechanisms for those excluded from labor for capitalist firms? Samers argued that exploitation (and, by implication, what is freely chosen economic activity) is not theorized, while small-scale, local economic activity is privileged with no investigation of its internal power relations, which might be very exploitative. Large-scale capitalist firms are ascribed an exploitative status, and there is no consideration of the extent to which local capitalism might be a xenophobic, inward-looking system of domination. Alternative economic practices might be possible only in spaces cut off from the power centers of capitalism, where competition or high property prices might crowd out more marginal alternatives.

In the second edition of their book, Gibson-Graham engaged a range of critics (Gibson-Graham 2006). Some insisted that "capitalism" and "class" are themselves Western concepts that do not apply in many Southern economies. At the other end of the spectrum, some see capitalism as so all-embracing that they have trouble envisioning anything escaping it. Others see capitalist commodification as so extensive that many economic activities claimed as alternative, such as the production of soya milk, can be seen as just the latest commodity generated by a constantly evolving capitalism. Businesses selling "alternative" goods are just responding to the latest market signals. Others called for a more critical assessment of the potential of economic alternatives: What are their limits? Are they just a "palliative to a deeper malaise" (Kelly 2005)? This is important, for a fundamental problem with the arguments of Gibson-Graham is, as we shall explore in some detail in this book, that they are not new. Groups of people have tried to create alternatives to capitalism from its dawn, and, some argue, have always failed. As Gibson-Graham related:

> We were aware of a senior Marxist geographer sitting in the back row, listening attentively. Near the end of the question and answer period, after some urging, he made his intervention. Our material was interesting, he said, but it wasn't compelling. We failed to acknowledge the power of global economic dynamics and the force of political conservatism that could squash alternative economic experiments of the kind we had described. We seemed oblivious to the many historical examples of local endeavors that had ended in disbandment, defeat, and disgrace....
>
> An incredulous Pacific historian derided us: "Do you really think that by earning $1,000 a year from selling village craft goods to international tourist resorts, rural Indonesian households will be able to prevent their daughters from being exploited in the Nike factory across the Straits?" (Gibson-Graham 2002, 25–26)

These criticisms rely on the intellectual pedigree of Marx and Engels's critiques of the nineteenth-century utopians (Engels 1968). Marx and Engels characterized the alternative economic practices of their day as a diversion from the big picture, class politics. These diversions look attractive when, after defeat, working people lack the confidence to make wider changes: "In part (the proletariat) throws itself into doctrinaire experiments, exchange banks and workers associations, hence into a movement in which it renounces the revolutionising of the old world by means of the latter's own great, combined resources, and seeks, rather, to achieve its salvation behind society's back, in private fashion, within its limited conditions of existence, and hence necessarily suffers shipwreck" (Marx 1852/1974). Working people start to develop "the chimeral game played with the future of society [which] ... can only be silly—silly, stale and basically reaction-ary" (Marx, quoted in Levitas 1990). Marx argued that social change comes from the struggle of millions to break through the restrictions to development caused by capitalism. For Marx, the proletariat's "task is no longer to manufacture a system of society as perfect as possible, but to ... discover in the economic conditions ... the means of ending the conflict" (Marx 1852/1974). Marx and Engels also argued that without the seizure of the productive wealth of society through revolution, the resources controlled by ordinary people will always be inadequate for large-scale change. It is problematic, Marx claimed, to seek social change at the level of the private, household economy through adopting a more cooperative economy from below.

Against this, in the constitution for the International Working-man's Association (the First International), Marx and Engels lauded the utopians and the cooperative movement as

> one of the great transforming forces of the present society based on class antagonisms. Its great merit is to practically show, that the present pau-perising and despotic system of the subordination of labour to capital can be superseded by the republican and beneficent system of the association of free and equal producers.

But they also went on to argue:

> Restricted, however, to the dwarfish forms to which the individual wage slaves can elaborate it by their private efforts, the co-operative system will never transform society. To convert social production into one large and harmonious system of free and co-operative labour, general social changes are wanted, changes in the general conditions of society, never to be realised save by the transfer of the organised forces of society, viz. the state power, from capitalists and to the producers themselves. (Fernbach 1974)

A contemporary version of this argument comes from the British Marxist newspaper *Socialist Worker:*

> Socialists cannot accept some of the political claims that are often made by people for their scene or lifestyle. . . . Nor, unfortunately, is it possible under capitalism to create permanent havens of alternative ways of living. It could not be done by Robert Owen and the utopian socialists of the 19th Century. It could not be done by the hippy communes in the 60s or by workers' cooperatives in the 70s and it cannot be done by traveller convoys or squatting communities today. Such alternative communities are never a practicable option for a large majority of working class people,

and even for the minority who join them they are seldom viable in the long term. *The pressures of the capitalist economy are too strong, too pervasive and too insidious to be resisted indefinitely this way.* (Molineux 1994; my emphasis)

These are valid arguments, but are they arguments that, while true for the nineteenth century, no longer hold in a world where, while many still struggle to survive, ordinary people in advanced capitalist societies often have access to resources that nineteenth-century proletarians could only dream of? Is the Marxist critique of utopianism still valid? This book is built on the hypothesis that this cannot be assumed a priori. It should be a research question that can be answered only through more rigorous examination of actually existing alternative economic practices. Gibson-Graham preferred to see these objections less as fundamental limits than as "challenges, problems, barriers, difficulties—in other words, as things to be struggled with, things that present themselves as more or less tractable obstacles in any political project" (Gibson-Graham 2006, xxv). They wanted to examine conditions of possibility rather than fundamental limits to possibility, and they stressed being hopeful rather than uncritically optimistic. This is the approach we take in this study.

Gibson-Graham's perspectives were explored more empirically in the collection edited by Andrew Leyshon, Roger Lee, and Colin C. Williams (2003), which looked at different forms of economic activity such as those of credit unions and cooperatives, the resale of secondhand clothes, and the use of alternative currencies. Other analyses within economic geography argued that attention should be paid to the specifics of the place, space, and culture in which economies are constructed and that the "social relations, in which we are all involved at a variety of scales and in a variety of forms are formatively crucial in everything we do as people" (Lee 2002, 339). Amin and Thrift (2000) wrote that geographers should draw attention to the role of society and culture in the construction of alternative, perhaps noncapitalist economic worlds or worlds in which the market is constructed differently than in the profit-loss nexus using different economic knowledges. Lee argued for "normative evaluation—whether judgements may be made about trajectories in which economies should go (or) an indication of how participants in economic geographies understand the criteria by which they are supposed to function" (Lee 2002, 339).

This book aims to work within this emerging corpus not by seeing "capitalism" as just a spook that we have unwittingly called out of the ether and can easily wish away, but by taking seriously the idea that we should not ascribe the term "capitalist" to market-based activities a priori. We should investigate, using a political economy approach, the extent to which, by paying attention to economic diversity, we might uncover or imagine new, more liberated alternatives to the exploitative and environmentally unsustainable economic activities that blight our planet. This book examines the experiences of those who have engaged in alternative economic practices through which new forms of money were created as alternatives to capitalism. Can new forms of money lead to new, more liberated noncapitalist practices based on money and markets created and regulated from below? Or should money be seen not as a representation, but as linked to the concrete, capitalist economy and as such, as part of the structure that enforces capitalist domination?

The Content of This Book

Chapter 1 will prepare us for thinking about money and liberation "otherwise" with a review of the key ways in which the relationship between money and the economy has been theorized. We shall review arguments that money emerges spontaneously from economies as a way to move beyond barter, that it is or is not a commodity or representation of real-world commodities. To what extent can money be created, and to what extent does it emerge from underlying economic social structures? Can we change the economy by changing the form of money, or does the form of money emerge from the economy? Chapter 2 examines how money has been conceptualized as contributing to freedom or, on the other hand, to domination. The chapter reviews political and sociological conceptions of the relationship between money and freedom before arguing that Foucauldian conceptions of money as a structuring discourse and as an autonomous system of domination not inevitably linked to capitalism help us operationalize a contention that unpacking how we think about money might lead to new political imaginations and practices.

Chapters 3 and 4 examine the history of political action from below around money. Chapter 3 examines the nineteenth-century experiences of utopian socialism, Robert Owen's labor notes, and Proudhon's arguments for a Bank of the People. In the late nineteenth century in the United States, Populists agitated for paper or silver money, although the secular rise of socialism focused on changing the economy rather than changing the money, and monetary contestation died out as a political strategy. Chapter 4 examines the twentieth-century experience, from the interest-free money and stamp scrip movements inspired by Silvio Gesell through the interwar Social Credit movement of Major C. H. Douglas, which inspired political parties in Canada and New Zealand and, in Britain, a militant uniformed wing, the Green Shirts. The Green Shirts enable us to examine connections between money reform, conspiracy theorists, and the anti-Semitic far right.

Chapter 5 begins the empirical section of the book, which focuses on contemporary forms of monetary contestation. In a discussion of local exchange trading schemes (LETS) in Manchester, U.K., the chapter examines competing rationales for their development: the actualization of alternative economic relations and livelihoods based on conviviality, ecological sustainability, free exchange, and unalienated labor. Chapter 6 examines the institution of Kör, or green money, in Hungary in the context of postsocialist change. Kör was introduced by green activists who saw it as a tool for building community in an environment where economic changes left many feeling isolated and left behind after a lifetime in a state that, while repressive to dissidents, did provide some security to those who did not challenge the system. Chapter 7 examines the performance of green dollar exchanges in New Zealand (Aotearoa) in a neoliberal environment where fiscal "imperatives" led to curtailment of the state's provision of welfare in favor of the delivery of welfare by organizations within civil society through self-help. The experience of New Zealand green dollars shows us that micropolitical alternatives to capitalist rationality can exist for some time in spaces where people committed to alternatives build them consistently over many years and where the political environment is not too toxic.

The crisis in Argentina that emerged in 2001 has been one of the highest-profile examples of recent years of resistance to the "disciplining" of a country by international financial organizations. In response to the crisis, literally millions of Argentines joined barter networks that were sufficiently extensive, for a time, for people's basic needs to be met. Therefore, Argentina has been the "poster child" of the alternative currency movement. Chapter 8 engages the debates on the role of alternative currencies as problems or solutions to a country in financial crisis, and argues that the mass levels of usage represent a popular refutation of the International Monetary Fund's recipe for Argentina. The conclusion examines the extent to which Marx's critique of building alternatives still stands. I will not answer that question now, but will rather leave the argument to be developed.

MONEY AND LIBERATION

Beyond the Veil?

MONEY AND ECONOMIES

W E DO NOT USUALLY THINK OF MONEY ITSELF AS AN OBJECT
of protest. There are critical lay views about money: that the
money system is "out of control"; that we are dominated by "the
man," money power, and conformity that makes us work; that people
who deal with money (especially credit) are at best dubious, at worst
parasitic; and that money is corrosive of character and community,
promoting selfishness and individualism (Leyshon and Thrift 1997,
32). We are perhaps opposed to those we think have more money than
we do and thus power over us, or we might just be jealous of them.
Money can be fairly earned or dirty money, but, remarkably in many
ways, we often do not problematize money itself. Money thus rarely
becomes an explicit focus for political contestation.

Consequently, apart from key moments when state-issued money
changes and money can drive social protest or mobilization, protest
is far more likely to challenge the way the economy is organized and
make moral claims about the validity of the way resources are allocated than to argue about the form or the nature of money. Political
contestation focuses on who wins and loses, on whether inequality is
immoral or a legitimate reward for entrepreneurialism and risk taking, and on differences in the levels of remuneration of, say, fat cats
and janitors. Debates about money are thus more likely to focus on its
effects than on money itself. For example, debates about the power
that money gives those who have it point to certain financial centers
(London, New York, and perhaps Tokyo) that act as "command and
control centers" for international capitalism (Sassen 1991, 1996), with

finance (rather than production) said to be directing capitalism. Globalization, hyperglobalizers claim, means that nation-states cannot control largely digitized, placeless flows of money disconnected from a "real world" of production and economies (Ohmae 1994; Leyshon and Thrift 1997). Anticapitalist campaigners argue that in southern countries money is controlled not by their governments, but by the International Monetary Fund and the World Bank, hence by U.S. and international finance (Bonefield and Holloway 1996; Wade 2003). Protesters at the 1999 World Trade Organization meeting in Seattle and at subsequent meetings of the international financial institutions argued that the globalization of finance leads to environmental degradation, loss of local control, annihilation of local cultures, and poverty for millions (Cockburn et al. 2000; Callinicos 2003). Entire countries are racked or disciplined on the altar of sound money, with Argentina perhaps the most recent and glaring example (Dinerstein 2001; Halevi 2002; Harman 2002; Rock 2002; López Levy 2004; North and Huber 2004). Money here forms the backdrop to wider debates. The nature of money itself, and the liberatory potential of different types of money, is rarely considered.

Lack of attention to the form and role of money is not really that surprising. Paying too much attention to it can cause one to be labeled a sad numismatist who has not grown out of his coin collecting days (and it is usually a "he"). But coin collectors catalogue rather than analyze money, something only economists are considered competent to engage in. Money reformers are often considered cranks, snake oil salesmen, shysters, and sharks who prey on the vulnerable in times of economic distress. As Hayek (1990, 12) so effectively put it: "Demands [for new types of money] have been raised over and over again by a long series of cranks with strong inflationist inclinations . . . [who] all agitated for free issue because they wanted more money. Often a suspicion that the government monopoly was inconsistent with the general principle of the freedom of enterprise underlay their argument, but without exception they all believed that monopoly had led to an undue restriction rather than to an excessive supply of money." Galbraith (1975, 51) said that money reformers were fools or thieves: "Those who supported sound money and the gold standard were good men. Those that did not were not. If they knew what they were about, they were only marginally better than thieves. If they did not, they were cranks. In neither case could they be accepted into the company of reputable citizens. [Socialists agreed:] They wanted to be revolutionaries, not knaves." Or money reformers can be conspiracy theorists, perhaps focusing too much on the symbolism of the pyramid and the "all-seeing eye" on the dollar bill, sometimes making fantastic claims about what they see as the role of masons, bankers, and financiers—or Jews—in dominating the world economy for what they allege are dubious purposes. An interest in money can lead to guilt by association: as we shall see in chapter 4, sometimes money reformers can move in unpleasant, anti-Semitic circles. An interest in money reform can be dubious or downright reprehensible, or can just invite ridicule. World Trade Organization Chairman Mike Moore abused antiglobalization activists in his native New Zealand as "wacko conspiracy types," "grumpy geriatric communists," "a mutant strain of the left . . . and weirdos from the   Social Credit types who tuck their shirts into their underpants" (quoted by Kelsey 1999, 14).

But mainly we do not consider money, either because it is "obvious" or because we see it as a distraction diverting attention away from the "real" issues. For laypeople, the problem is often the amount one has, not how it works or where it comes from. For some economists, money itself is so unproblematic that, as the monetarist economist Milton Friedman argued, we might as well assume that it was dropped by helicopter and proceed from there to an examination of how the stock of money affects economic performance. If money is just an unproblematic way of facilitating trade between people with incommensurate needs, it need detain us no longer. Put another way: I want a chair. You have a chair to sell and want a table. I do not have a table to sell. Our needs are incommensurate unless we use money so you can buy a table from someone else with the money I give you for the chair. Therefore, the volume of money matters, not its form or how it gets there. Some economists consequently see money as a representation of a "real" economy that exists behind it, what Schumpeter called a "a 'garb' or 'veil' over things that really matter." According to Schumpeter, "Not only can [money] be discarded when we are analysing the fundamental features of the economic process but *it must be discarded just as a veil must be drawn aside to see what is behind it*" (quoted by Ingham 2004, 17; my emphasis). Focusing on money,

then, is a distraction from the real issues, addressing the symptoms —
not the cause.

If money *is* worth study in its own right, and there is some relationship between money and the economy, there is no agreement
about what it is. While classical equilibrium theory assumed that
the amount of money in an economy would always be enough to lubricate transactions and could thus be ignored in economic analysis,
Keynes later argued that too little money in the economy could lead
to a lack of demand and underconsumption, which should be countered by government action to boost demand through government
spending. By the 1970s, monetarists such as New Right propagan-
dist Sir Keith Joseph argued, contra Keynes, that in the United Kingdom "inflation has been the result of the creation of new money out
of proportion to the goods and services available. When the money
supply grows too quickly, inflation results. This has been known for
centuries" (Smith 1987, 73). Keynesians countered that, because it
cannot be assumed that people will spend their money (as opposed
to holding it idle in savings accounts), there is no automatic relationship between the amount of money and economic activity. The
Japanese found this out to their detriment when they issued bonds
to all citizens to promote spending in an effort to overcome the de-
flation of the 1990s: they were just added to savings accounts. At
the other end of the spectrum, small amounts of money can move
quickly, servicing large volumes of economic activity. Large volumes
of money can appear, seemingly from nowhere, such as the liras that
emerged from under mattresses in Italy prior to the introduction of
the euro.

Consequently, the debate about the relationship between money
and the economy is unresolved: does economic change originate
from the way money is issued and functions (money as a *cause* of economic activity), or does economic change relate to business activity,
prices, levels of production, and the consequent demand for money
(money as a *response* to economic activity)? Does changing the supply
of money set off an inflationary bubble, with too much money chas-
ing too few goods and money consequently losing its value and prices
rising, or can there be too little money in circulation to meet demand,
with rising prices a consequence of limited money's gaining value as a
result of unmet demand for goods and services (Galbraith 1975, 47)?

[4]

If liberation is sought through changing money, the extent to which money is a cause of or an effect of economic activity is obviously crucial. If it is an effect of economic activity, changing the form of money will not change the form of the economy; changing it will be a diversion from the real problem.

Economic analyses of money take four approaches; some suggest that money can be seen as open to contestation from below, but some do not. First, the evolutionary school of Adam Smith, John Stuart Mill, and Carl Menger conceptualizes money as a "natural" tool that emerged as a method for overcoming the absence of the "double coincidence of wants," described earlier, which restricts barter in order to promote more effective markets (Smith 1776/1981). The value of money is therefore related to the volume of goods and services traded in that market. Second, Ricardian "commodity money" theorists argue that money is a universally exchangeable commodity that acts as a method of valuing other inequivalent commodities. A third economic analysis, taking account of the delinking of modern money from the gold standard, in the United Kingdom in 1931 and in the United States in 1973, is of paper capitalist credit money that acquires its value from our confidence that we will be able to redeem it in the future for real commodities or services because it is issued by a reliable source (Ingham 2001). Finally, we have the debates between Keynes and the monetarist school about the extent to which money is related to the workings of the real economy insofar as states can or cannot influence economic activity by managing its quantity or by public spending. These economic analyses can be complemented by sociological and political analyses that argue that money is a political or social construct created by states or through social interaction rather than something that arises from the workings of capitalist market economies. We shall examine these conceptions in the next chapter before taking a Foucauldian approach to money: examining it as a system of domination in its own right, not linked to wider economic, political, or social explanations. But first we shall examine what economic conceptualisations of the relationship between money and the wider economy tell us about a strategy of creating new forms of money as a strategy for social change.

The Evolutionary School

The evolutionary school sees money as arising from the natural tendencies of economic actors to "barter, truck, and exchange" in order to trade with each other on a "higher" rational, pecuniary basis, ignoring irrational, emotive, sacred, or social beliefs. If we all do what we do best—baking bread, writing books—and use money to exchange these goods and services, all will benefit. For this school money goes beyond inefficient barter to lubricate economic transactions, and it emerged spontaneously when, through millions of independent trades, one form of money emerged as a universal. In time this universal came to be gold or silver, but it has also been conch shells, tobacco, furs, and the like. While there are anthropological debates about the extent to which this view truly represents how money emerged (Ingham 1999; Hart 2001, 264, 272), the important point for this analysis is the claim that money emerged spontaneously from the market and will always work in ways that tend toward (Walrasian) market equilibrium—that is, efficient markets allocating resources in the optimal way, with prices finding their own level through market competition. Competition and market allocation is what is important, not the nature of money, as long as there is *some* relationship between the amount of money and the volume of goods and services in the market. For Mill, what was important was that money should be relatively scarce in relation to goods and services; its intrinsic value is less important.

The perspectives of the evolutionary school suggest that opportunities for creating money are fairly open. Money emerges spontaneously through market mechanisms, and the optimum form of money will win out, so new forms of money will emerge as market forms evolve over time. Thus, in this argument, financial innovations gave us banknotes, deposit accounts, and fractional lending and now give us new forms of financial innovation such as air miles or the *hawala* system that facilitates international money transfer between Muslims. For some, such as LETSystem originator Michael Linton, the alternative currency networks that we discuss in this book are as politically neutral as other new forms of financial innovation. Banks emerged to finance new markets, rising and declining according to their success in generating economic activity. At times this would be a loose system where money was made available as required to finance economic activity, such as in the nineteenth-century American West, where approximately sixteen hundred local banks issued some seven thousand paper currencies to meet market conditions. The pioneer establishing his farm could be assured of cheap credit from a local bank that could easily go bust, leaving him with his farm and no debts (Galbraith 1975, 97–98). At other times, harder, more limited money was required: commodity money.

The Commodity School

The Ricardian "commodity school" argued that it is possible for money to be overissued such that its volume is out of relationship with the volume of goods and services in the economy, and that paper money is not reliable. So not all innovations are welcome, and the evolution of paper money unconnected to specie was particularly dangerous. Hard commodity money (as opposed to soft paper money) is a direct commodity that emerges as a "universal equivalent" commodity that traders agree to accept from each other to facilitate the circulation of commodities (Lapavitsas 2003). It can be a direct commodity—for instance, a gold coin—or a commodity that acts as a token or symbol that is a proxy for the value of that commodity (for example, a pound sterling banknote issued when Britain was using the gold standard). Gold emerged as a standard because it is a commodity that both is limited and embodies many of the intrinsic values that money should have: portability, indestructibility, homogeneity, divisibility, and cognizability (Jevons, quoted by Dodd 1994). From this perspective, ice cream might be a commodity at the opposite end of the spectrum (Lapavitsas 2003). In these conditions, money has a value that relates to the ratio of the volume of tokens or symbols in circulation in relation to that commodity; if there are too many symbols in circulation in relation to the commodity that backs them, the value falls. If there are too few, the value rises. For this reason, money should be issued according to a conservative estimation of the needs of the "real" economy, or perhaps even only when backed, 100 percent, by a commodity or another "hard" currency. In the 1990s Argentina's peso was "pegged" to the U.S. dollar such that a peso could be printed only when it was backed by a dollar held by the Argentine treasury.

The important issue for this analysis is that if, as commodity theorists argue, money is a representation of the "universal equivalent" commodity, the possibility of changing it is limited if its value is primarily underpinned by the production of valuable yet limited commodities monopolized by those who control the means of production (Lapavitsas 2003, 49–67). If the commodities that underpin money are widely shared, this will be less of an issue, but commodity theorists would argue that it may then be too soft a currency. Thus the adoption of hard commodity money in the United Kingdom was accompanied by a destruction of the local banks and of poor people's small coinage (Gilbert and Helleiner 1999, 7), which had the effects of massively increasing the efficiency of the economy and of creating and extending markets, but it also acted as a supremely powerful tool in forcing those who did not own the means of production to sell their labor to obtain money with which to provide for their material reproduction. The soft paper money that funded smallholdings and small farms in the United States was similarly shut off. Here money acted as a tool for capitalist discipline, and those who controlled the commodities it represented controlled the value of commodity money.

Commodity money, if its value is related to limited commodities controlled by elites, is not amenable to change from below unless the elites give up this specific advantage, which is unlikely. Moreover, if money is a representation of abstract commodities and the logic of the system is to produce these commodities at a profit by extracting surplus value from working people, capital will have no interest in facilitating the elimination of a key technique of this domination. Subaltern groups might be able to create forms of exchange as they see fit, and in fact they have done so where money was poorly developed, such as in frontier societies, but if the forms of exchange generated by subaltern groups cannot be exchanged for the commodities controlled by capital, liberation cannot go far. Liberation will be limited to the exchange of goods consumed by subaltern groups or their petty production, which Marx claimed would be primitive. It will be absent from the entire realm of production, the dynamic and created element of the economy. This is a key problem with proposals for commodity money based on a basket of everyday commodities (Solomon 1996, 68–70).

[8]

The commodity conception of money is the one that Marx used in *Capital*—"Throughout this work I assume that gold is the money commodity, for the sake of simplicity," he wrote (Marx 1867/1976, 188)—and from this he moved quickly to an analysis of the circulation of commodities given value through human labor and abstractly represented for the purposes of exchange by money (Lapavitsas 2003, 9). In seeing money as a symbol of commodities Marx was drawing on the Smithian understanding of markets as emerging from a natural predisposition of humanity to barter, truck, and exchange, differing from Smith in his understanding of this exchange not as being undertaken between free producers or artisans but as structured by the tendency of some producers eventually to take over the others and to employ labor in an exploitative relationship based on the extraction of surplus labor. With the exception of de Brunhoff (1971), Harvey (1982), and Bonefield and Holloway (1996), Marxists generally pass over the form of money in favor of an analysis of the workings of the capitalist system. In *The Limits to Capital* Harvey attempts to fill this gap by reviewing forms of money from gold through credit money, disconnected from specie, that can be created by individuals and banks to meet necessary volumes of exchange in the real economy provided that enough discipline is applied to it, but he does not examine how forms of money have been contested (Harvey 1982, 242).

Beyond this, the form of money and contestation over it is not a major focus of Marxism. Fine and Lapavitsas (2000) argue that Marx's insistence on the labor theory of value meant that he did not entertain the possibility that more liberatory value systems might emerge from the social constriction of money, while Dodd argued that, by focusing on production, Marx failed to examine the other side of the coin—how people spend their money—and the political implications of consumption choices (Dodd 1994, 22). Marx argued that even those with money were still captured by the wider economic system: they could not spend their way out of it, which for Dodd reduces monetary transactors to the level of "economic automata" whose motivation can be reduced to that of a rational utility maximizer. If rationalism is assumed, the political or moral reasons that people spend money become irrelevant, and the form of money will not affect rational choices. Leyshon and Thrift (1997, 55, 57) argue that Marx can be supplemented to take account of changes in the form and use of money in the twentieth century. They argue that we can go beyond a focus on the "real" economy as commodity production, with money seen as an analytically more limited process that facilitates the circulation of what really matters—commodities—without losing any of Marx's insights. They argue that this is for four reasons. First, finance capital has emerged as an increasingly independent form of capitalism, disconnected from production, and should be treated as such analytically (as Lenin, Bukharin, and Hilferding did). Second, they argue that the state has an increasing role in the creation and maintenance of money, which again suggests that money should be examined independently. The role of the state in maintaining capitalist reproduction is a key issue in the work of Miliband and the regulation school, and money should thus be investigated as an allied but independent element in the functioning of economies. Leyshon and Thrift's third and fourth objections are of greater use to this analysis: third, that credit as an independent force in the constitution of economies needs analysis in its own right and cannot be reduced to a method for facilitating the exchange of commodities, and fourth, that money plays an important social and cultural role in the creation of livelihoods, which we shall examine in more detail later.

Finally, some Marxist commentators have taken forward Marx's conception of "commodity fetishism" to include a conception of money and finance as fetishized (Holloway 2002). Marx argued that under capitalism life is increasingly commodified—prices are put on everything—and social relations are increasingly organized to facilitate the production of commodities and maintain their value. This is the key logic of the capitalist market. Commodities supersede or become more important than human needs, and humans end up worshiping or "fetishizing" commodities and are valued by their capacity to labor to produce these commodities. Holloway has argued that in mature capitalist economies this fetishization can be applied to money as a commodity that has grown beyond Marx's conception of it as a tool for facilitating the exchange of "real" commodities. Money as a commodity has become fetishized in that the need to safeguard its value is put above human needs such that livelihoods are created and destroyed according to the needs of money and monetary stability. The success of economies is expressed in money terms, not in terms of commodities ("inflation is low = good," not "*x* tons of pig iron was produced = good"). Economies crash if the debt, the balance of payments, or inflation is "too high." Financial stability is imposed on economies by structural adjustment, not by the promotion of livelihoods or human happiness. If all else is subjugated to a fetishization of stability expressed in money terms, irrespective of the number of livelihoods lost and needs unmet, this "stability" can be characterized as a form of violence that values human life and livelihoods below money, at least as a way of organizing human life that does not very highly value happiness and fulfilment. Dinerstein (2001, 2002) argued that during the period when the Argentine peso was pegged to the dollar and in the 2001/2 financial crisis millions of livelihoods were sacrificed to this "violence of stability."

Making less of a fetish of stable money might make possible livelihoods that might otherwise be sacrificed on the altar of stability. Further, if Holloway is right, by resisting this fetishization of the commodity expressed in money terms that is at the heart of the capitalism system, we can break one of the key technologies of domination through what Dinerstein characterizes as the "politics of life," which puts need and human happiness first. Alternative currency networks might be an example of this liberatory politics, and new forms of money might be a key technology for resisting commodity fetishism. Indeed, Williams (2005) argues that the commodification thesis is taken too far, that (following Gibson-Graham and the CEC [Community Economies Collective]) many areas of life are not commodified, and that alternative currencies can be seen as part of an uncommodified sector of the economy along with mutual aid, family provisioning, and the like. As we shall see later, Zelizer (2005) also questions the extent to which emotional and family life is commodified. Against this, if money is a representation of commodities, concrete things objectively circulating between people, and not a social construction, playing with the representation will not change the referent. The value of money is a function of real things, commodities. Lapavitsas (2003, 21) believes it is important to remember the objective nature of money "if Marxist economics is not to degenerate into flights of fancy about the 'true' essence of the capitalist economy as relations among human beings."

Capitalist Credit Money

Ingham (2001, 2004) thinks Marx should be seen as a person of his time, with a wholly conventional analysis of money as a universal equivalent abstract commodity. Ingham argues that capitalist credit money is not a representation of existing commodities; it is a claim on commodities to be produced in the future, issued by banks and other trustworthy institutions. Its value cannot be reduced to a commodity because it is in essence a claim on future production that we believe will be met because it is issued by a reputable institution, such as a bank issuing loans. These loans facilitate production. Ingham argues that Marx was limited by Smithian conceptions of money emerging from barter, ignoring the role of societies and institutions in validating what we see as money and, in particular, failing to understand the change in the social relations that underpin monetary production that arose with the growth of capitalism. This change saw money grow, through financial innovation, from a representation of commodities into a "promise to pay" (i.e., to receive goods in the future) issued by a trustworthy institution, because this was a better form of money than more limited commodity money. Thus banks, as trusted institutions, put money into the economy in the form of credit given to trusted customers, in a process that is autonomous from commodity production. These networks of trust create money in ways that go beyond the conceptions of the commodity school. While Marx did argue that capitalist credit money could grow beyond the needs or limits of production, leading to "crisis and swindle," he did not see capitalist bank-created credit money as a constitutive element of capitalism, alongside labor and plant, not reducible to commodities (Ingham 2001).

Ingham thus sees capitalist credit money as an innovation distinct from commodity money, an innovation created by an autonomous element of capitalism—the finance sector—that cannot be reduced to the production or exchange of commodities. Capitalism is thus characterized by a power struggle between those who produce money (the finance sector), those who produce commodities (the productive sector and labor), and state regulation (Ingham 2001, 318). While the finance sector and states can create money, they cannot set its value; this is "sociologically enacted" by the owners, controllers, and producers of both money and commodities. Money and commodities are separate concepts. This characterization of money as subject to a power struggle opens up space for social action about the creation of forms of money closed off by conceptions of money as a representation of limited commodities controlled by elites; here, the elites are challenged.

The Quantity School: Monetarism and Its Critics

A fourth conception of money as related to the "real" economy is the quantity theory and its critics. From Mill's conception that money should be limited forward, there has been a consensus that there is *some* sort of relationship between the form and volume of money and economic performance and that scarce money is "better." When money was direct commodity money—gold coins—its form and volume were easy to control, whereas capitalist credit money in the form of overdrafts, loans, mortgages, and checks is harder to regulate or restrict. The debate between quantity theorists (more recently, monetarists) and Keynesians has centered on debates about exactly what money *is,* and about how much is too much. For example, while quantity theorists argued that the supply of money is a function of the amount of money in circulation and its velocity (how many times a given note lubricates transactions) in relation to the volume of goods and services, Keynes argued that this ignores whether people choose to spend money or hold onto it in what he called "idle balances." Having money does not mean that one spends it, so printing more money can be like "pushing on a piece of string." A better way to boost spending would be through fiscal rather than financial measures—through government spending, not through printing money that might end up in idle balances (Smith 1987). In contrast, monetarists argued that there is a demonstrable relationship between the stock of money and the long-term health of the economy, with depressions arising when the stock of money is too low and inflation when it is too high (Friedman 1963).

The debate then focuses on the extent to which money can and should be created when the supply is too tight (as the Argentines felt it was in the 1990s) or limited when it is too loose (as in Argentina in 2002), and whether changes in the quality of money will affect the economy. Monetarists argue that the amount of money will have an effect on the economy, with Keynesians doubting that there will necessarily be any close relationship. The debate between monetarists and Keynesians indicates that it can be hard either to define what money is (coins and notes? bank deposits on immediate call, or available in thirty days? mortgages and loans? air miles? luncheon vouchers? IOUs?) and the extent to which states (as opposed to private economic agents) have any control over it. Do states create money, or do economic agents create it through their decisions to create or apply for credit, to spend, and to accept money, and what forms of money do they create and accept? Can they create too much, and does too little restrict economic activity? Smith argued that most economists agree that there is *some* relationship between the form and quantity of money and economic performance, but there is no agreement about the extent to which changes in money lead to changes in the economy or whether changes in the economy lead to changes in money (Smith 1987, 147). Thus, from a Keynesian viewpoint, because there is no agreement on what money is or any guarantee that new forms of money issued will be spent (rather than saved), it would be better to focus on fiscal spending, while a quantity theorist might approve of alternative forms of money when the supply is artificially limited. For this reason, quantity theorist Irving Fisher supported stamp scrip (discussed in chapter 4) during the U.S. Depression (Fisher 1933, 1934) while the Keynesian Roosevelt replaced it with state spending to boost demand—the New Deal.

At times, monetarist Milton Friedman's professed attachment to liberalism and markets and opposition to big government suggests that he would support a liberalization of forms of money. In *Capitalism and Freedom* (1962, 39) he argued:

> A liberal is fearful of concentrated power. His objective is to preserve the maximum freedom for each individual separately that is compatible with one man's freedom not interfering with another man's freedom. He believes that this objective means that power should be dispersed. He is suspicious of assigning to government any functions that can be performed through the market, both because this substitutes coercion for voluntary co-operation in the area in question and because, by giving government an increased role, it threatens freedom in other areas.

Consequently:

> The need for the dispersal of power raises an especially difficult problem in the field of money. There is widespread agreement that government must have some responsibility for monetary matters. There is also widespread recognition that control over money can be a potent tool for controlling and shaping the economy. . . . The problem is to establish institutional arrangements that will enable government to exercise responsibility for money, yet at the same time limit the power thereby given to government and prevent this power from being used in ways that will tend to weaken rather than strengthen a free society.

Nevertheless, Friedman does not follow through on his professed attachment to freedom, preferring inflexible preset "monetary rules" to govern money issuance irrespective of the economic climate (Friedman 1962). This rules out the creation of alternative forms of money, something Friedman would have seen as printing money to solve problems rather than getting the economic fundamentals right.

In contrast, fellow monetarist Hayek (1990) argued for free banking, with money issued by private banks, not states. He argued that money issuance was not one of the three tasks Adam Smith assigned to states and that, like law, morality, and language, money can emerge spontaneously. He argued that money is no different from other commodities and should therefore be subject to the same market disciplines. Consumers should be able to select the best form of money from those on offer from private banks in the market; states should not legislate the form of legal tender. Following Smith, Hayek argued that self-interest would be a better guarantee of sound money than government action, for issuers would be incentivized to limit their issuance or lose their business. In Hayek's view, there should be no prescription against subaltern groups' creating their own forms of money, but Hayek also argued that market forces would force out the weaker currencies and promote the strongest, so in order to survive, a conservative approach to money creation would need to be taken. In the debate between monetarists, Friedman doubted that in practice private money would force out state money, while Hayek (1990, 85) found it surprising that Friedman "of all people" had such little faith in competition.

Laidler, coming from a monetarist perspective, supported Friedman against Hayek. He conceptualized money as a public good for which governments should have responsibility and argued for the construction of the right institutional environment to maintain price and monetary stability (Laidler 1990, 105–10). Because we cannot assume that government will do this effectively, he believed, arguments for free banking "have a lot to be said for them" (108). But Laidler had problems with the credibility of an unregulated private sector issuing reliable and stable money that was unrelated to some commodity or bundle of goods stored at a bank. He then argued that all private banks are likely to rely on the same bundle of commodities, that private banks would not compete with each other in actuality, and that, consequently, taken as a whole, the private money-issuing banking sector would end up as an unstable private monopoly. This, he argued, was not a robust structure on which to base the functioning of a modern capitalist economy.

Laidler also argued that it is unlikely that individuals would have the information they need to "discipline" an overissuing private bank, so regulation would be necessary for the efficient functioning of markets in order to avoid an anarchic system in which the provenance and reliability of privately issued money was unknowable. Stiglitz's work on information asymmetries demonstrates that even with regulation people cannot easily identify the corrupt or vulnerable companies—the Enrons; they do not have the information they need, because those who have it do not pass it on (Stiglitz 2003). They would similarly struggle to identify the bad banks. They could not do so in the free banking era of the United States between 1814 and 1836 (Galbraith 1975, 79–97), nor could they foretell the collapse of BCCI or Barings. Although Hayek argued that a "thousand hounds" would be after any banker who did not maintain the value of his currency (Hayek 1990, 53–54), work on information asymmetries suggests that one cannot rely on the press to identify problems. Thus, unless society was happy to pay the social cost of regular banking failures, Laidler argued, a central bank would be necessary to act as regulator and lender of last resort "if a social institution, namely the system of monetary exchange, is threatened by bank failures and there is a case to be made for public intervention. This does not mean that every badly run bank must be bailed out, but it does mean that a public interest must always be weighed when a decision is taken about such an issue" (Laidler 1990, 109). In time, Laidler argued, the money-issuing private banking sector is likely to become a highly regulated private or public enterprise, much in accord with the status quo, perhaps a state-regulated central bank licensing private banks to issue currency, much as Scottish and Northern Irish banks do in the United Kingdom at present. Unless the money supply is conceptualized as leading automatically to a Walrasian equilibrium, economic problems are in some way affected by the functioning of money and cannot be reduced to "the consequences of capricious intervention by an incompetent government that is the enemy of economic efficiency." Hence, "government is after all an inherent part of an economically efficient solution to monetary problems" (Laidler 1990, 110).

Other arguments against free banking include Gresham's law, which states that bad money will drive good money out of circulation, and consequently competing currencies will lead to a deterioration of the money supply, because people hold onto money from the sources they trust the most and spend that issued by agents in which they have less confidence. Hayek argued that Gresham's law is not applicable, because the currencies he envisaged are not convertible to each other at equivalence and will consequently have different values. People will not, then, have an equivalently valued poor currency that they can pass on, keeping the better. Rather, contra Laidler's argument that all private banks would rely on the same basket of commodities and be indistinguishable, Hayek believed that individuals will identify the most solid forms of currency and refuse to accept the poorer ones, which will be eliminated and die (Hayek 1990, 43). The final problem with Hayek's suggestions is one that will loom large in this analysis: balkanization. Hayek suggested free banking as an alternative to a state-imposed euro. However, according to Cohen, rather than moving toward competition in money, the general drive seems to be toward centralization as the euro is adopted in Europe, while some Latin American countries (Argentina in the 1990s, Ecuador in the 2000s) have experimented with dollarization (Cohen 1998, 68–91). A diversity of currencies entails transaction costs and is consequently likely to be unattractive from a purely economic perspective.

Conclusion

Economic conceptualizations of money have different implications for the project of social change through creating new forms of money. First, we have to assume that money is worthy of analysis in

its own right and is not an irrelevant or uninteresting tool for facilitating what really matters, the circulation of commodities. We also
have to assume that it is more than a veil that we have to draw aside
to get at what really matters. Further, we need to assume that money
has some impact on the wider economy and that changing the form
of money will lead to changes in economic relationships. There is no
consensus on this. If money is in fact worthy of study and matters in
terms of influencing the way economies are constructed, the question is "Can subaltern groups create it?" The evolutionary school
would see subaltern-created currencies as another financial innovation that will last to the extent that they "work"; they would see the
issue as technical, not economic or political. Commodity theorists
would see the attempt as doomed, because subaltern groups by definition do not own the valuable commodities that back commodity
money and elites would be uninterested in relinquishing a tool that
ensures their domination. Credit money theorists would see alternative forms of currency as personal credit money, but would question
whether those issuing them really have a reliable call on commodities
with which to back the currency in the future. Quantity theorists are
split, with Fisher an advocate of scrip in the 1930s, when credit was
too tight; Hayek advocating privatized money; and Friedman in favor
of tight monetary rules. Quantity theorists would be opposed to issuance of money unconnected to real goods and services as a panacea.
The lessons are mixed. But before we can take the analysis further,
we need to examine political and sociological approaches to money,
given that we see markets as sociologically enacted rather than as a
series of rules that work the same everywhere.

The Politics of
Monetary Contestation

——

ALTERNATIVE CURRENCY ACTIVISTS ARGUE THAT "MONEY only has the value we give it." They have a point. Money does have meaning only when it is located in a wider social setting, without which it would have no *intrinsic* value. Bread feeds us, and clothes keep us warm, but, as Lapavitsas wrote, "If the social dimension of money were taken away, only metal disks, pieces of paper and book entries would remain. Money must be immediately and directly social, otherwise it would not be money" (Lapavitsas 2003, 50–51). Money, then, has social and economic functions that give it meaning. But to what extent are these malleable? Sociological conceptions of money locate its role less in facilitating the circulation of commodities between optimizing self-interested individuals (the economistic model) than in contributing to the construction of society and helping us navigate our way through complexity and diversity. While Smith saw money as emerging through the "natural" human desire to trade, that is, through economics, sociologists would locate money in society or in politics. Malinowski and Mauss examined gifts and potlatches as nonmonetized forms of exchange and reciprocity in which the givers, far from being self-interested and rational, achieved status through their generosity. Mauss pointed to the prevalence of gifts and reciprocity in modern life in phenomena such as weddings, Christmas giving, or the exchange of love tokens, through which objects are inscribed with value through giving and sentiment (Hart 2001, 192–93). This suggests that exchange can be uncoupled from Smithian

individual self-interest and examined in ways that take more cognizance of cultural, social, and affective aspects. In contrast, money is
often though to be a key tool for moving beyond exchange based on
sentiment and obligation to exchange based on instrumental rationality; Hart (2001, 193) recalls the Innuit proverb "Gifts make slaves as
whips make dogs." This chapter examines relationships between
money and social change.

Universal Money as Freedom

Simmel (1908/1978) saw money as a key constitutive feature of modern society because it homogenizes: it cleans up our economic relationships in a complex society based on the division of labor. In contrast with Marx, Simmel saw the possession and the institution of
money as freeing those who had it from social restrictions. If I pay for
a service with money, the obligation ends there and then. I need no
longer be bound to exchange relationships and can be free to move on
to the next exchange in what is at the same time a liberating yet isolating world of purposive rather than affective relationships. A peasant who has to provide a bushel of wheat is tied to wheat production,
whereas a peasant who has to pay tax can make his livelihood as he
sees fit, as long as he pays his taxes. Money is objective and fair. I do
not need to like you to trade with you; I just need your money, and
my money is as good as yours. If I do not like someone, I can take my
money elsewhere, and this ability to change our relationships, lubricated by money rather than favors, hierarchies or obligations, makes
us free. Social class, status, tradition, and affectation are all irrelevant
clutter that can be cleaned out through the use of money. Strangers
can get what they need from each other if they can pay for it (Simmel 1908/1978, 222). We get what we need from a complex interde-
pendence based on what people can do, not on their personalities,
morals, or status. Money allows us to join a group without giving up
our freedom because we can limit our involvement with a monetary
contribution. Money, then, for Simmel, is a tool for freedom and independence in a complex society made up of thousands of incom-
mensurable transactions. Simmel also saw money as a tool that, when
allied with human intelligence, allows us to make the incommensu-
rable commensurable and to weigh what would happen as a conse-

quence of our choices in accepting one thing and sacrificing another. Money is a token that enables us to apportion value and play "what if" games in deciding what to do and how to obtain the best value from our transactions.

In these analyses, then, money is a tool of modernization and rationality. Talcott Parsons saw money as a tool for transmitting information within a modernity characterized by complexity and social differentiation without complex and time-consuming negotiation, while Habermas saw it as another example of the internal colonization of the "lifeworld" by instrumental rationality. For Habermas, money acts as a substitute for language or communication to reproduce the rational systems of domination of the social system by acting as a communicative tool that enables its users to avoid the interpretive complexities in securing exchange relationships (Dodd 1994, 59–81). Thus for Habermas, money is a tool not for freedom (as it is for Simmel) but for domination. For Marx it can be both in that it uproots old systems of domination (religion, status, feudalism), re placing them with domination of the market. Lapavitsas argued that money is both hostile to social distinction *and* undemocratic. It is the great leveller, ignoring inherited power or custom. The lowborn with money are the same as their "betters." Money has no time for intellectual or moral distinctions or for matters of taste or culture. But it is also undemocratic. It accepts not human equality, but only the equality of everyone's money. It gives economic, social, and political power to those who have it and denies it to those without. If we have money, our power in a market is greater. It creates new distinctions, such as the ability to buy a spouse or a place at the right school for our children. It perpetuates social division and hardens attitudes toward the needy (Lapavitsas 2003, 53). Money as rationalism (comprising freedom or domination) is Polanyi's complex multipurpose money, which can be contrasted with "primitive" special-purpose monies.

Simmel did not want to disconnect money from the realities of grounded exchange of real commodities. Paper money is a symbol, but it is not a symbol completely delinked from the "real" values it represents. It is thus more a representation that needs to be related in some way to a form of intrinsic value, and it has no value if what it can buy is valueless. It must be related, at the end of the day, to an exchange that meets our material needs. While some try to make money into "the ideal of a pure symbol which is never attained," as it moves away from its relationship with commodities it "cannot cast off a residue of material value" (Simmel 1908/1978, 157). That is, in the substitution of symbolic for intrinsic value there does need to be some relationship between the supply of the symbols of value—money—and the supply of valued goods and services. Money needs to be an effective representation of value with an observable connection between a commodity and a sum of money. Simmel argued that moving to token money unconnected to any form of precious metal would invite its misuse. He argued that money performs best when it is more than just an abstraction, a symbol. Gold is also valued because of its function and performance—its glister, its usefulness in making jewelry; plastic would not perform the same function. For this reason, considerable effort is put into the design of banknotes so that we can feel they will perform well, so that others will also value them and they will not rip, get too dirty, or decay. Thus, while money may be a representation created by and set within social structures, it must have an effective economic function or it will exist only in a Platonic world beyond space and time (Simmel 1908/1978, 157). Money is thus less an abstract symbol than a representation of something real, and for Simmel at the end of the day this something real was a commodity. This cuts against conceptions of money as just a performance or representation that does not exist *prior* to discursive interpretations, but is created as a discourse by which we decide to inscribe it with powers unrelated to any underlying reality (De Goede 2005, xxii)—as Gibson-Graham argued is the case with conceptions of "capitalism." Rather, money is a representation that through performance in meeting real economic needs becomes real itself. If it does not meet real needs, the representation is valueless, like paper "Monopoly money."

Zelizer's Multiple Money

In contrast with Simmel, Marx, and Parsons, Viviana Zelizer (1997, 2005) saw money as more diverse and multiple. Focusing on how people give value to and use money, she rejected it as a tool for rationalization (let alone domination). Zelizer accepted arguments about the role of money in helping us navigate through complex modern society by making life fungible, liquid, or divisible, but she argued that the rationalizing tendency of money can be mitigated by social and cultural factors that limit the extent to which modern life is being commodified. She argued for multiple social monies, arguing that because people give different values to the exchange relationships they enter into, we cannot see one form of money as dominating others or one form of exchange logic—commodification—as dominating others based, for example, on affection, politics, or emotion. We react against the use of the "wrong" sort of money or a "wrong" use of money, such as giving money as a gift or as a declaration of love or paying for sex. Money can be tainted as "ill-gotten gains" or it can be gained through "honest toil." Can "tainted money" be cleaned up, for example, when a Mafia boss makes a donation to his church? Do we pay more for a picture we like? So, Zelizer argued, money may be indivisible, nonfungible, nonportable, and deeply subjective. It is not universal, but heterogeneous. She argued that we "earmark" money, ascribing a special purpose to it, such as saving to pay a bill or for a celebration:

> By earmarking money, people . . . create their own spectra [of money] in place of those provided by government and banks. . . . [They create] a complex social economy. As money entered the household, gift exchanges and charitable donations, individuals and organisations invented an extensive array of currencies, ranging from housekeeping allowances, pin money and spending money to money gifts, gift certificates, remittances, tips, Penny Provident savings, mother's pensions, and food stamps. They sorted ostensibly homogenous legal tender into distinct categories, and created other currencies that lacked backing from the state. (Zelizer 1997, 201–2)

Zelizer also rejected Simmel's argument that money is a rationalizer, removing sentiment from economy relations. Examining family economies as well as social mores around sex and dating and around caring for the sick or elderly, she argued that money and sentiment neither inhabited separate worlds nor were inextricably mixed. Rather, she argued that any relationship is based on a negotiated mixture of sentiment and monetary exchange:

> Household economic relations involve an intricate mix of intimacy and economic activity. They interweave long term commitment, continuous demands of co-ordination and reciprocity, relations to kin, friends and others outside the household. They impose shared vulnerability to

the failures, mistakes and malfeasance of other household members . . .
[and] when households get into financial trouble or break up, economic
interactions of family members add yet another layer of complexity: kin
help the unemployed, and financial roles often reverse, with children, for
instance, now supporting their parents. Intimacy and economic activity
continue to intersect. (Zelizer 2005, 284)

Thus Zelizer rejected the commodification thesis. In contrast with
Habermas, she argued that money and emotion lubricate each other
and that consequently society and culture can limit commodification.
Economic relations lubricated by money need not be commodified
relationships if the objective of the exchange is not financial gain.

This is not something that Marxist scholars have rejected out of
hand. Lapavitsas (2003) argued that the value of commodities, as abstract labor, is a function of *negotiated and contested* class relations
based on conflict over, for example, how much workers are prepared
to be exploited or what is perceived to be an acceptable rate of pay or
profit. In this case, the value of commodities, and hence the nature of
an economy comprised of circulating commodities, is far from "objective" or socially neutral. This is even more the case when we consider the value of commodities whose value does not relate closely to
human labor, such as cultural or religious artifacts. Lapavitsas (2003,
13) also agreed with Zelizer that while capitalist markets are the key
organizing principles for capitalist societies, this does not mean that
all markets are capitalist. Noncapitalist markets cannot be expected
to function in the same way as markets of commodities; for example,
the logic behind the circulation of gifts will not be the same as that
behind motorcars. Money created by and circulating between people who wish to exchange their time and resources using more social,
affective, or ecological criteria will not work in the same way as that
between businesspeople working within the traditional rational economic paradigm of efficiency and profit maximization. The logic of
these markets will be different if their scale is less extensive by nature
of the limited number of goods and services circulating in noncapitalist markets.

While Marx, the supreme modernist, saw capitalism as in some way
progressive and rational and expected capitalist forms to overwhelm
what he saw as more backward economic relations, if we see noncapitalist relations as different, not backward, other opportunities for lib-

[*24*]

eration become possible—the key claim of Gibson-Graham. This is not the approach of Marxist critics of Zelizer's social constructivist analysis, such as Fine and Lapavitsas (2000), who argue that Zelizer has chosen limited and esoteric examples of particular forms of market relations, without getting to the heart of the "market." This, they argue, is still focused on the exchange of limited commodities produced by alienated labor and controlled by capitalist elites. Yes, the way that commodity production occurs has a social element, but focusing on consumption rather than production, and rather unusual forms of consumption at that, does not get to the heart of capitalist markets (Fine and Lapavitsas 2000, 373). Money at heart represents relations of trust and power in capitalist markets that facilitate profit making, and it is thus a foundation of social power and domination (Lapavitsas 2003, 49).

Chartalist or State-Centered Perspectives

The German chartalist or nominalist school argued that from the beginning money was an arbitrary quantification of purchasing power or unit of account legislated by states (Ingham 2004, 47–49). Someone decided what the currency would be, and it was states that conferred the quality of "valuableness" on what emerged as money. Ingham (2001, 311) argued that money emerged not from the actions of self-interested individualistic traders with an inherent tendency to trade, but from more communal, tribal societies as *wergeld,* a way of quantifying "worth" when making compensation for wrongs, insults, and injuries (a view challenged by quantity theorists; see Lapavitsas 2005). Later it was established by states to facilitate long-range trade and to gain control of national territory. Money is thus culturally and politically sedimented, historically grounded, not socially produced as one would produce a work of art (Ingham 1999, 2004). States legislated the use of money to gain control of national territory and to raise taxes to pay for wars and later for collective goods. This is why money generally circulates in nationally determined spaces, not economically determined spaces—unless the state is weak (for example, contemporary Ecuador or the former Yugoslavia in the 1990s) or in border areas where the national currencies of two or more states might just as easily circulate (Cohen 1998). Money is used to create national consciousness, and that is why feelings are so high about money (along with stamps and flags) as a symbol of national sovereignty (Gilbert and Helleiner 1999, 1). States give legitimacy to what is essentially valueless paper currency by inscribing it with the nation's power:

> The state's ability to guarantee the legitimacy of its money—facilitated by the homogenisation of the currency, centralisation as well as the rise of policing capabilities—made possible the use of token currencies such as paper money that are of no intrinsic value but which circulate because of the economic and political power inscribed on them by their issuing institutions. Money's relationship to the state was thus mutually reinforcing for not only did this trust lend the state legitimacy, but it also compelled the public to become dependent on the state's authority for fulfilling their financial obligations. (Gilbert 1999, 26)

Money is thus a social fact given reality by states (Ingham 2001, 314). States need not create money, but their legitimation is necessary if it is to have valuableness.

Critics of the chartalist position argue that while in modern capitalist economies thinking about money without considering the state that adorns most money forms seems inconceivable, the state can set the form of money only if it fits with deeper social and economic realities (Lapavitsas 2005). States can legislate that the unit of account is the pound, but not at how much a pound is valued, that is, how many yards of cloth a pound buys. The state may be weak and its form of money not valued, a perennial problem in Argentina in the twentieth century (Ingham 2004, 165–74). Consequently, while states may declare the unit of account in which people must pay taxes, they cannot give it value or ensure that everyone will use it. Money is thus characterized by a power struggle between states and markets, producers of money, producers of commodities (both capital and labor), and (as this book shows) subaltern groups excluded from access to commodities (Ingham 2001, 318). We can see this battle in decisions to move from soft paper money issued by local banks during the formation of early capitalism, which were later supplanted by decisions to use hard money to enforce labor discipline as capitalism matured, as theorized by Polanyi. The substantive value of money is thus sociologically enacted through struggle. As Weber (quoted by Ingham 2001, 328) put it, "Money is primarily a weapon in the struggle for economic existence."

Debates about the effects of international financial crises and the nature of speculative currency markets suggest that nations no longer fully control the nature of money in their territory (Bello et al. 2000). Currency market traders/speculators spectacularly bet against national currencies, as incidents such as the United Kingdom's ejection from the European Exchange Rate Mechanism in 1992 graphically show. Long-term trends in the growth of international capital markets, disconnected from national circuits of production and international forms of currency like the euro and dollar, suggest that the era of the national domination of money—if it ever existed—is over (Leyshon and Thrift 1997). A question, then, arises as to the extent to which the end of state monopolies of monetary provision provides a space for new forms of monetary innovation by subaltern groups or whether states are the only institutions sufficiently trusted to give valuableness to money and to enforce its acceptance.

Money as an Autonomous System of Domination

The previous discussions relate money to other economic, political, or sociological systems of power. Some conceptions (the evolutionary school, Zelizer's multiple monies) suggest that a number of actors can create money, while the commodity, capitalist credit, and chartalist schools suggest that only economic elites and states, respectively, can give money valuableness. Simmel sees modern multiple money as a tool for achieving freedom; Marxists see a system for ensuring domination. The extent to which money can or should be created by subaltern groups is thus limited by whichever conceptualization is preferred.

However useful these theorists are, perhaps a more productive way of looking at political action for alternative forms of money might be to take a Foucauldian approach to money as a structuring discourse, a system of domination that operates through its own logic, not as a subsystem of a wider system of power, economics, or society. The "modernist" conceptions of money, above all, saw money as part of a "total" analysis of the economy, of society, or of state power. Perhaps more fruitful ways of thinking about money and liberation might be found if we did not discipline our thinking by relating it to "totalising metanarratives" (Foucault 1980, 83). As part of a wider project to understand power, Foucault undertook a number of genealogical enquiries into what he saw as autonomous systems of domination: prisons and other disciplinary forms, mental illness and health, sexuality, and the like. Polanyi saw enclosure in the United Kingdom as a specific, state-induced policy to create industrial capitalism by removing alternatives—self-provisioning in the country-side. E. P. Thompson (1963/1980) points to the huge multiplication in crimes in general, and in the use of the death penalty in particular, in early nineteenth-century Britain as part of a wider strategy for enforcing the introduction of capitalism. In contrast, Foucault would wish to understand events like enclosure or France's great confinement processes of incarceration and normalization, which cannot be understood by relating them to another system of domination, say, capitalism. They should be understood in terms of their own logics and rationales. If we take a Foucauldian approach, we would examine money as a system of domination "where it is in direct and immediate relationship with that which we can provisionally call its object, its target, its field of application . . . where it installs itself and produces its real effects" (Foucault 1980, 97). We would relate money not to any other system of power, but to its own object, target, or field of application.

Foucault took this approach because of his conception of power. He conceptualized power as operating within a decentered net or grid in which we are all simultaneously entrapped, yet also resist. Rather than theorizing power as hegemonic, held by some (who have it all) over others (who have none), Foucault believed that power is found in all relations, and is anonymous and all-pervasive (1980, 89). It is not unitary or organized according to one metanarrative, but is found in multiple, local, decentered forms of subjugation that operate by their own logic (1980, 96). Thus (for example), working people are not powerless in the face of capital, but they are also subject to other forms of domination through legal and sexual codes, disciplinary forms, codes of conduct, and the like, which operate according to their own rules as well as being disciplined by capitalist systems of domination in the disciplinary field or the grid of paid work. If our worker is a female, has been found guilty of what the state calls a crime, is gay or ill, she will also be subject to gendered, criminal, sexual, or medical systems of domination as well as systems of domination around paid work. None of these systems comes first, and no system of domination—political, economic, or social—is the prime system. Arguing that these systems of domination are autonomous means that their production was undertaken by their own logic, not in relation to any other system of domination that they were meant to enforce. Criminality was increasingly defined as a response to unruliness, not just to force workers into factories, although obviously it had that effect, and that is one reason, but not the only one, why elites supported it. For example, Foucault was clear that economic elites had a great interest in developing a more effective policing and penal policy for the London docks (Gordon 2002, xiv), but he was also clear that the development and deployment of forms of power cannot be reduced to an unimportant adjunct of capitalism; they have their own existence. He was very much aware, for example, that the French Communist Party was silent on the existence of the gulag (Foucault 1984, 53). That communist and capitalist regimes used similar systems of domination was at the heart of Foucault's analysis of how technologies of domination work in their own terms.

Foucault wanted to show how human beings are created as subjects through three "modes of objectification" (Rabinow 1984b, 7–11). First, Foucault identified the "dividing practices" that separate the "criminal," the "mad," "deviants," and the "ill" from "respectable" society. Second, he identified the methods of scientific classification that organize society and privilege or disqualify ways of thinking about it, objectifying the subject into, for example, a laborer or a lawyer, powerful or weak, and organize knowledge through language. Third, Foucault described subjectification: how the divided and classified subject created her identity as, say, a woman, as gay, as a worker. His sympathies were with those in the "borderlands," unconstrained and unclassified, and he wanted to value their ways of looking at the world rather than pronounce on whether they were right or wrong.

These structuring discourses work so well, for Foucault, precisely because they are portrayed not as systems of domination, but as common sense. The phenomena or the ways of thinking about phenomena that emerged are portrayed as the ones that always would emerge, probably as they were the best ideas or most effective phenomena. Science, technology, and rationality are deployed as apolitical organizational mechanisms for complex societies. Alternatively, eminently challengeable phenomena are naturalized: "That's the way it's always been, isn't it obvious?" Criminals need to be punished so good people are safe; the mentally ill or those with "deviant" sexualities need to be cured so they are "happy." The limits of what is criticizable are thus set, what is commonsense defined, and the language we use to define it is set in ways that benefit the powerful (De Goede 2005, 9). Whole areas of life are depoliticized, removed from debate by all but cranks.

Because systems of domination are discourses that are constructed such that they act in ways that we feel are unchallengeable, the contingent nature of the process whereby these dominating discourses were constructed is obscured. Not all of these systems were established as part of a big, predestined plan: other routes could have been taken, other battles against domination fought on their own terms, with wildly different outcomes. History is not smooth and continuous transformation. Rather, at times it advances rapidly, while at others there are sharp discontinuities: nothing is set, nothing inevitable (Foucault 1984, 54). For Foucault, the key issue is that examining the origins and construction of human subjects categorized by discourses of criminality, illness, or sexuality in their own terms and in their historical context might identify other roads that could have been taken. For Foucault, "the real political task in a society such as ours is to criticize the working of institutions which appear to be neutral and independent, to criticise them in such a manner that the political violence that has always exercised itself obscurely through them will be unmasked, so that we can fight them" (quoted by Rabinow 1984b, 6). Foucault, therefore, wanted to value "autonomous, non-centralised kind(s) of theoretical production . . . whose validity is not dependent on the approval of the established regimes of thought" (Foucault 1980, 81). If we were to take this Foucauldian approach rather than labeling money reformers a priori as cranks who do not see the big picture or as crooks selling us snake oil, it would valorize heterogeneity above totalizing thought by valuing and illuminating hidden, dominated, antirational discourses that subvert dominant hegemony. Foucault sought to value even "knowledges that have been disqualified as inadequate to their task or insufficiently elaborated: native knowledges located low down on the hierarchy . . . even directly disqualified knowledges" such as those of the "mad" (1980, 82). This concern with the other, the hidden, the marginal is for critics like Harvey (1992, 47–48) "the most liberative and therefore the most appealing aspect of postmodern thought . . . [against] the imperialism of an enlightened modernity that presumed to speak for others . . . with a unified voice." Looking at subaltern views on money might illuminate other paths to take.

Following Foucault, we can therefore also analyze money as a phenomenon that has its own claims of truth and modes of power and gives rise to processes of subject formation (Rabinow 1984a, 386) whereby subjects construct themselves and their economic life through the money they create. That is not to say that money is completely disconnected from politics, economics, or society; that would obviously be absurd. But it is to investigate the extent to which money forms a "local" system of domination that, while contributing to wider systems of domination, also operates within its own forms of logic and local practices. Taking this approach to money would be to write a genealogy of finance following Foucault's historical work on criminality, sexuality, and mental health (see De Goede 2005). The problem with writing a genealogy, however, and with the general tone of Foucault's work, would be to see society as a spider's web of domination characterized by all-powerful systems of control, discipline, and surveillance (Best and Kellner 1991, 96–97). Power would be seen as an all-inclusive "capillary" flow (Gledhill 1994, 150), and it seems that whichever way we struggle we remain caught, like a fly in a spider's web. Focusing on phenomena as systems of domination in their own right could too quickly lead to a pessimistic view on the extent to which these power relations could be challenged, and Foucault consequently ended up refusing to offer prescriptions for challenging them—arguing at one point, "I am not going to fall into the trap of offering solutions" (Best and Kellner 1990, 96–97), and at another refusing to "imagin[e] an ideal social model for the functioning of our scientific or technological society" (Rabinow 1984b, 5). That is fine: Foucault wanted to study power and did not want to provide the sort of metanarrative, total solutions advanced by his former comrades in the French Communist Party. He wanted to historicize and contextualize all claims for abstract or universal truths, including utopian claims.

But the problem remains: Foucault uncovers discourses of power "so we can fight them" but does not show us how, beyond a highly individualistic strategy of subject formation focused on the body. Given Foucault's sexuality, the context of the emergence of the gay liberation movement uncovering and challenging discourses of domination around sexuality, and Foucault's location in San Francisco in the years when he moved from an analysis of domination to an analysis of subject formation, a focus on the body as a site from which liberartory politics can be developed is highly appropriate. But subjectification must not become a new metanarrative. Outside struggles in which the body is central, it has less micropolitical effectiveness. We must also remember that the gay liberation movement also deployed far more collective forms of political action, such as Stonewall and gay pride festivals, while the rise of AIDS made a focus on unconstrained sexual exploration and expression a biologically untenable strategy in and of itself, with awful consequences for some of its protagonists (including Foucault himself). Consequently, the gay liberation movement today focuses more on inclusion, equal rights, and collective organization than on the right to present and use the body as the subject sees fit, although the presentation of the body and consumption choices continue to form a vibrant part of gay politics.

A second problem with a genealogical approach is that while it is right to see that the systems of domination Foucault analyzes had their own rationality and that precapitalist and communist systems also used them, in the context of a resurgent neoliberalism (which Foucault did not live to see, dying as he did in 1984), we do need to pay more attention to how capitalist systems of rationality are enforced. Foucault never insisted that the modes of objectification he examined were unconnected from capitalism, and certainly capitalism has operated effectively with very different attitudes toward how the "mad" are conceptualized and disciplined, with the "dysfunctional genius dot-com entrepreneur" replacing the desiccated, rational IBM company man (Frank 2002), "care in the community" replacing the great confinement, and closed-circuit television becoming a new confinement. Capitalism no longer requires women to undertake privatized child care and unpaid household work and has no problem with an entrepreneur's sexuality. But other systems of domination are constitutive of capitalism: for example, forms of remuneration, conditions of work, and prices of commodities. Foucault recognized this, but the economy or capitalism was never central to his analysis. I would make it more central given that the alternative currency systems under investigation in this book do engage with the construction of markets and exchange relationships.

The alternative is that, while attention to the "other" is valuable, in uncritical advocacy of such microstruggles there is a danger of over-emphasizing exceptionalism and valorizing the "different" that can be little more than a "naive" (Boyte and Rattansi 1990, 39) or "*laissez-faire* 'anything goes' market eclecticism" (Harvey 1992, 42). A purely local conception of power as an anonymous and impersonal grid can be a poor guide to political action. Foucault points to the existence of universal power relations without identifying the strong and weak parts of the power grid, and fails to explain why, if power is so omnipotent, resistance arises (Callinicos 1989, 83). In this book I therefore want to ask if Foucault's way of looking at things, with money as a system of domination in its own right and a challengeable structuring discourse rather than as part of the structure of capitalist domination, helps us identify more liberatory forms of political action. The jury is still out: Foucault provides a hypothesis, not an epistemology to be accepted a priori, then later applied to money through a genealogical investigation. I also want to spend more time on resistance than on domination. Consequently, a second Foucauldian contribution to this analysis will be that of micropolitics.

Micropolitical Resistance

A micropolitical analysis of alternative forms of money would be founded on a Foucauldian understanding of money as a local system of domination, alongside many others, in which we are trapped *but which we also resist.* Money is a structuring but constructed discourse that we may be able to challenge locally. Multiple systems of domination mean that there is also the possibility of multiple challenges to power relations in which the logic of local systems of domination is first made visible, and then creative micropolitical technologies are developed that combat the particular ways in which these local power systems manifest themselves (Callinicos 1989, 84). Foucault argued that "where there is power, there is resistance" (Foucault 1998, 94–96), but also that it is not possible to escape from power or be outside it. Because power is not just domination, but ways that phenomena and ways of understanding are shaped and formed, we cannot escape its effects. The effects of power are everywhere, but, consequently, so is resistance to it. But this resistance is in the form not of one "great refusal, no soul of revolt, source of all rebellions." Rather, there is "a plurality of resistances, each of them a special case: resistances that are possible, necessary, improbable; others that are savage, solitary, concerted, rampant, or violent; still others that are quick to compromise, interested, or sacrificial" (Foucault 1998, 96). Occasionally there are radical ruptures, "but more often, one is dealing with mobile and transitionary points of resistance, producing cleavages in society that shift about, fracturing unities and effecting regroupings, furrowing across individuals themselves, cutting them up and remoulding them . . . the swarm of points of resistance transverses across social stratifications and individual unities" (Foucault 1998, 96).

Taking Foucault's work on resistance further is the concept of "heterotopia," or the coexistence of an "impossible space," of a large number of "fragmentary possible worlds" existing in the same space simultaneously (Harvey 1992, 48). Rather than conceptualizing political challenge as attempts to produce any single metanarrative or recipe for a more perfect organization of society, heterotopia engages with an understanding that there may be many visions of and aspirations to the "good life" that are contradictory, mutually exclusive, or unsustainable in the long term. Liberatory politics should be happy with this: surely, in an age where religion has not withered away in the face of modernism; where some prefer decentralization, others centralization; where some have faith in technology while others are skeptical; where some prefer the urban, others the rural; and where sexuality is seen more as a spectrum than as something binary, we no longer believe in any one, unified conception of utopia. The concept of heterotopia engages with this. Here heterotopia is a multiple space in which different political relationships can exist side by side, neither privileged nor any less or more real in a hetero(geneous ut)opia. Heterotopia might be a resistant space that operates for a sustainable length of time or across a significant space by means of changed rules, but without superseding capitalism or imposing its values on other heterotopian spaces. Heterotopia might then mean the existence of multiple temporal, lasting alternative spaces existing alongside each other, living by different rules, but not able to impose their values more widely. Heterotopia might also be a fleeting or purely cognitive heterotopia operating as what Bey (1991) called a "temporary autonomous zone," a momentary effervescence, a fleeting liberation, effective only "below the threshold where the systematic imperatives of power and money become so dominant" (White, quoted by Harvey 1993, 54). Finally, it might be a "utopian space," a declaration of resistance to money power, a vision of an alternative, unrealizable yet inspiring "mobilising utopia."

Again, there are limits to the heterotopian approach. Foucault focused on heterotopias both as a way of avoiding a focus on meta-narratives and because he saw power ascending from individual bodies rather than descending from structures (Foucault 1980, 98), and thus he held that we can best understand and change power locally (Best and Kellner 1990, 57). He concentrated on the processes of subject formation (Foucault 1980, 97) and focused on the body as the site where repression is centered and therefore as the site most appropriate to break from systems of domination, arguing for people to "resist what we are" (Foucault 1982, 216) and to "recreate yourself as work of art" (Foucault 1982, 237). The problem is that Foucault unfortunately left his analysis of power there and did not go on to develop any understanding either of resistance (Best and Kellner 1990, 69) or of the circumstances in which resistance might be successful, areas that were as theoretically rich as his studies of domination. In developing conceptions of microresistance to local systems of domination, we consequently need to go beyond Foucault.

Deleuze and Guattari shared Foucault's concerns with otherness, micropolitics, and difference, but as active political militants they went past Foucault's stress on domination to the identification of creative "lines of flight" (Best and Kellner 1990, 96–97), to what they called positive reterritorializations of unconstrained and undominated territory through creative local political action (Callinicos 1989, 84; Best and Kellner 1990, 101). They emphasized innovation and the ability of political actors to create their future over resistance to preexisting and constraining power relations. Therefore, unlike Foucault, they did not reject the need for macro-level challenges,

arguing for macro and micro political struggles to go on simultaneously while challenging Foucauldian "phobias of the macro" or Marxist distinctions between the "center" (the real economy) and the
margins (ephemeral micropolitical protests) (Best and Kellner 1990,
94–95). In collaboration with the Italian autonomist Antonio Negri,
Guattari called for "a thousand machines of art, life and solidarity to
sweep away the stupid and sclerotic arrogance of the old organisa-
tions!" (quoted in Best and Kellner 1990, 93).

Finally, Deleuze and Guattari added to Foucault's conception of
power by arguing that "power centres are defined much more by what
escapes them or by their impotence than by their zone of power" (Deleuze and Guattari 1987, 217). They believed that there are just as many
free, unterritorialized spaces that innovative political action can re-
territorialize and that there are "multiple lines of flight" that can be
followed in a quest for the development of new strategies and organizations that do not re-create the dominations of capitalism. All social
systems, they argued, "leak in all directions," and they promoted what
Best and Kellner (1990, 103) call a "postmodern 'warfare'" in which
political actors seek to "liberate difference and intensities from the
grip of the state machine." They advocated following these lines of
flight, these leakages away from social structure and power fields, by
learning from nomadic tribes such as Genghis Khan's Mongols, who
resisted attempts by states to control them (Best and Kellner 1990,
102). This they called "*Nomadism.*"

A second set of conceptions that help us develop ideas of micropolitical resistances come from James C. Scott's work on subaltern resistances (Scott 1985, 1990). Scott conceptualized microresistance as
practices whereby local systems of domination are resisted by those
who do not feel powerful enough to smash them entirely. Micropolitical resistance may be material, such as taking grain from the merchant's store, poaching from the landlord's newly enclosed woods,
engaging in strikes and slowdowns, producing poor-quality work,
overcharging or underpaying, or avoiding paying taxes; or it may be
found in symbolic forms, such as refusing to be deferent, assuming a
resistant demeanor behind the backs of the powerful, or using inappropriate or disrespectful language. Scott argued that every system
of domination or appropriation has its own ritual of subordination,
and microresistance is therefore a set of down-to-earth, low-profile

material stratagems designed to resist specific forms of local domination and minimize appropriation. In this conception, micropolitics as the "weapon of the weak" is less utopian than approaches that look for total, perhaps unattainable or unrealizable solutions and Marxist approaches to social change as fundamental transformation becomes the real utopianism. This is something that the weak feel is beyond them. Here, alternative money schemes could be seen as weapons for the weak to use to overcome particular facets of day-to-day domination through, for example, producing alternatives to paid employment or clientelist political practices, or they may be a way for people who do not believe that wider systemic changes are viable to make smaller, day-to-day changes that nonetheless have significant material effects in challenging discourses of domination.

The use of alternative forms of money as micropolitical resistances can be seen as a creative effervescence, as a technology of liberation, rather than as a defensive resistance to a Foucauldian system of overarching domination. A micropolitical analysis would be founded on an understanding of the possibility of the existence of multiple challenges to power relations, with money seen as one facet of the power relations that underpin a capitalism that is to some extent, as Lapavitsas (2003) has shown, a socially mediated and constructed discourse of domination. It would emphasize the proactive creativity and dynamism of political action. Before we begin this task, we should first engage a number of critiques of the micropolitical approach.

First, if no normative statements about what is and is not acceptable behavior are made, an uncritical acceptance of "difference" and "resistance" as of value in and of themselves, without any analysis of what *difference* or *resistance* means, can lead to the valorization of reactionary resistances, such as racist or antiabortion mobilization, or a failure to think through the challenges of movements such as Sendero Luminoso or Islamic fundamentalism, whose praxis might be "problematic" for Western audiences. As we shall see later, some political action around money reform degenerated into anti-Semitism. Is this to be lauded as resistance? No, it must be condemned. Foucault was particularly uncritical of the concept of resistance without developing what he held to be successful or unsuccessful resistance. His rejection of all metanarratives means that the reasons for change get lost in a nihilistic inability to defend the need for change or to identify what the mechanics of change might be. Outside his chosen genealogies Foucault failed to think through the complexities of structure and agency, how the macro and micro levels of domination and resistance that he focused on reinforce and support each other (Best and Kellner 1991, 69). His overemphasis on local struggles therefore disconnects them from macro-level processes such as the operation of the state or of capitalism (Crooke 1990, 59). Callinicos (1989, 83), from a Marxist tradition, asked if local knowledges are any different from local variants of a single "other" opposed to the prevailing apparatus of power, part of a wider, unified, and coherent challenge to the prevailing orthodoxy. Foucault condemned large-scale mobilizations for radical political change as totalizing metanarratives, and thus provided no guide as to when the "old order" collapses, such as the 1989 wave of East European revolutions. Consequently, Foucault heard subaltern voices but denied them the chance to find allies, failed to examine the building of political organizations to struggle against power relations (Boyne and Rattansi 1990, 37), and offered political solutions that were individualistic to the extreme (Best and Kellner 1991, 70). In failing to address problems of building collectivities, Foucault, almost certainly unintentionally, ensured that the strong dominate by a prescription against the drawing of resistant voices into wider, perhaps more powerful, formations:

> While it opens up a radical prospect by acknowledging the authenticity of other voices . . . postmodernism immediately shuts off those other voices from access to more universal sources of power by ghettoising them with an opaque otherness, the specificity of this or that language game. It therefore disempowers those voices . . . in a world of lop-sided power relations. . . . It avoids confronting the realities of political economy and the circumstances of global power. (Harvey 1992, 117)

This results in the disempowering of the very voices Foucault hoped to amplify and has the effect of stressing domination over resistance. It fails to identify which strategies for overthrowing or resisting power relations might be locally effective "militant particularisms" (Harvey 2001) that need the construction of wider conceptions of social change and of solidarity among distant others at the macro level to be fully effective. Foucault therefore effectively set up the thing he most hated, a metanarrative that reifies domination over resistance and defines subaltern communities purely in terms of power relations, rather than letting them speak with their own voices as political actors (Gledhill 1994, 147).

From Foucault we therefore take a recognition of "non-class sites of domination" (Harvey 1992, 40) and the possibility of more creative endeavors such as the construction of noncapitalist markets, noncapitalist practices, and alternative forms of subaltern-created money without wishing to cut micropolitical approaches off from wider metanarrative approaches. Understanding that there might be micropolitical noncapitalist practices that have liberatory potential does not mean that "capitalism" can be wished away in a puff of poststructuralist smoke as a structuring discourse rather than as a structural form of domination existing beyond the limits of individual human perception and ability to challenge. Besides, as Gledhill (1994, 123–50) cautions, the unproblematic valorization of local struggles and of interesting "others" is inadequate without grounded research iden rifying the nature of the resistance and the domination it opposes, along with an understanding of the capacity of the actors to, in Marx's evocative term, "make history." A micropolitical analysis of political action around money must engage the objections previously raised through grounded analysis of its performance in real political environments. Grounded analysis of the creativity of alternative forms of money as nomadic micropolitics will uncover the capacity they have to make the changes they seek to make. Analysis would therefore be of the extent to which alternative money programs illuminate local power circulations and are an effective means of local struggle against this local power, valid on its own terms (inspired by Deleuze and Guatarri's nomadic approach), as opposed to Foucault's more pessimistic conceptualization of political action as defensive resistance to all powerful systems of domination. They may be one of Guattari and Negri's "thousand machines of art, life and solidarity."

This analysis is the task for this book, where we shall examine movements that have developed alternative forms of money, from Owenism in early nineteenth-century England through populist farmer radicalism in the United States and from the use of European stamp scrip between the wars and Social Credit in Canada and New Zealand through the contemporary alternative money "movement" in the United Kingdom, Hungary, New Zealand, and Argentina. In each case we shall examine the hypothesis that what those developing these alternative systems have been doing can best be thought of as engaging in a micropolitical struggle against money thought of as an autonomous system of domination. The question we shall examine is the extent to which their political strategy might or might not open up new forms of liberatory potential.

Utopians, Anarchists, and Populists

THE POLITICS OF MONEY IN THE NINETEENTH CENTURY

———

IDENTIFYING MOVEMENTS FOR MONEY REFORM CAN BE TRICKY. Individuals, theorists, and gurus have developed arguments about money, but here we limit analysis to where we can identify collective actors who have developed resistant conceptions of money and, more important, attempted to act on them. We leave out academics who have theorized, politicians who have legislated, central bankers who have governed, or gurus who have fulminated (but without attracting some measure of collective support) unless we are discussing the impact they had on collective action for new forms of money.[1] Focusing on arguments about money has its problems, for such arguments cannot easily be disentangled from the wider economic and political value systems of which they are a part. This review will consequently focus on those who have made claims about the need for alternative forms of money in the nineteenth and twentieth centuries and their success or otherwise in putting them into practice, necessarily assuming that the reader has a wider understanding of the politics of these wider movements. In this chapter we consider the nineteenth-century movements, while chapter 4 covers the twentieth century up to the emergence of the current wave of resistant monetary innovation in the 1990s and the first years of the twenty-first century.

Resistant conceptions of money are also interconnected with

wider debates about finance, forms of credit, and banking; about the nature of and value of work; and about the nature of connections between labor, value, and money. Any review must be linked to these arguments, but cannot hope to do them justice. We consequently take a wide approach to what constitutes "money" as a tool or institution, more properly discussing what Ingham (2004, 60–74) calls the more generic quality of "moneyness," how what is thought of as money performs the tasks and roles ascribed to it. We explicitly reject a rather sterile analysis of whether the resistant forms of money that have historically been generated are really money or a tool that performs the "softer" tasks of money (as a means of exchange or measure of value) but is less able to perform "harder" functions of money (as a store of value or a means of settling debts, particularly those to the state). The test will be of the liberatory potential of the generation of new money forms, not whether they fit any checklist of what constitutes money.

Utopian Socialism: Fourier, Owenism, and Proudhon's Bank of the People

Arguments about money emerged alongside and in resistance to the development of capitalism within the emergence of socialist thought. The utopian socialists Fourier, Saint-Simon, and Blanc called for liberated forms of work facilitated by free credit. For example, in his extraordinarily detailed account of the future ideal form of society, the beehivelike Phalanstery, Fourier argued for work to be organized at a daily "exchange," held at nightfall, where "every individual must go . . . to arrange his work and pleasure sessions for the following days. It is there he makes plans concerning his gastronomic and amorous meetings and, especially, his work sessions in the shops and fields. Everyone has at least twenty sessions to arrange, since he makes definite plans for the following day and tentative ones for the day after" (Fourier 1971, 253–55). Remuneration would be through the issuance of (1728) exchangeable shares, backed by the property of the Phalanx, to supplement wages paid in proportion to a worker's contribution in capital, work, and talent. Four classes of food would be provided communally, with minimum standards guaranteed.

Blanc (1840/1975) argued for "the principle of association and the organisation of work according to the rules of reason, justice and humanity" through social workshops for workers "who offer guarantees of morality" and are paid wages according to a hierarchy of functions, with the wages at least guaranteeing the livelihood of the worker. The hierarchy of functions would be organized by the workers themselves, while profit would be distributed to the workers, to the old and sick, and for capital investment, in proportions of one-third each. Capitalists could invest in the social workshops, which, Blanc argued, would inevitably supersede private enterprise due to their superior organization. Credit would be provided by the state, redistributing a share of the social workshops and thus usurping the role of banks. Blanc argued:

> What should credit be? A means of furnishing the instruments of work to the worker. Today . . . credit is something entirely different. The banks lend only to the rich. If they wished to lend to the poor, they could not do so without running to ruin. The banks established from the individual point of view could never be other than they are, an admirably conceived procedure for making the rich richer and the powerful more powerful. Always monopoly under the appearance of liberty, always tyranny under the guise of progress! The proposed organisation would cut short so many iniquities. This share of profits, especially and invariably devoted to the expansion of the social workshop by the recruitment of workers—that is credit. Now do you need banks? Suppress them. (Blanc 1840/1975, 76–77)

Critiques of banking and arguments for socialized credit and for equitable remuneration and the socialized management of work were central to the utopian prescriptions. Small-scale communities would remunerate work with shares based on labor time. But these were proposals only.

Robert Owen developed the first practical examples of alternative currencies as a political challenge. Inspired by the French socialists, Owen argued that the source of all value was labor. In his *New View of Society* he argued: "Those who have reflected on the nature of public revenue, and who possess minds capable of comprehending the subject, know that revenue has but one legitimate source, that it is derived directly or indirectly from the labour of man, and that it may be more or less from any given number of men (other circumstances being similar), in proportion to their strength, industry, and capacity" (Owen 1816). Among the many social reforms Owen advocated was the adoption of money denominated in hours of labor. In 1820 he produced a report proposing the alleviation of poverty through labor notes, issued labor tickets in his New Lanark Mill, and used labor notes to underpin the Fourier-inspired cooperative communities he funded in the United States, such as New Harmony (Donnachie 2000, 259).

In the 1820s, at the same time that Owen was working with intentional communities in the United States, in the United Kingdom the cooperative movement was emerging in Rochdale. By the 1830s, the cooperative societies were more than grocery stores selling goods at a fair price and distributing the profits to members: they organized propaganda, raised funds to establish intentional communities, and acted as networks in which artisans in the same trade who wished to cooperate could pool small amounts of capital to provide employment in hard times for their members. It was emphasized that each would receive just reward for his labor. At first these associations could trade locally, but after a while they found they needed a mechanism to exchange with other like-minded cooperative associations, perhaps ones producing different goods. In 1830 the forty or so cooperative societies in London established an Exchange Bazaar, with others following in Liverpool and Birmingham.

While the early cooperatives had emphasized fair prices and the redistribution of profits, the idea that the only true source of value was labor (and the labor of the working classes at that) had grown, so the bazaars, or exchanges, decided to make time the unit of wealth. Owen's newspaper for the cooperative movement, *The Crisis,* argued: "All wealth proceeds from labour and knowledge. And labour and knowledge are generally remunerated according to time employed. Hence it is proposed to make time the standard or measure of wealth" (Podmore 1903/1966, 406). The exchanges, therefore, issued labor notes, while prices were calculated using a formula that took into account the cost of materials and labor priced in cash, divided by an average daily rate that was set at ten hours at the rate of 6 pence per hour (Cole 1925/1965, 263). By 1832, four to five hundred cooperatives had been established across the country, and on this wave of cooperative fervor Owen set up his famous National Equitable Labour Exchange on an informal basis in the rather splendid premises on Gray's Inn Road, London, from which he published *The Crisis.*

The exchanges were, for a time, very successful, turning over twelve thousand to fourteen thousand labor notes a week (Podmore 1903/1966, 403). Jones (1890, 32) argued that the doors of the bazaar often needed to be closed, given the crush of traders. Owen addressed mass meetings in which he exhorted the "non-industrious classes" (shopkeepers, distributors) to cross the bridge into a better world before it was too late. However, the failure to put the Gray's Inn premises on a firm financial footing eventually came back to haunt the exchange when the landlord, an admirer of Owen who had been willing to forego rent for a limited period, on seeing the quantity of business conducted, demanded rent in amounts Owen thought excessive. In January 1833 the exchange was evicted and moved to new premises, moving again in May. The cooperative societies that traded through the bazaar took control from an increasingly diverted Owen, who had met many trade unionists through the exchanges and was increasingly asked to speak at their meetings. From Owen's perspective, the spectacular growth of cooperatives and the overnight success of the exchanges, the crisis associated with the 1832 Great Reform Act, and a massive growth of social struggles for trade union rights meant that the new cooperative millennium was dawning and everyday problems could wait.

Through 1833 the exchanges seemed to be working well, but by the beginning of 1834 business dropped off to 5,000 hours a week (down from 14,000 at the beginning), but with the exchanges holding unsold stock valued at 55,000 hours and only 23,000 hours in circulation. Goods could be produced in return for labor notes, but could the income be spent? Did the exchanges end up holding lots of poorly produced, unsellable stock? It seems that the answer to each of these questions was no. By March 1834, some 2,300 hours were in circulation, but now with only 8,000 hours of unsold stock; the business was saved from bankruptcy by receipts from festivals and Owen's lectures. The last evidence we have on the exchanges is a letter written to Owen in June 1834 recommending that, because the investors in the exchange had lost £500, the labor notes be called in and the debt paid off over time. We do not know what happened after that. We do know that by 1834 Owen, who as a former factory owner was probably never fully committed to labor notes, was wholeheartedly focusing on large-scale changes in society through trade union struggle. Cole (1925/1965, 266) argued that the other exchanges quickly came "crashing down," although Podmore claimed that the Birmingham

Exchange traded successfully for a year in 1833/34 before being wound up due to lack of support, but with an operating surplus of £8 that was given to the Birmingham General Hospital.

Why did the exchanges not succeed? Was it the result of local conditions (perhaps errors were made in the way they were organized that might have been corrected in a different environment), or were the problems more fundamental (perhaps labor notes were a flawed concept)? Certainly the way the exchanges were set up was less than perfect, reflecting the fevered political and economic conditions of nineteenth-century London, characterized by mass unemployment and destitution, mass social struggles around Chartism and the Great Reform Act of 1832, and the political repression of the post–Napoleonic War period that Polanyi associated with the construction of capitalism. This was only fifteen years after Peterloo. Jones (1890, 29) argued that the exchanges were established hastily with little planning and were seriously undercapitalized. This may have been a result of disputes between Owen and the wider cooperative movement over the planning of the bazaars reported by Moreton (1969, 50). Moreton argued that Owen believed that what was required was a large-scale, well-funded operation run by himself (the only one with the skills necessary) and funded by the stock exchange, while others in the cooperative movement preferred small-scale experiments, working from the bottom up. Owen believed that working-class people with few resources would be unlikely to generate the capital required to establish viable cooperatives and exchanges, but as a rather autocratic factory boss he was unused to persuading the fiercely independent London artisans toughened by decades of struggle of the strength of his ideas. Where he could not command, he failed to persuade. He may have suspended his concerns based on a conviction that because the new cooperative dawn was nigh, details could wait. Against this, Podmore pointed out that Owen later argued that he had not supported establishing an exchange at the time and in the manner suggested, but had been forced to act by "impatient friends who were not sufficiently experienced or farsighted enough to realise that long and careful preparation was needed to ensure the success of such an enterprise" (Podmore 1903/1966, 422). This may be an understandable post hoc rationalization; given the ferment of the time, Owen would have seemed curmudgeonly and sectarian for standing aside.

Either way, the result of these disagreements was that a plan to levy £30 on each local cooperative society to establish new cooperatives and exchanges, passed at an 1830 conference, produced only a few pounds, and the necessary funds were not raised. Owen had to rely on his own finances, and he had by this time spent most of his own money on his intentional communities in the United States. Owen's ability to alienate also became a problem once the London exchange had been established; on his return from the United States, he gave a series of Sunday morning lectures in which he voiced such uncompromising atheism that a significant number of traders left the exchange. The theme of a charismatic but autocratic leader committed to large-scale plans failing to convince grassroots followers committed to organic plans is one that recurs in the alternative currency movement, as is that of the inability of poor people to put cooperation into practice given limited resources.

As a result of this undercapitalization, the exchanges were vulnerable. Not only were they unable to pay the rent for the grandiose property in which the London Exchange was based; the costs of exchanging labor notes that could not be spent as cash on goods proved to be greater than expected, and many people who worked administering the exchange found it impossible to live on labor notes alone. They required some payment in cash in order to pay for staples not available for labor notes, and cash was scarce. Jones (1890, 36) also argued that a lack of capital meant that the bazaars were casual, unincorporated institutions, which made them vulnerable to eviction, and unable to defend their name against others who established bazaars without the ethical stance of Owen and his supporters. Jones says such bazaars were widespread and resulted in serious fraud. Limited funds and poor planning meant that administration was poor and there was too little regulation of trading custom and practice, resulting in frequent disputes between traders unaccustomed to dealing with unfamiliar units of value, such as time. Podmore argued that local magistrates refused to adjudicate claims because the exchanges were unincorporated and labor notes were not regarded as legal tender.

A fundamental problem seems to have been gender. William Lovett identified "the prejudice of the members' wives against the stores": "Whether it was their love of shopping, or their dislike that their husbands should know the exact nature of their dealings, which were booked against them, I know not, but certain it was that they often left the unadulterated and genuine article in search of what was often questionable" (quoted by Podmore 1903/1966, 424). He also claimed that women did not like being confined to one shop for their purchases. This seems a resolvable issue: it is not surprising that the women would resist male surveillance of how they spend their money, a phenomenon that is not restricted to the use of alternative currencies. Zelizer (1997) provides myriad examples of women's struggles to achieve and maintain control of their own money and how family budgets are spent. She identifies ways in which women put away small sums of money for their own purposes or just to survive in case a male breadwinner did not pass on enough money to feed and clothe the family. Labor notes reflected the household economies of patriarchal artisan households of the time. They were organized by male artisans in the interest of male artisans relying on the unpaid reproductive labor of their wives supporting them. They generally circulated between craftsmen, but daily staples were not available in the same variety. If the exchanges had grown, especially out of the Gray's Inn premises, which appear to have been close to Bentham's panopticon, women would no doubt have been able to find a variety of places to shop where their consumption choices, especially for food, were not observed by men. Besides, because the artisans were usually men, women did not have access to their own supply of labor notes, but relied on their husbands for them. But there is nothing about time-based currency that means it cannot be used to value work done by women; in fact, as we shall see later, it can often be a better indicator of work done by women than cash. Labor notes reflected the patriarchal relations of early nineteenth-century London, and the problems of gender justice there.

If gender was not an unsurmountable problem, Moreton (1969, 48) argued that a crucial failing of the exchanges was that although there was some estimation of the market valuation of a laborer's time in coming to a price, the bazaars accepted the artisan's own estimate of the time taken to make an item. Consequently, there was no attempt to differentiate between more and less efficient forms of production, so the moral or political decision to assign an hourly rate based on an average between high and low pay did not work well in practice. Therefore, some items were valued over market valuations and some under, with the result that overvalued goods accumulated at the store. In contrast, Podmore argued that the London Exchange was reducing its store of uncirculated goods; the fundamental problem was a general lack of interest in the concept of exchanging based on the time of the artisans. Suffering from a lack of support, the exchanges were closed. This suggests that the problem was not that the exchanges could not work, but that they were unattractive.

Jones (1890) argued that there were two crucial faults with the exchanges. First, there was no means to provide workers with capital to get started. The poorest had nothing to exchange, so were excluded. In addition to the artisan's skills and time, food and raw materials should have been provided if the exchanges were to meet the needs of the many destitute of the time. In particular, a lack of availability of food, coupled with the propensity of food vendors outside the exchanges to discount labor notes heavily, meant that the notes could not meet basic needs and that the purchasing power of labor notes was disadvantaged in comparison with cash. This phenomenon, the poor purchasing power of poor people, is a recurring issue. The failure to provide up-front food and raw materials is another facet of the underfunded nature of the exchanges. Of course the lack of food supply was compounded by the resistance of women to buying food under a male gaze, as discussed earlier. This does seem to have been a fundamental problem, but perhaps one that could have been solved with more planning, although again we come up against the limits of ordinary people to provide for themselves, excluded from access to resources.

Second, Jones points to the vigor of the attacks on the bazaars by political enemies, despite Owen's claim that the exchanges threatened no entrenched interests. This was probably because powerful groups understood that Owen saw the exchanges as but a step to freer economic relations, something he argued for in *The Crisis*. Political attacks on the exchanges as communistic and atheistic in the context of the political repression of 1830s London probably had something to do with dramatic fall-off in the levels of trading, while those committed to organizing exchanges concentrated on less threatening forms of cooperation, fair exchange, and social change through self-help, such as the cooperative trading shops, the building societies, and other mutual aid and benevolent societies. Others were radicalized and became involved in political action aimed at changes at the macro level, such as trade unionism and Chartism.

Outside the United Kingdom, the labor note concept continued to be popular in anarchist circles. In the 1850s, Josiah Warren ran a time bank for three years in Cincinnati, and later set up two intentional communities in America (Modern Times and Utopia), which traded labor notes (Woodcock 1963, 391; Kantor 1972, 6). They both lasted twenty years. In the 1840s, Proudhon developed ideas of mutual exchange based on labor theories of value from local experiments into a fully-fledged proposal for the organization of society with his proposals for a Bank of the People. Rejecting an economy where, seemingly by accident, some received much higher remuneration for their work than others, irrespective of the quality of the work done (with a skillful cleaner receiving much less than a lazy or inefficient lawyer), Proudhon wished to develop an economy based on the exchange of goods and services between free producers, which, he argued, would develop into one based on mutualism and real equality. He contrasted a strategy of building the mutual economy with the Marxist strategy of revolution, which he argued was "an appeal to force, to arbitrariness" (Proudhon to Marx, 1846, quoted by Woodcock 1963, 101).

Proudhon took part in the revolution of 1948, but believed that the revolutionaries had no conception of how to build a better society. In order for free association between producers to work, money and some form of credit would be required. Proudhon was critical of money based on precious metals, arguing that elite groups would inevitably control it in their own interests, so "whoever can get control of the specie of the world can rule the markets with despotic hand, and may work his will upon communities and nations" (Dana 1896). Similarly, elites would use interest to keep those to whom they had lent in peonage. To challenge this unjust system, he argued for credit- and money-issuing power to be in the hands of the "laboring classes." Credit and money should just facilitate exchange, not be a tool for capital accumulation. To facilitate this, a Bank of the People, composed of artisans, would issue democratically regulated credit on the principle of reciprocity or mutualism to meet social need, without speculation or interest (which Proudhon called usury).

Proudhon's banks would be confederations of fifty thousand to one hundred thousand free producers who would agree to issue exchange notes and guarantee their reciprocity. In 1848, as a deputy in the French Constituent Assembly, he agitated, unsuccessfully, for the Bank of France to be transformed into the Bank of the People, arguing that an interest rate of 2 to 3 percent would cover all the government's expenses, allowing taxation to be abolished. In this respect, his ideas were a panacea. Throughout the revolutionary year of 1848, Proudhon agitated daily for his bank, but because the reaction of 1849 saw the defeat of the revolution and the construction of the Bonapartist dictatorship, he ended up in prison for sedition. Although the bank was incorporated in January 1848, it never traded, and it was liquidated on Proudhon's arrest and incarceration. However, ideas for communal control of credit would reemerge in the Social Credit movement in the twentieth century, as well as in socialist demands for the nationalization of banks.

After Proudhon, the bulk of anarchist philosophy moved from the cooperative mutualism of Proudhon to the more violent terroristic or revolutionary approaches of Bakunin, while the politics of money reform became entangled with struggles against specie currency based on precious metals and for various forms of paper currency. The Chartist Birmingham Political Union called for the introduction of paper currency (Thompson 1981, 65–66) as did, on the other side of the class divide, the proto-Keynesian Birmingham School, which looked to free up money issuance to meet the interests of the growing manufacturing class. The Birmingham School argued that credit should be created to the point that "the general demand for labour, in all the great departments of industry, becomes permanently greater than its supply" (Thomas Attwood, quoted by Ingham 2004, 42).

In drawing lessons from the experiences of the utopians and anarchists, we need to draw on Marx and Engels's critique of the utopians (Engels 1968). As we saw in the introduction, they doubted that ordinary people had the resources they needed to create their own alternative economic relations. They also rejected the quick fix, the panacea of changing society by making a technical change in the money system. Recall that Marx thought that the money system is created to serve the needs of the accumulation system, not the other way around. Money is created to facilitate the efficient development of the capitalist system and is a reflection of the economy, not a factor in its creation. If we change the money system (the veil), we do not change the "real" economic system (Marx 1852/1974). Marx and Engels also argued that social change comes not from clever plans but from changes in productive forces, not "an accidental discovery of this or that brain, but the necessary outcome of the struggle between two historically developed classes — the proletariat and the bourgeoisie." If social change were so easy, Marx and Engels said, presumably we could have been saved the bother of having to go through the agonies of exploitation under capitalism. One clever soul, showing us the way a lot earlier, would have saved us a lot of trouble. Unfortunately, they argued that there are no shortcuts and society needs to develop its productive forces on a large scale before a new society can be born from the actions of the overwhelming majority of people (Engels 1968). The problem of seeing social change coming from quick technological fixes rather than from class struggle was that the utopians stressed persuading elites that their proposals amounted to a painless, apolitical change that would benefit all rather than an attack on entrenched class interests.

The liberal approach to social change at the heart of the utopian social change strategy can be delinked from that of building cooperation from below. Of course, if we restrict these innovations to small numbers of people attempting to persuade elites of the truth behind their proposals for new forms of money, Marx and Engels's argument holds true. But if large numbers of people are using alternative forms of money in their daily lives so that we can identify actual liberated real economies, the Marxist critique might have been right in regard to nineteenth century utopianism, but not in regard to the present. This remains a question for empirical investigation. Before we address it, we shall turn to a genuinely mass movement for alternative forms of money: the Populist movement.

Fighting "The Man": Farmer Radicalism in the United States

In times of crisis, financial rectitude becomes secondary to national survival. The American Revolution was funded by forty-two issues of $241 million in paper continental notes, which Franklin described as "a wonderful machine. It performs its office when we issue it: it pays and clothes Troops and provides Victuals and Ammunition; and when we are obliged to issue a quantity excessive, it pays itself off in depreciation" (quoted by Galbraith 1975, 68). Similarly, the American Civil War was fought and won through the "irresponsible" (in the conventional view) issuance of "greenbacks," some $450 million of green-inked paper money delinked from the gold standard. The experience was mixed. While "excessive issuance" did lead to inflation, paper money also allowed the Revolution and the Civil War to be financed (Galbraith 1975, 70, 71), a lesson not lost on those who argued that government issuance of paper money should continue.

The Greenback Party called for paper money to remain the currency of the United States at a time when, after wartime exigencies had passed, business and financial "gold bug" interests called for a return to the gold standard. They argued that an increasing money supply was needed to keep pace with population and economic growth and that hard money linked to specie was an unnecessary hindrance to prosperity (Goodwyn 1976, 14). The Greenbackers' substantive call was for democratic fiat money. Theirs was a chartalist call for money that was money because the government said it was money. By extension, Greenbackers argued, because the people elect the government, state-designated money was money to which the people had democratically given value: "We make our own money: we issue it, we control it" (Ingham 2004, 44). For Greenbackers, this was "the people's currency, elastic, cheap and inexportable, based on the real wealth of the country" (Goodwyn 1976, 14). In other words, Greenbackers saw paper money as a social construction, "a creation of law, a simple representation of value, and instrument of exchange, and not in any sense a commodity" (Goodwyn 1976, 371). Like Proudhon, they argued that money whose issuance was controlled by its relationship to gold meant that one financial class dominated others. They counterpoised this with another form of money, based solely on a social construction of value. Their gold bug opponents wanted the United States to withdraw greenbacks and immediately return to the gold standard from what they saw as an aberration from sound money. Few things troubled the nineteenth-century conservative mind more than revolutionary paper money (Galbraith 1975, 70).

The Greenbackers lost the debate after the war, for greenbacks were withdrawn slowly, while the overall money supply was not increased. The Greenback Party failed, partly because calls for financial reform were too abstract and did not speak to sectional interests, be these the interests of farmers or of workers (Goodwyn 1976, 17), while its leaders were effectively painted as fools and charlatans, widely derided by nicknames such as "calamity" so that it "drew no more than ridicule from respectable society" (Goodwyn 1976, 22). Money was further tightened when the silver dollar was withdrawn as a result of technological advances in the 1860s that significantly increased the silver supply (and thus lowered its price); meanwhile, until the discovery of the South African fields in the 1890s, gold was increasingly scarce, expensive, and thus "hard." In the "crime of '73," finance interests successfully demonetized relatively soft silver in favor of scarce, expensive, hard gold, thus keeping tight control of credit; all this was done in a bill that was not even subject to a vote in Congress. "Sound" money triumphed. Scarce money after 1873 saw a new agricultural recession as demand slackened, unemployment rose, and commodity prices collapsed. The United States rejoined the gold standard in 1879, although the needs of frontier societies for credit were to some extent met through what Galbraith called the "great compromise." Small, unregulated local banks, many of them fraudulent, were able to keep fairly lax credit polices to meet local conditions in the West, although hard money ruled the East.

Fifteen years later, a real money–based insurgency emerged in Populism, which was, until the early twenty-first century in Argentina, perhaps the only example of a mass movement organizing around forms of money and discourses on finance. In the war-ravaged and impoverished American South, where Confederate dollars were outlawed and vast areas had no financial infrastructure whatsoever, subsistence farmers increasingly had to rely on the lien credit system. Food and other household necessities would be advanced by what creditors called a furnishing man, often truncated to "The Man," later an all-encompassing symbol of authority. The brutalizing micropolitics of the relationship between the poor farmer and The Man are important:

> Acted out at a thousand merchant counters in the American South after the Civil War, these scenes were so ubiquitous that to describe one is to describe them all. The farmer, his eyes downcast and his hat sometimes literally in his hand, approached the merchant with a list of his needs. The man behind the counter consulted his ledger, and after a mumbled exchange moved to his shelves to select the goods that would satisfy at

least a part of his customer's wants. Rarely did the farmer receive the
full range or even the full quantity of one item he requested. No money
changed hands; the merchant merely made brief notations in his ledger.
Two weeks or a month later, the farmer would return, the consultation
with the ledger would recur, the mumbled exchange and careful selection
of goods would ensue, and new additions would be added to the ledger.
(Goodwyn 1976, 26)

These marked-up goods would be furnished on credit in exchange for
a "lien" on the farmer's expected crop, at exploitative interest rates.
Because farm prices were depreciating as greenbacks were removed
from circulation, farmers never paid off their growing debt and had
to remortgage themselves again and again, year in, year out. As often as not, the end came only when The Man refused to reissue a line
of credit. Bankrupted, many went west. The only alternative to this
was the "Grange" system of cash-only cooperative stores modeled on
Rochdale that had spread across the Midwest in the 1870s. However,
not offering credit, the Grange was of little use to the poorest
farmers, who lived from hand to mouth on credit until their crop was
delivered. The result was that only relatively wealthy farmers could
participate, and the Grange declared that it was not "as some have
falsely claimed, a crusade against the moneyed capitalist . . . [but] a
farmers organisation for self improvement and self help." By 1879, the
Grange described itself as "essentially *conservative* . . . in contrast to
the lawless, desperate attempts at communism" (Goodwyn 1976, 46;
emphasis in original).

The failure of the Rochdale model for all but the cash rich in the
Midwest led to the emergence of the Texas-based Farmers Alliance,
which denounced "credit merchants, railroads, trusts, money power
and capitalists" (Goodwyn 1976, 39) in favor of cooperative buying
and selling collectives, of which by the mid-1880s there were over two
thousand with one hundred thousand members. In Dakota a terri-
torywide cooperative exchange was established, while cooperative
experiments spread widely across Kansas as well as elsewhere across
the American South and West between 1887 and 1892. Again, however, the cooperatives ran up against problems when manufacturers refused to sell direct to the purchasing cooperatives, with the effect that Alliance members decided to establish selling cooperatives
which, through efficiencies of scale, did win enhanced incomes for

their members and enable them to buy out of the lien system. Selling cooperatives became a common feature in many states, although in others collective action by merchants meant that the bulk purchases were boycotted and attempts were made to drive the exchanges out of business by price cutting. Rumors were spread about quality and so on. Relying on poor farmers and boycotted by the banks, many exchanges were seriously undercapitalized. A lack of cash continued to be a problem in the period before the crop was sold, while farmers who had signed their crop over to a creditor did not have a crop to sell and were completely excluded. Attempts by the Texas Alliance to cooperatively bundle up their members' credit requirements and raise loans based on their collective collateral in order to buy everyone out of the lien system were, predictably enough, rebuffed by a finance capital that refused to grant the requested loans.

Interestingly from Marx's perspective on cooperation, the Alliance responded to their difficulties by radicalizing, developing their critique of credit and what they called money power, building links with the newly organized Knights of Labor, and entering the political realm (Foner 1955, 300, 326). In direct contrast to the rightward drift of the Grange, which increasingly described the alliance as "an unruly and objectionable element," cooperative farmer radicalism evolved into Populism in the 1890s, much as Owenism had been one of the founding strands of the British trade union movement. Yeomen farmers no longer saw themselves as on friendly terms with capital; their allies were workers, against capital. Cooperation would be formalized into a Southern state–wide cooperative exchange network of state exchanges to enable farmers to escape "the tyranny of organised capital" (Goodwyn 1976, 90). The state exchanges would be able to loan money to moneyless farmers at appropriate rates, sell the state's cotton crop in bulk, and hold back part of the crop at harvest time to get a higher price later. Demands were made for government-issued flexible money, greenbacks, and the immediate issuance of unlimited silver and gold coinage to remedy the severely contracted money supply and the resulting depressed commodity prices. These and other demands and visions hammered out by the leagues became the "Omaha platform," which was communicated widely across the South and West of the United States by farmer-lecturers who, linking up with the cooperative networks in Kansas and the Dakotas and with assorted Greenbackers, created the Populist agrarian revolt that spread like wildfire across the American South and West in the 1890s. It seemed that there was "almost a universal conviction that financial salvation [had] come" (Goodwyn 1976, 93).

The Populist explosion can be explained in part by the lecturers' daily exposure to the persistent, grinding poverty encountered in the remotest parts of the United States: a poverty to which they had no immediate solution given the failure of either local cooperative experiments or the larger cooperative exchange networks to meet the needs of the very poor due to their lack of resources and opposition from financial and manufacturing elites. The lecturers had to explain the constant delays to desperate people, fired up by visions of change. Proposals that the exchanges overcome the credit problem by issuing their own currency to enable poor farmers to hold their crops off the market when the prices were lowest, thus enabling them to buy themselves out of the lien, "however ingenious, [proved to be] beyond the means of the penniless farmers of Texas" (Goodwyn 1976, 137). The Texas Exchange withdrew from the battle against the credit system and insisted that all purchases be in cash, before collapsing in 1889. This was a major defeat.

Two solutions to the evident failure of cooperation could be proposed. First, given that poor farmers could not generate the credit they needed, the exchanges needed help. The response was a more widespread attempt to create money, the subtreasury plan, which aimed to marshal the currency-issuing power of government on behalf of the poorest farmers and urban workers by issuing greenbacks to provide credit issued through government-owned warehouses or "subtreasuries" in which farmers would store their produce before sale. The plan would be submitted to Congress; political action was not seen as necessary because this was self-evidently a sensible plan that would help in the harmonization of the classes. Again, an ingenious plan submitted for approval to sensible elites would be called "one of the wildest and most fantastic projects ever seriously produced by sober man" by the *New York Times* (Goodwyn 1976, 271). America's Gilded Age elites recognized that the socialistic plans for government-owned warehouses and credit issuance would have shattered the credit system on which Southern patterns of class domination were founded.

Others located the problems with cooperation in the opposition of financial and commercial elites. Cooperation, they argued, cut against self-interested gold standard financiers who refused to capitalize the exchanges. Whenever a cooperative failed through a lack of credit, the solution seemed to change the money system to enable the cooperative commonwealth to thrive. This was fully fledged Greenbackism, taking the subtreasury plan to its logical conclusion. As commodity prices fell from an equivalent of a dollar a bushel in 1870 to 60 cents in 1890 (or 35 cents in Dakota, 10 cents in Kansas), the Knights of Labor were smashed and the Greenback Party was ridiculed out of existence. Alliance radicals argued that persuasion was not enough. Political action was required to wrest the money system out of the hands of Eastern financial elites, and the Alliance partisans carried this politics into the new People's Party that emerged between 1892 and the 1896 "Battle of the (Gold and Silver) Standards."

While the People's Party in the South focused on cooperation and the subtreasury plan, monetary politics in the new states of the West focused on the need for free silver coinage, an argument that obviously resonated with miners but was also driven by mining interests. The Honest Money League argued for silver currency, claiming, "There is all the difference between true money, real money and paper money [as] there is for your land and a deed for it. Money is a reality, a weight, of a certain metal of a certain fineness. But a paper dollar is simply a deed" (Ingham 2004, 44). Just as the politics of bimetallism developed as a response to the Populist insurgency and the recession of 1893, the new People's Party managed to elect a significant number of representatives to Congress in 1892 and 1894, leaving "big money"—both Republican and Democratic varieties—severely rattled. The People's Party, however, failed to reach the magic 51 percent necessary in a two-party, "first past the post" system, and those for whom winning power through election was the aim of the movement consequently increasingly argued that a single platform, for free silver coinage, would unite Populism with the growing numbers of Silver Democrats and sweep all before it. The "wild theories" of the Omaha platform should be renounced. Their opponents argued that this would mean giving in to the Democrats, seen as half of the money power, just at the time when the new People's Party was at the height of its success, for a policy that Populism's Greenbackers felt was a diversion. It would mean giving up on the subtreasury plan and leaving the banking system, seen at the heart of the oppressive lien system, intact. Populism was split.

The silverites were strengthened when the Bimetallic Leagues comprehensively outorganized the Populist farmer-lecturers after 1894–95 with bestselling pamphlets arguing for silver (as well as Dana's pamphlet on Proudhon, quoted earlier), which were sold on every rail train and in every cigar shop. These apparently sent everyone "wildly insane on this subject . . . the farmers are especially unruly . . . you just can't do anything with them — just got to let them go" (Goodwyn 1976, 243). With silver capturing the imagination, the silverite Populists decided to ensure that Populist forces would support a prosilver Democratic platform in 1896, while the Silver Democrat organization systematically captured the party in time for the 1896 convention to overwhelmingly nominate the prosilver William Jennings Bryan as Democratic candidate for the U.S. presidency. Populists ensured that Bryan was also nominated as the People's Party candidate, and Populism collapsed as an independent force. Nothing more was heard of the subtreasury plan or of alternative currencies for thirty years.

Bryan's defeat by the pro–gold standard Republican McKinley[2] was helped by finance from the new Gilded Age plutocrats and thousands of flag-waving members of the Sound Money Clubs, who, together with employers, carried out what can only be called a reign of terror to reimpose the violence of financial stability on a nation. Railways, shops, mills, lumber companies, and factories were closed down on the day of the election, with the owners saying that they would not reopen if Bryan was victorious. Manufacturers received letters from dealers saying that they would no longer supply them if the vote went the wrong way, with the letters posted for the workers to see, while another employer told his workers that their pay would be $10 if Bryan won, $26 if the victor was McKinley. Goodyear workers were told that a vote for Bryan would be seen as an attack on the values of the company (Foner 1955, 337–42). Although the evidence seems to indicate that the majority of rural and urban workers and farmers supported Bryan, they could not cope with the violence, intimidation, corruption, and endless flows of money the Republicans controlled, and Bryan's defeat settled the money question until the

Wall Street crash of 1929. No mass party would ever question U.S. capitalism as fundamentally as did Populism, for sound money and common sense became axiomatic, while "populism" was reinscribed as suspect speechifying to plebeian masses with no intention of following through on extravagant promises.

Nonetheless, Populism was not a dream propagated by cynical leaders who said what was needed to get elected. It was a profoundly democratic attempt to strike at the heart of systems of domination in the nineteenth-century U.S. South and West. The Populists were also ahead of their time, for fiat money has been the norm since 1973, and the world did not cave in when money became just a representation instituted by government (or other) fiat. The Populists also claimed that the true value of a currency rested on the wealth of a country as defined by its productivity, not by the intrinsic value of metal. Again, this is now an uncontested claim.

Populism's success owed more to the experience of cooperative experimentation—even when it was thwarted—than it did to theorizing about money. When farmers who were not completely subjugated by the lien system cooperated in buying and selling collectively, they were often successful, and by the mid-1890s had some thirteen years' experience with practical cooperation. They used many micropolitical commitment building mechanisms: mile-long processions of carts decorated with evergreen to symbolize the "living issues" of the Alliance, brass bands, crowds so large that four farmer-lecturers were needed to keep them occupied, flags in carts after a successful bulk sale, and twilight meals feeding thousands. At the core of the movement were the countless discussions and explanations of the subtreasury plan and the need for greenbacks, for abolition of the lien and of usury, and for mobilizations to defend threatened exchanges and the like from finance capital, a mobilization made possible by the selfless, indefatigable work of the farmer-lecturers who systematically covered the country spreading the word of the cooperative commonwealth. This was more than dwarfish, ephemeral cooperation: it was a mass movement. However, it could not meet the needs of the poorest. Where the farmer-lecturer infrastructure was less well developed or where it encountered local micropolitical resistance, it foundered; for example, what was good micropolitics for rural farmers spoke less to urban workers, while lecturers in the Deep South

were attacked by Democratic mobs and night riders reinforcing racist structures of domination. Miners in the far West were more attracted to demands for free silver—if they could mine it. Populism
was thus limited to agrarian America; a broader, lasting movement
against "money power" was not built.

By the late nineteenth century, the socialist movement and the
rise of trade unions focusing on the economy rather than on finance
had replaced money reform as a serious political movement for all
but a few enthusiasts. Money would be used for human liberation
as the state was taken over either by reform or by revolution. The
form of money was neutral, although we would probably replace the
image of the monarch (in the United Kingdom, at least) with more
stirring socialist symbols to reinforce socialist consciousness. In fact,
following the failure of war communism in the early days of the Soviet
experience, where toilet paper became more valuable than money,
socialists would be as keen on "hard" money as the most conservative
central banker (Galbraith 1975, 76).

4

Twentieth-Century Utopians
GESELL AND DOUGLAS

W HILE THE MAINSTREAM OF SOCIALIST THINKING
focused on changing the economy wholesale, either by reform or by revolution, the monetary strand was kept alive by the
twentieth-century Distributists (Findlay 1972). Originally inspired by
the romantic writings of Morris and Ruskin as well as Kropotkinite
anarchism, but also by an antisocialist rejection of collectivism as destructive of liberty and private property, Distributism looked to a return to a medievalist economy controlled by guilds and governed by
use values rather than by exchange values. The pathologies of finance
capitalism were a major element of Distributist thinking, and, inspired by Quaker banking practices built on relations of trust rather
than pure financial speculation, Distributism advocated the nationalization of credit and the imposition of a "just price."

After the First World War, the Distributists' most visible advocates, Hilaire Belloc and G. K. Chesterton, focused on the need to
defend the "little man" from, on the left, socialism (which they saw as
destructive of individual freedom) and the welfare state (which they
viewed as encouraging dependency on governments to solve problems) and from, on the right, "monopoly capitalism." By 1924, Distributism had its own newspaper and some twenty-four local chapters in the United Kingdom, although it did not survive the death
of Chesterton in 1936. Besides, arguments for the nationalization of
credit and a just price were taken up by Social Credit. A concern with
the pathologies of finance capital also verged on the anti-Semitic.
Distributism, with its antisocialist concern with the individual small

man, thus also formed one of the currents from which the British Union of Fascists emerged.

To the left of Distributism, Guild Socialism attacked the wage system, arguing that wages represented only part of what the worker was entitled to and rejecting the right of capitalists to make a profit. They rejected the disconnection between wages paid and the value of the product produced by labor, thereby dehumanizing labor as merely one of a number of factors of production (Hutchinson, Mellor, and Olsen 2002). Wages were contrasted with "salaries," which ensure that salaried employees are paid at the same rate irrespective of how hard they work on a particular day, and with pay in the armed forces, where soldiers are paid irrespective of whether they fight or not. Building on this logic, Guild Socialists advocated production for need, and, through mechanization, a reduction in labor time, hinting at a role for the state in organizing production for need that was later taken up by Social Credit. Others took a more decentralized approach, proposing that workers take control of production through their guilds, running industry democratically and providing their own welfare services, as a direct challenge to state socialism. Guild Socialism split when the Russian Revolution forced those who had been critical of state socialism to support an existing socialist experiment under major attack from the capitalist powers. Some went off to join the British Communist Party, such as Willie Gallagher and J. T. Murphy, while others later became attracted to Social Credit (Findlay 1972, 76–84).

Silvio Gesell and Stamp Scrip

The anarchist stream in money reform was continued by the Argentine-based German money reformer Silvio Gesell, who developed arguments for the abolition of interest and for "free money" (Gesell 1958). Gesell identified interest as the prime pathology of the capitalist system and advocated interest-free banking. His ideas remained at the theoretical level during his lifetime; apart from serving a one-week term as minister in the Munich Soviet in 1918, he did little to implement his plans. After his death, a "Freework" movement in postwar Germany established the Wära Exchange Association (a word compounded from the German words for goods, *Wara,* and currency,

Wärung), which issued its own currency notes, interest free as a response to Germany's financial collapse and experiences of hyperinflation (Fisher 1933). With the arrival of the Depression in 1929 the owner of a coal mine in Schwanenkirchen, Bavaria, used Wära notes to reopen his mine, with the Wära passed on to local merchants, then to the wholesalers, then on to the manufacturers who returned to the coal mine for coal. Fisher (1933) estimates that during 1930–31 no more than twenty thousand Wära were issued, but some two million people used them.

Gesell-inspired scrip notes issued by local authorities or business associations spread to other towns in Germany, Austria, and Switzerland. In 1932, the town of Wörgl, Austria, used them to fund public works for unemployed people, who spent the notes with local merchants who then paid the notes back to the local authority in local taxes (Dauncey 1988, 282–83). Local state employees were paid 50 percent of their salary in scrip inscribed with the words "They Alleviate Want, Give Work and Bread." The notes could be exchanged for cash, but a service charge was levied that was greater than the costs of passing the note on. Stamp scrip took on Gesell's ideas for *demurrage*: scrip could be banked or spent locally, like ordinary cash, but it had to be "validated" with a stamp purchased each week. After fifty-two weeks the note could be exchanged for cash by the local authority, using the receipts from the weekly stamps. If the note was not passed on, the holder of the note would still have to purchase the weekly stamps or the note would be worthless, so it was obviously in his or her interest to purchase something with it rather than hold onto it. Demurrage was intended to increase the velocity of circulation; "slow money," horded rather than spent, was regarded as the cause of the Depression. The politics of the Wörgl notes are clear from the inscription on the back of each note:

> To all. Slowly circulating money has thrown the world into an unheard of crisis, and millions of working people are in a terrible need. From the economic viewpoint, the decline of the world has begun with horrible consequences for all. Only a clear recognition of these facts, and decisive action can stop the breakdown of the economic machine, and save mankind from another war, confusion and dissolution.
>
> Men live from the exchange of what they can do. Through slow money circulation this exchange has been crippled to a large extent, and thus

millions of men who are willing to work have lost their right to live in our economic system. The exchange of what we can do must, therefore, be again improved and the right to live regained for all of those who have been cast out. (Fisher 1933, 25)

Gesell's ideas inspired other financial responses to the Great Depression of the 1930s. In the United States, economically distressed farmers began swapping their surpluses with each other, and the movement developed from individual swaps to organized barter exchanges and swap bulletins and newspapers (Fisher 1934, 149). Contemporary reports claimed that the "Swap Movement" had some fifty thousand participants in four hundred exchanges across twenty-nine states (*New York Herald Tribune,* 15 January 1933). Eventually, warehouse receipts were issued by the barter exchanges; when denominated in dollars, these began to circulate as money and were loaned as money (Fisher 1933, 6). As news of the European scrip movement crossed the Atlantic, in no small part due to its popularization by respected Nobel Prize–winning economist Irving Fisher (1933), local authorities and business associations in the United States also began to issue their own local currency notes, denominated in dollars, and barter grew from an informal movement run by poor farmers into a more formalized stamp scrip system (Fisher 1934, 147–68). The EPIC (End Poverty in California) movement of the Populist socialist Upton Sinclair supported widespread use of scrip as a means of exchange between cooperatives (Sinclair 1963, 282–92). This support provoked claims that scrip was ruining the value of the currency during Sinclair's 1933 race for the governorship of California. The Roosevelt administration then used Keynesian demand management to do at the macro level what stamp scrip had attempted to do at the local level, and the movement was superseded.

The European scrip movement provoked more intense opposition as Fascism emerged. The Wörgl experiment was shut down by the Austrian central bank (Dauncey 1988, 283). The German experiments were halted by the November 1931 Reich Banking Law, which established the state monopoly over currency issue (Godschalk 1985), although the Gesell-inspired Wir business-to-business barter network in Switzerland continued into the twenty-first century (Douthwaite 1996). However, the lesson of the 1930s is that scrip was seen as an alternative for use in desperate times when the state refused to intervene, often through an ideological commitment to laissez-faire economics and, crucially, when taking scrip was the only alternative to no business at all. When the state adopted Keynesianism, be it of the democratic or Nazi variety, scrip was superseded as an ad hoc, uneven, and rather inadequate alternative to demand management. The revival of the economy meant that merchants who were never happy with scrip could demand hard cash again. It was not until the breakdown of the Keynesian consensus in the late 1960s that the first stirrings of a new local currency "movement from below" was seen, and not until the revival of laissez-faire in the 1990s that a really large-scale movement emerged. Meanwhile, the move toward state intervention represented by Keynesianism meant that from the 1930s on, the state became the focus for monetary reform.

Social Credit

Although most critics of the capitalist system became socialists, especially after the 1917 Russian Revolution (with the United Kingdom's Socialist Party, the country's oldest socialist group, explicitly focusing on the role of money and wage slavery in ensuring the perpetuation of capitalism), a second strand emerged in the early twentieth century that focused on the inability of liberal, free-trade capitalism to distribute its rewards fairly. Movements for currency reform in the 1920s were inspired by the first successful experiences of state planning of industry and of price controls, which contrasted with the dubious role of the financial sector in profiteering from the debt taken on to wage the First World War and the rapid onset of crisis with the abolition of state control in 1920. This, coupled with the technological optimism that accompanied the mass use of electric power and industrialization, made what critics called "poverty in the midst of plenty," seemingly overproduction coupled with poverty for millions, unacceptable in a land supposed, after the war, to be "fit for heroes." Romantic attachments to medieval guilds in Distributist and Guild Socialist thinking seemed inadequate now that the state had shown itself able to organize production to win the war.

Social Credit emerged when Major C. H. Douglas developed another panacea for solving economic problems overnight: the "A + B theorem" (Douglas 1937; Hutchinson et al. 2002, 123–41). A factory manager, Douglas noted the difference between the wages he paid (he called them "A" payments) and all the other costs of his production—for raw materials, plant, bank payments, power costs, marketing, and so on ("B" payments). The price of the goods he produced was obviously constructed from his costs, made up of wages (and dividends to shareholders) and all other costs, A + B. The A payments his workers received were always, by definition, less than the price of the goods in the shops, made up of A + B. Scaling this up, the whole economy is the totality of all A + B payments and combined purchasing power (the totality of A payments is less than the combined value of goods on sale, or B payments). Douglas argued that the result is overproduction and poverty amid plenty because it is a mathematical impossibility for workers to purchase the goods they have produced with the wages they have received if these are less than the price of the products they have made. Either they do not consume, or they make up the difference with credit from banks, charged at interest, so they become slaves to banks. The solution should be the distribution to each citizen of a national dividend that would be the difference between A and B. Technocrats in a national credit agency would calculate the value of the dividend, and, to avoid inflation, prices would be controlled at a "just" or "scientific" price.

Although Douglas was antagonistic to political organization, Social Credit "study circles" emerged in the United Kingdom in the early 1920s out of the fractured Guild Socialist movement, composed of those who rejected the communists (Findlay 1972). Douglas's ideas were popularized by the *New Age,* an influential bohemian journal that gave Guild Socialists, Distributists, and supporters of many esoteric, mystical, and eclectic ideas a voice and intellectual credibility in bohemian political circles. However, after a promising start in the early 1920s, outside centers such as Coventry the movement did not really grow beyond 278 paid-up members by the end of the 1920s, with perhaps 1,000 supporters, partly because Douglas himself opposed it. Many of its members eventually became Marxists by the 1930s, while some joined the British Union of Fascists and others joined other movements for monetary reform, such as the Economic Freedom League, dining groups, or local associations such as the West Riding Association. In 1935, Social Crediters endeavored to persuade the main political parties to adopt the "National Dividend," while Douglas, who had embarked on extensive travels throughout the Commonwealth, was increasingly being seen as dogmatic and authoritarian.

Money Protest Militant:
The Green Shirts in the United Kingdom

In the United Kingdom, Social Credit had a more successful militant wing, the Green Shirt Movement for Social Credit led by the charismatic John Gordon Hargrave (Findlay 1972, 147–66; Drakeford 1997). Hargrave had made his name in the scouting movement and had been seen at one time as a successor to Baden-Powell. However, as a convinced pacifist, Hargrave was repelled by the use of scouting to stir up patriotism in the First World War and set up his own alternative, the Kibbo Kift. Like other postwar outdoor movements, Kibbo Kift organized all ages around a philosophy of outdoor life, pacifism, and a rejection of an urban, mechanical society which, it felt, had led to the regimentation of society, a disconnection with ecology, and, eventually, war. This was wrapped up in a rather esoteric mysticism that mixed Anglo-Saxon mythology with a form of deep ecology; a Spencerian commitment to the creation, through training, of a new elite held to be fully formed human beings; and a uniform consisting of a green and brown Saxon jerkin and cloak. Perhaps as a result of this esoteric presentation, Kibbo Kift did not grow to more than a couple of hundred members before a large number of members opposed to Hargrave's authoritarianism left to set up the Woodcraft Folk in 1924.[1]

In true guru style, Hargrave undertook a two-week retreat into the mountains of Wales with a lieutenant in 1927. On his return, he informed Kibbo Kift that it had adopted Social Credit as its guiding philosophy, and with this change it began to be more successful. Hargrave was then inspired by John Strachey to focus his strong propaganda skills on the unemployed rather than bourgeois radical *New Age* readers, and Kibbo Kift began to sign up groups of unemployed people who swore to fight for "One National Demand for the proper supply of Money to buy the Goods produced by the Community . . . by means of Unarmed Mass Pressure; and to this end I place myself here and now willingly under the strict discipline and direct leadership of the Kindred" (Findlay 1972, 154). Responding to the Great Depression and the failure of the first Labour government, unemployed people in Coventry were organized into a uniformed Crusader League by Social Crediters and Catholic priests. In 1930–31 this league spread to other cities before being subsumed into the Kibbo Kift. The kift updated its uniform, cleaned away the Saxon mythology, and changed its name to the Green Shirt Movement for Social Credit. The Green Shirts were a uniformed party led in an authoritarian manner by Hargrave (who styled himself Grey Fox) that aimed to build a new elite of a thousand members and commanded the unquestioning allegiance of another quarter of a million followers. This elite would impose Social Credit on the confused, huddled masses for their own benefit; they could not be expected to make the necessary changes themselves. The Green Shirts attempted to build this cadre through uniformed street parades with drums and colorful banners inscribed with the movement's swastika-like logo of crossed keys, as the crossed keys would open the door to the Social Credit future.[2] Domination of the streets, intimidation of opponents, and the presentation of overwhelming power by men marching amid noise, music, banners, and logos is, of course, the micropolitical strategy of fascist and racist movements everywhere. But this is not to say that the Green Shirts were totalitarian.

Micropolitically, providing hierarchy, security, and structure to the lives of unemployed people was as much a factor in the success of the Green Shirts as it was in that of other uniformed political organizations such as the Nazi Brownshirts or the British Union of Fascists (BUF). The Green Shirts involved their members six days a week, with two nights for drill and street patrols, one for business, one for recreation, Saturday for selling literature, and one evening for study of Social Credit. The movement was popular, with sixteen local branches in the major industrial centers, while its newspaper, *Attack,* sold seven thousand copies a week at its high point in 1932–33 (Drakeford 1997, 131). The Green Shirts provided food and clothing for the hungry, camping opportunities, excitement, and solidarity to unemployed people in grave economic times as well as a philosophy that explained a way to a better future and, it must be said, a convenient scapegoat—high finance and the banks. Its program was clear, concise, and simple:

1. Take control.
2. Close the "chatterbox" at Westminster.
3. Take over the Bank of England in the name of the people.
4. Open the National Credit Office.
5. Issue the National Dividend to every citizen.
6. Enforce the scientific price.
7. Set up Local Hundreds (constituent assemblies) in every district to give expression to the will of the people throughout the country.
8. Put down any counter revolutionary "fascist" activity, or attempts to overthrow the party of the people's credit (the Green Shirts).
9. Defend the victorious Social Credit revolution from international financial sabotage. (Zavos 1981, 203)

The Green Shirts saw the Communist Party as their major competitor for the allegiance of those suffering from the Great Depression, while the BUF were their opponents. Like the communists, they engaged in street battles against the BUF and carried out direct action such as defacing a wax statue of Hitler, painting the Bank of England green (quite regularly), throwing a brick at No. 11 Downing Street,[3] burning Bank of England Chairman Montagu Norman in effigy, burning a sheaf of wheat outside a meeting of the Wheat Commission (with the slogan "They burn the wheat we want to eat!"), and marching in formation at demonstrations. The levels of organization achieved were, Findlay (1972, 159) argues, such that even the fascists were impressed: up to October 1934, the Green Shirts held 3,426 open-air meetings and 32 demonstrations, sold 56,000 newspapers, and distributed 223,000 leaflets. Their newspaper *Attack* was published regularly between 1933 and 1937.

In 1935, the movement was transformed into the Social Credit Party of Great Britain and Northern Ireland and decided to run a candidate for Parliament in a bye-election. It won 11 percent of the vote, but after a falling out with Douglas it rejected respectability and began an internecine war with the tiny Douglasite Social Credit movement, smashing up its meetings, with Hargrave now rather hysterically calling for calling for "drums, drums, more drums!" The 1937 Public Order Act outlawed political uniforms, and the Green Shirts were effectively finished before the Second World War terminated its activities. It did not revive after the war.

Was the Green Shirt movement fascist? Certainly the banners, logo, parades, and authoritarian micropolitical practice suggested so. But it also promised equality and security for all and rejected the organic state, although Sheppard (1981) argues that proposals for local hundreds to replace political parties were corporatist. Its marches were peaceful, and violence was either rare or expressed in creative political stunts that prefigure the sort of demonstrative direct action tactics used by organizations like Greenpeace. It was never anti-Semitic, opposing Douglas on this issue and insisting on sending a prominent Jewish member to the headquarters of the BUF in response to BUF complaints about Green Shirt antifascist propaganda. It involved and gave dignity to ordinary people something the elitist technocrat Douglas opposed. It actively opposed the BUF, both physically and through agitation, and a fascist attack on the Green Shirt headquarters in Liverpool in 1935 was one of the triggers for the banning of political uniforms in 1936 (Drakeford 1997, 182). It was opposed to both fascism *and* communism, and we should resist looking at the Green Shirts through the lens of the later experience of fascism in the Second World War.

Social Credit Enters the Mainstream:
Canada and New Zealand

Outside the United Kingdom, Douglas was an enthusiastic advocate of his views, traveling through the British Commonwealth and America meeting politicians and doing radio broadcasts. He received a much warmer welcome in those places than in the United Kingdom, especially as the Depression worsened. But he remained uninterested in political organization, continuing to regard his solution as a technical change to the nation's accounting system. In Alberta, Canada, the populist radio preacher Aberhardt, running for the office of premier, called for "reliable, honourable, bribe-proof businessmen who have definitely laid aside their party politic affiliations . . . to represent Social Credit in every constituency" (Zavos 1979, 58). In a landslide, Social Credit won 89 percent of the vote and Aberhardt became the premier, with Douglas (and then Hargrave) briefly serving as advisers. However, perhaps recognizing the difficulty of implementing Social Credit in practice, especially because Canadian provinces did not control fiscal policies, Aberhardt resisted introducing legislation and instead issued provincial scrip,

[*71*]

subject to demurrage, which Douglas opposed. But because the Social Credit government itself would not accept scrip notes for taxes,
businesses and unions boycotted them (Zavos 1979, 204–5). The
war intervened, and Social Credit then lost the next election. Aberhardt was then reduced to making radio broadcasts railing against
the banks, which he said wanted to set up a "worldwide slave state."
When Aberhardt died, another preacher, Manning, replaced him,
and Social Credit won the 1952 election. A combination of oil wealth,
antisocialism, and religious piety meant that Social Credit stayed in
power until 1976 as a rural, sound-money conservative party that attracted the support of small farmers and small businesspeople, but
with no Douglasite politics whatsoever. A similar Social Credit Party
was in power in British Columbia from 1952 to 1972 and then again
from 1975 to 1986, but was an explicitly pro–small business antisocialist party with no connection to Douglas's ideas at any time. In
Quebec in 1962, a Poujadist Parti Creditiste stood on a Douglasite
program and won twenty-nine seats.

In New Zealand, Douglas also received a hearing from the New
Zealand Labour Party, which had won power in 1935 with a strident
campaign against the banks and a slogan of "Poverty in a Land of
Plenty." Douglas was invited to appear before a parliamentary commission that successfully debunked his A + B theorem, and Social
Credit ideas were not implemented, although a welfare state was.[4]
Nevertheless, a Social Credit League was established and survived as
a minor force, winning between 5 and 10 percent of the vote through
the 1950s and into the 1960s. In 1966 it won a parliamentary seat,
appealing again to farmers, small businesspeople and lower-middle-
class professionals, often with strong religious beliefs. Looking as
if it might be able to hold the balance of power in the 1980s after
two spectacular bye-election victories, by the 1990s Social Credit
faded when it was exposed as having little more to offer than the
now rather discredited A + B theorem. Little was achieved beyond
proposals for a local currency in one city, Hamilton, and a heavily
defeated bill to nationalize the banks and centralize credit into a
New Zealand Credit Authority offering credit at cost in a modern
version of Proudhon's Bank of the People. In New Zealand, Social
Credit was annihilated at the polls in 1984 for, of all things, having
supported the National government's controversial plans to build a

dam; campaigns against dams like that planned for Lake Manapouri on South Island helped New Zealand's green movement coalesce (King 2003, 440–45).

From Money Reform to Anti-Semitism: The Dark Side

Having traveled the world showing off his "wonderful new discovery," Douglas seems to have become an embittered, ill, isolated man who held a grudge against a world that did not accept the salvation he believed he was bringing. He degenerated into conspiracy theories, imagining that he had been prevented from implementing the simple reform that would solve all economic problems by an international banking conspiracy (Wall 2003). Taking conspiracy theories further, Douglas opened Social Credit up to the accusation that its supporters were closet fascists when he argued that there was a "a coherent Jewish policy everywhere" to control (both) international finance and Bolshevism. Douglas argued:

> No consideration of this subject would be complete without recognising the bearing on it of what is known as the Jewish Question, a question rendered doubly difficult by the conspiracy of silence that surrounds it. At the moment it can only be pointed out that the theory of rewards and punishments is Mosaic in origin, that finance and law derive their inspiration from the same course, and that countries such as pre-war Germany and post war Russian [sic], which exhibit the logical consequences of unchecked collectivism, have done so under the direct influence of Jewish leaders. Of the Jews itself [sic] it may be said that they exhibit the race consciousness to an extent unapproached elsewhere, and it is fair to say that their success is due to their adaptation in an environment that has been moulded in their own ideal. That is, as far as seems useful to go, and there may be a great deal to be said on the other side. It has not yet, I think, been said in such a way as to dispose of the suggestion, which need not necessarily be an offensive suggestion, that the Jews are protagonists of collectivism in all its forms, whether it is camouflaged under the name of socialism, or big business. It should be emphasised that it is the Jews as a group, and not as individuals, who are on trial and the remedy if required is to break up the group activity." (Quoted by Sheppard 1981, 37)

Alongside other esoteric material, the *New Age* had published anti-Semitic attacks on "Jewish Finance" from Distributists Cecil Chesterton and Belloc and other anti-Semites such as Ezra Pound (Surette 1999). For example, Orage (the editor) wrote: "It would be

deplorable if anti-Semitism were revived in England. But so alarm-
ing is the combination of Jewish international financiers against Democracy that some such movement may be identified." Against this,
Finlay argues, "There is no suggestion that this anti-Semitism was directed at the Jews as persons: many Jews wrote for the paper, notably
the prominent Zionist, Israel Zangwill, and one of the most striking
attacks . . . on Jewish financiers came from M. D. Eder, himself a Jew"
(Findlay 1972, 71–73). Douglas himself attacked both "a very deeply
laid and well considered plot of enslaving the industrial world by Ger-
man-American-Jewish financiers" and argued, contra, that "the very
last thing which I should desire . . . would be the association of the
Social Credit movement with Jew-baiting" (Findlay 1972, 102). Later,
however, Douglas does seem to have degenerated into outright anti-
Semitism, arguing:

> I have, for my own part, come to believe that there is a fundamental rela-
> tionship between the troubles which affect Europe and what is known as
> the Jewish problem. I have formed that view/opinion [with] reluctance.
> . . . Perhaps the first necessity is to explain beyond any risk of misunder-
> standing the nature of the charge and why it is a racial and not personal
> indictment. In this connection, Disraeli's description of his people as a
> "splendidly organised race" is significant. Organisation has much of the
> tragedy of life to its debt; and organisation is a Jewish speciality. (Quoted
> by Findlay 1972, 104)

Douglas believed that the Jewish people were an exclusive,
homogeneous race, thinking the same way and therefore susceptible
to or perhaps the unknowing dupes of a dominating conspiracy of
financiers, some of whom were Jewish, others not. Freemasonry, he
argued, operated the same way. But he did not seek to discriminate
against Jewish people in any way, and believed that they should be
entitled to the National Dividend as were any other citizens. Douglas's
position was similar to that of the eccentric former U.K. Green Party
coleader of the 1990s, David Icke, who, among other things, had
claimed for himself a special relationship with the supernatural, and
argued that the anti-Semitic forgery *The Protocols of the Elders of Zion*
was in fact an uncovering of an international conspiracy by financiers
which had been deflected onto the Jews.[5] The outrage that rightly
greeted this revisionism further discredited Icke and caused his ideas
to be ridiculed. The extent to which Douglas's (and Icke's) positions

were anti-Semitic is debatable, but the evidence is strong. In any case, they gave succor to anti-Semites.

Consequently, Sheppard reports that New Zealand Social Credit supporters of the 1930s debated the origins of bankers with Jewish names, and one supporter published a sympathetic article on Hitler, calling himself "pro-Nazi." Even in the 1980s, a Jewish Social Credit candidate received a phone call: "Mr. Sheppard, I thought I would phone you to thank you for standing for Social Credit in this election and for standing up to these people." "Who?" Sheppard asked. "The world Jewish conspiracy, of course" (Sheppard 1981, 31). Sheppard argues that anti-Semitic books about the "Jewish financial conspiracy" and the "Rothschilds' control of Europe" circulated widely.

Of course, it is as much of a fallacy to ascribe fascist tendencies to Social Credit as a whole as it is to ascribe finance to a Jewish conspiracy (although Wall [2003] takes a stronger line on this). Post-Holocaust readers have a sharper understanding of the indefensibility of anti-Semitism than those speaking before that indescribable abomination. But the politics of money reform have many strands, some of them dark, or at least giving succor to fascist or reactionary thought. Silver Democrat and Populist presidential candidate Bryan alienated many working-class supporters, who did not respond well to reports that when he closed his speech at the 1896 Democratic Convention with the words "You shall not press down on the brow of labor this crown of thorns; you shall not crucify mankind on a cross of gold," the audience, recognizing the anti-Semitic undertone to this, chanted, "Down with gold! Down with the hook-nosed Shylocks of Wall Street! Down with the Christ-killing goldbugs!" in the fifteen minutes of pandemonium that followed (Foner 1955, 335). It should also be remembered that Strasserite versions of Nazism railed against banks as did many advocates of money reform.

Another problem with Social Credit is that the A + B theorem is wrong; few Social Credit supporters now embrace it. Obviously, for a business to make a profit, its wages and dividends (A payments) must be less than the full price charged, reflecting other costs (B payments). Douglas was right to observe that capitalist production does mean depriving the worker of part of his production, and that this is exploitative. He was right to argue that often wages will be so low that consumption of the very things the worker produces is beyond the means of the individual worker, and right to be on the side of the exploited and in favor of production. But this does not mean that workers will *inevitably* be unable to purchase the goods they produce, for many B payments go on to form wages for others—the people who work in banks, produce the raw materials, market the goods, and so on. Money circulates, so a small amount of money can fund much economic activity; therefore, judgments that the economy has little income in total are simplistic. Interest and credit, if at reasonable rates, need not play such a pathological role in an economy, and in market theory it is considered fair that a fee, interest, is paid for money borrowed, or rented, from its owner (Zavos 1981, 80).

Another problem with Social Credit is that it is a rather statist solution. In northern countries especially, the forms of social control envisaged to ensure a "just" or "scientific" price might have been acceptable in the Depression-hit 1930s, but are unlikely to be credible post-1989 given what is regarded as the historical defeat of state planning as typified by the Soviet Union—assuming, that is, that technocrats can identify such a price. Hayek's premise about the inability of bureaucracies to predict the millions of consumption choices in complex markets seems strong, although it could equally be argued that prices are set through processes of private planning guided by real-time data through electronic point-of-sale technology that allows, say, a supermarket to know to the pound how many carrots it sells a week. This technology, it could be argued, could be used for a modern version of Social Credit, now more likely to be called a citizens' income program. Finally, and perhaps most damning, the nationalization of credit and finance has been a powerful attack on the capitalist system, going completely against the deregulation of financial markets introduced in the late 1980s and beyond. Social Credit is thus not an apolitical change in the nation's accounting, but a powerful critique of private enterprise. Critics of the New Zealand Social Credit League, Social Credit's most effective political force, likened it to state socialism. By 1990, Social Credit was a spent force in New Zealand, its aging membership joining the left-wing Alliance, which became a junior coalition partner in the Labour-led government of 1999, although by 2005 it was attempting to revitalize itself as the Democrats for Social Credit.[6]

Alternative Forms of Money: The Lessons of History

If we review the experiences of radical movements for alternative forms of money that have emerged since the rise of capitalism, the experience is mixed. Two movements, Populism and the stamp scrip movement, emerged as mass movements as a result of economic crises, with Social Credit in New Zealand and Canada becoming a minority, though still a significant presence. This suggests that subaltern groups are able to generate large-scale mobilizations, if only fleetingly (1880s–90s, early 1930s). We see that in the past Marx's objections were well made: that too often alternative forms of money were advanced as apolitical panaceas by self-proclaimed gurus (the utopians, Proudhon, Gessel, Douglas, Hargarve, Aberhardt), but also that participation in the politics of money could lead to a more generalized radicalism (Owenism, Populism, the Distributists and Social Credit ers who joined the Communist Party, the Green Shirts).

The Populists and Green Shirts adopted effective micropolitical mobilization strategies, which Owen, Proudhon, and Douglas rejected in favor of persuading elites. We saw that Owenism and Populism did not involve the poorest, who lacked the resources to participate. The Populists attempted to buy out their members' debts, and the Green Shirts provided support and comradeship to their unemployed comrades. We saw Owenism as a micropolitical response to the advent of capitalism in the United Kingdom, Populism to the degradation of tenant farmers in the United States, and stamp scrip and Social Credit to the presence of both great need and overproduction during the Great Depression. In all four cases, alternative forms of money developed from below as creative forms of micropolitical resistance (taking the Green Shirt movement as a form of grassroots Social Credit) did seem to offer participants an alternative to a world that offered them no way out, while attempts at reform fell on deaf ears. There was resistance below the surface, with interesting forms of economic alterity being developed, if only fleetingly. But we also saw resistance from elites: middlemen and the banks to Owenism; middlemen, banks, Sound Money Clubs, employers, and Democratic mobs to Populism, with Keynesianism superseding stamp scrip and Social Credit seen as cranky, superseded by communism and to some extent fascism. The experience of the past is that subaltern groups can create forms of money from below, but the extent to which such micropolitical innovations will last is limited. By the Second World War, subaltern forms of money had died out as modernist state planning became the new norm. It was not until the breakdown of the Keynesian settlement in the late 1980s that we saw new forms of money generated from below: and it is to that experience that we shall now move.

5

New Money, New Work?

LETS IN THE UNITED KINGDOM

THIS CHAPTER BEGINS OUR DISCUSSION OF THE MODERN alternative currency movement with an analysis of local exchange trading schemes (LETS) in the United Kingdom. Recall that the United Kingdom's local money schemes emerged in the late 1980s and early 1990s, when Britain was expelled from the European exchange rate mechanism and the economy went into a deep recession. Claims for the extent of growth of LETS in the United Kingdom in the 1990s vary. LETSLink UK claimed there were some 350 schemes of varying sizes in existence by 1996. Williams (1996b, 3) suggested they may have involved thirty thousand participants, with a turnover of 2.1 million units. In 1999, research by the team led by Colin Williams (Williams et al. 2001) identified 303 LETS, while 186 LETS were registered on LETSLink UK's Web site in 2005. In this chapter we focus on hearts and minds. Why did people join LETS? What did they hope to achieve from it? To what extent did participants see LETS as the kind of alternative, anticapitalist practices that we examine in this book?

Manchester LETS, founded in 1992, will be the focus of our discussion of LETS in the United Kingdom. It was not typical of U.K. schemes; it was far better organized and much larger than most. But it is appropriate for use as an example of a successful LETS where the possibilities of social change through alternative forms of money were discussed in some detail. Given its level of organization and the existence within it of a large number of people with different rationales for participation, debates that would have been heard elsewhere were taken further in Manchester. The LETS had large numbers of members (approximately 550 at its height) and a system turnover of 183,842 bobbins (the unit of currency used) in the three years to October 1995. It was relatively long lasting in that by 2004 it still had a hard-core membership of approximately 170 members before shutting down in 2005. It had a diversity of members with different views about how money should be denominated, valued, issued, and spent. Manchester LETS was the focus of my doctoral study in 1993–95, and I revisited it in 2001 and 2005 (North 2006).

LETS in Manchester

Four interconnected groups came together to form the initial network of 120 people who formed Manchester LETS. One was a group of Quakers and Labour Party members. At the same time, the Manchester Green Party was discussing LETS, and the two networks combined resources with Green Party members connected to a third network interested in DIY (Do It Yourself) politics, the myriad green and anarchist social change and protest projects that later formed part of the anticapitalist movement that emerged into wider public consciousness after the 1999 World Trade Organization interministerial meeting in Seattle (see Wall 1990; McKay 1996; Carter and Moreland 2004). These networks spread out into the fourth mutual aid network, composed of people interested in conflict resolution projects, self-help, co-counseling, and, more enjoyable, circle dancing. Thus, while many U.K. LETS systems were based on a limited social network or were in a particular part of a city, in Manchester one citywide system was established. Combining resources from many networks (or, as members put it, "going where the energy is"), Manchester LETS sprang from a number of micropolitical resistance networks with an aim of facilitating trade, developing economic alternatives, and supporting mutual aid.

Manchester LETS was also different from many LETS systems in that the early joiners hoped and believed that LETS was a revolutionary new financial innovation that would be able to bring about significant social change and cure many of the pathologies from which the capitalist economy suffered. They wanted to be taken seriously. To achieve this potential, a LETS should be established as a serious, competent, and efficient organization operating to high standards. A core ethos insisted that members take responsibility for ensuring that they did what they agreed to do. Core group meetings were held regularly to coordinate organization, a manual specified what jobs were to be done by whom, and work teams coordinated the various tasks. A premium was put on what Rosabeth Moss Kantor (1972) called "commitment building mechanisms" that bind individuals to the group and ensure that it functions effectively. Care was taken to project, from the start, a professional image, and the organization produced a forty-four-page directory that came out on time, was accurate, and included advertisements from one or two local business members. This level of organization obviously relied on the involvement, often for many hours a week, of many committed individuals. The network was not launched until a large community of prospective traders had been established that would form a robust network delivering concrete benefits from the start, with trading starting at a ceremonial launch meeting at which, as on the stock exchange, with the ringing of a bell.

However, this core ethos came strongly from one of the founder networks and was contested to the extent that it came close to alienating those who wanted a more explicitly micropolitical or counter cultural focus that did not emphasize a professional and mainstream image. These members, from the green and anticapitalist networks, wanted to value everyone's contributions equally by establishing some accepted hourly labor rate. Others wished simply to share their skills with others without using any form of currency. Some wanted to be able to acknowledge other people by paying them a local currency, but not receive any themselves. Yet others wanted simply to charge one unit per job. So from the beginning the ethos of Manchester LETS was contested and the network was composed of members with wildly varying conceptions of how to use and value the currency and of the extent to which what they had joined was an anticapitalist movement or an unproblematic financial innovation of benefit to all that would save the world from imminent ecological and financial catastrophe. As we saw earlier, this was an issue that Owen and Douglas had to grapple with in their day.

To keep members of both tendencies together, a libertarian

compromise was brokered that would ensure that no one group could dominate:

> The vision was, and is, one where LETSystems remain "light" in their administration and avoid becoming organisations themselves. The focus of a LETSystem is its trading. The administration of a LETSystem is only there to facilitate the trading activities of its members by the provision of accounts and the directory. If we keep things light, then all sorts of initiatives can happen from within the network, like the "LETS get together,"[1] and local trading events,[2] or imaginative community development ideas. (Internal document, 4 January 95)

Therefore, the Manchester LETS core group saw it as a "free association" of members using LETS as a "tool" that was little more than an accounting package and directory. They thought nothing should be done centrally except to deliver this tool to members to use as they saw fit. The implication of this was that LETS was not necessarily a resistant movement with a specific set of values, and that any one ethos was likely to discourage participation from those that did not agree with it. Mass usage of this financial innovation was more likely, they thought, if no core set of values was insisted on beyond the ethos of acting professionally and keeping one's promises to other members. Manchester LETS aimed to enable those with a countercultural focus and those who saw more mainstream potential to interact on the basis of shared interest in exchange.

The name of the unit of local currency—the "bobbin"—was also a libertarian attempt to avoid investing the currency with any one set ethos. The name was chosen "because of the historical connection of Manchester with the textile industry . . . [but also] because the expression 'it's bobbins' is sometimes used locally to mean 'it's of little or no value' or 'it's worthless.' We considered if this might be a drawback, but decided that it is accurate since the bobbins themselves really are worth nothing—it's the talents and resources of the members that matter!" (Internal document, "Manchester LETS Policy"). Manchester LETS chose a name for its currency that, it hoped, made it clear that it had no value in and of itself. The ascription of value was left to individual innovation:

> What's a bobbin worth? It's entirely a matter for you and the person you are trading with.

Businesses usually opt to treat 1 bobbin as equivalent to a pound sterling because it's easy for them to administer. The people who work for LETS usually claim 6 bobbins an hour. People for whom social contact is an important part of their trades might charge a flat rate of 1 bobbin for any job.

Each trade has its own unique characteristics. No single exchange formula is satisfactory for everyone. You can try out one of the methods above or have fun trying out your own ideas. Feel free!

Thus members were free to decide how to value their work, how to value the bobbin, and how much sterling to charge, and individual members with differing sets of values were left free to interact. The core group "decid[ed] to give no guidelines or restrictions, since the heart of LETS is to encourage people to take control of their economic life" (Internal Document, "Manchester LETS Policy"). Unfortunately, to the everyday Mancunian the phrase "that's bobbins" really does mean "that's useless" and consequently cuts against some of the inherent qualities that an effective form of money, whatever it is used for, should have. It suggests not trust, but defection—"I wouldn't pay him in bobbins" (for shoddy work). It does not suggest that the token that this group has adopted is reliable, that it is serious, or that it will hold its value in the future. In short, it does not suggest "moneyness."

The alternative was the "Manchester pound," adopted by another Manchester-based local money network that focused more explicitly on business participation, but this would have demotivated the more countercultural members, who were excited by the inherently resistant qualities of calling the money the "bobbin." These members argued that focusing on recruiting businesses promoted the continuation of a destructive economy and introduced exploitation into the system (Wall 1990; Coleman 1994, 133–34). Advocates of the bobbin wanted to celebrate money as no more than a unit of measurement, with a name that did not in reality mean anything. This is not as strange as it seems: Lapavitsas (2005, 9) points to other theorists who have argued on similar lines, such as Innes, who wrote: "The eye has never seen, nor the hand touched a dollar. All that we can touch or see is a promise to pay or satisfy a debt for an amount called a dollar. . . . The theory of the abstract standard is not so extraordinary as it first appears, and it presents no difficulty to those scientific men with whom I have discussed the theory. All our measures are the same. No one has ever seen an ounce or a foot or an hour." Or even Marx, (1867/1976, 190), who wrote: "Since the expression of the value of the commodities in gold is a purely ideal act, we may use purely imaginary or ideal gold to perform this operation. Every owner of commodities knows that he is nowhere near turning them into gold when he has given their value in the form of a price or of imaginary gold, and that it does not require the tiniest particle of real gold to give a valuation in gold of millions of pounds of commodities." Manchester LETS chose a name that stressed the role of money as numerary, as a unit of measurement unconnected with anything real, and not as a store of value with intrinsic value. The bobbin was as far from a hard currency as ice cream is from gold.

The core group also wanted people to "encourage people to take control of their economic life" and "try out one of the methods above or have fun trying out your own ideas. Feel free!" This also is not value free. It cuts against Simmelian conceptions of money as modernity, money that cleans up economic life and detaches questions of personal morality or sentiment from exchange in complex economies. It is a claim for free economic life that cuts against the need for wage slaves to have to sell their labor in disadvantageous and alienated economic relationships. Manchester LETS was therefore, from the beginning, a rather schizophrenic organization, proclaiming from the top a libertarian ethos that most members did not (really) subscribe to and a form of money that was explicitly resistant while claims for universality were made.

"Transformers" and "Heterotopians": Contested Values in LETS

Recall that the main object of this chapter for our wider study is to examine the differing value bases that inspire participation in LETS and the extent to which LETS can be conceived of as micropolitical resistance to capitalist systems of domination, here in a mature capitalist state (the United Kingdom). During fieldwork in Manchester in 1995–96 I developed a fourfold typology of alternative values placed on a scale, with those who saw LETS as an uncontroversial financial innovation at one end (Transformers) and those who saw it as micro-political resistance at the other (Heterotopians).[3] These are "ob-server-generated" categories (Hammersley and Atkinson 1983, 178).

The LETSystem: "LETS is Value-Free"

The "LETSystem" is the name for Michael Linton's original scheme from Comox Valley, Canada, which was organized according to a "value-free," libertarian ethos and forms the extreme "transfor matory" end of our spectrum. LETSystem designer Linton locates LETS as a monetary system firmly within the evolutionary school, as the latest in a long line of financial innovations that uses personal computing and other new information technologies to enable every one to act as their own bank issuing their own personal credit money. Participants back this with a commitment to earn back the credit they have issued at a later date. According to Linton, "This is com pletely neutral—a bank account . . . like store budget vouchers or air miles. If we can say to people, 'Have a card that saves you cash,' do we have to educate them, morally? No. Do they have to understand the system? No. They have to understand that it's saving them cash, and if they understand that, they're happy, and I'm happy" (Michael Linton, Comox Valley LETS, 1996).[4] This echoes Douglas's claim that it is no more necessary for everyone to understand finance than it is to understand, say, the intricacies of electricity generation to use power. No preexisting values are needed before one can use this new tool. This was certainly a claim that resonated with many ordinary members of Manchester LETS, who saw it as an uncontroversial new financial innovation that they found useful in their day-to-day lives:

> A friend suggested that she thought [LETS] was me, and I do a lot of soft furnishing type things. I've got someone to do all my ironing, cleaning my windows. I give piano lessons, so my main interest is the contact with other people. You do make good friends, you know, meet lots of interest-ing people. . . . I don't see it as Green Party, I don't saw it as any party. I think I see it as going back in time, and it's how people used to, you know, exchange goods: a loaf of bread for a lettuce, or a pound of tomatoes for a cucumber. It's just how people used to be. (Margaret, Manchester LETS)

> I didn't get involved in LETS as I believed in it for a political reason. I don't have a strong feeling that we need to develop an alternative to the

money system—I don't think it's possible to be honest. I just don't. I think
that the power of the money system is just phenomenal. (Bob, Manchester
LETS)

A couple who described themselves, jokingly, as "the only Tories in
the LETS scheme" argued that there is plenty about entrepreneurialism and self-help that would have appealed to nineteenth-century
self-help guru Samuel Smiles (1866/1966). Others, echoing Simmel,
saw LETS as a way of cleaning up relations previously based on reciprocity that they felt were not balanced. For example, one single par-
ent rejoiced in the fact that she could afford to pay to get things done
she needed, and did not have to cadge favors.

Taking a Smithian line, LETS can be seen as no more than the latest example of financial evolution that facilitates humanity's natural
tendency to truck, barter, and exchange when, as in the United Kingdom in the mid-1990s, the capitalist economy was undergoing one
of its periodic crises. The first problem with this claim was, however,
the small size of Manchester LETS—one of the United Kingdom's
largest schemes—which limited the amount of trading possible, and
the second, as we saw later, was the nearly total lack of business participation (problems not restricted to Manchester LETS; see Aldridge and Patterson 2002; North 1996, 1998a, 1999b). Both of these
limited the effectiveness of bobbins as a form of money. Besides,
while LETS can be seen as the latest in a long line of financial innovations, this is not the same as seeing it as a welcome innovation.
Quantity theorists would be concerned if individuals issued credit
they did not then earn back, for the amount of money in circulation would quickly be out of balance with the volume of goods and
services and, they would argue, lead to inflation (although remember that Keynes would have argued that if money stayed in people's
LETS accounts, as savings, it wouldn't necessarily be inflationary).
Finally, enabling individuals to issue their own money to others in
order to meet their needs (assuming there are enough people, skills,
and resources available) fundamentally cuts against capitalist labor
discipline. Enabling people to avoid selling their labor power in disadvantageous exchange relationships is far from value free. In fact, it
is micropolitical dynamite.

Humanizing the Economy

Transformers publicly promoted LETS as an apolitical innovation that should be seen as a legitimate attempt to maximize participation from as diverse a group of people as possible in order to build a robust trading network with as many resources as possible. Their message was "All are welcome": those who join for instrumental rationality as well as those who are true believers. I call this approach "transforming" because advocates of LETS argued that through their everyday interactions with others traders would be subjected to a number of social, market, and micropolitical signals that would transform their outlook for the better. They would be "humanized" and "greened." Linton argued that, because these effects are designed in, LETS is a powerful tool for transforming the quality of relationships between economic actors (what LETS members call "relationship trading"), building economic alternatives, and constructing localized economies

LETS participants often say that they joined because they "want to get away from the money economy." By this they mean that they want an economy that values people more than profit, need more than efficiency, and quality more than cheapness. The humanizers therefore sought to "humanize" the economy by connecting spiritual and economic values, primarily by redefining and revaluing work—especially that often attributed to women, the young, and the old—by refusing to define its value in narrowly instrumental cost-benefit terms. Humanist economic thought traditionally categorized conceptions of the economy into Schumacher's (1973) idea of "Buddhist economics," contrasting mainstream HE (high-tech, exploitative) values with those of a humane or SHE (sane, humane, and ecological) economy. Dobson (1993) saw LETS as bringing the economy "home." Consequently, proponents claim that LETS is a more balanced economy that values the affective, emotional, and cooperative as well as efficiency, organization and the achievement of goals: "I saw it as a balanced economy—a balance between men and women, between the masculine and feminine in each of us.... An economy that calls on each of us to practice in that kind of way is more likely to soften people than this horrendous situation that frightens so many people—men as much as women" (Rose, Manchester LETS). Humanizers hoped to redefine work away from the nine-to-five and away from a world of full-time employment to a blur of work and leisure. They valued a freer, more informal economy with opportunities for a portfolio of varied work opportunities as a real alternative to conventional employment patterns. Humanizers emphasized the contribution and value of those who are not valued in the conventional economy (young people, older people, people with special needs, people recovering from mental illness). They sought to redefine work away from the concept of a "job" to that of a "valued activity." As two humanizers explained:

> I became more and more interested in how people can actually participate in valued activities without actually calling it employment. Because, for a lot of people, the opportunity to be involved in valued activity in the community is as important as a job. I believed that there are a lot of dormant skills in the community which people don't use, people don't value. People value experience in terms of putting a suit on or going to a job, or calling themselves "a teacher" or calling themselves "a road sweeper." People ignore the fact that . . . we've all got huge quantities of shareable talents and skills. (Gilli, Manchester LETS)

> We have an economy at the moment and all we are doing is changing the way it is transacted, and a lot more besides, the means of control, the choices, the aims and whether they can be more green aims. Changing the word economy for creativity. We don't talk about economic growth, we talk about happiness growth, creativity growth. The fact that there is all this creativity going on, it won't be undermining anyone, it's just changing shape slowly. It's like pizza bubbling away—there are little bubbles turning up here and there. It's just changing, yes? (Kos, Manchester LETS)

Humanizers argued that rational economic actors will be "humanized" through participation in LETS, for they will find that for optimum efficiency in their exchanges they will need to pay attention to the quality of their relationships with those with whom they trade, ensuring that they treat their fellows in a convivial, supportive, and nonexploitative fashion, for they have no other way of enforcing participation or the provision of a quality service: "The LETS community does look at a transaction as a relationship, whereas the commercial world looks upon a transaction as a transaction. You need some respect for the person you are dealing with, as you know they don't have to do it. It's got to be mutually beneficial, whereas a transaction in the real world does not have to be. . . . There's an imbalance of power" (John P, Manchester LETS).

In a LETS, currency is unlimited; there are neither credit limits, debt charges, nor disciplinary methods of forcing people to work. Participants will see through the way money acts as a local system of domination supporting capitalist rationality:

> It throws a light onto what money actually is, and you actually see it as the trick it is. . . . It's quite a notion that we are collectively fooled by the flickering value of money as being how we value ourselves. If we looked at things in a different way, if we give things of beauty which currently have no money value—I saw it as part of that movement, and of course this goes against the status quo quite a lot. (Malcolm, Manchester LETS)

> I think it's one of the mechanisms by which capitalism can be subverted, because capitalism rests on a system of power relations. I don't think LETS has the same capacity for those power relations. . . . There are two things wrong with capitalism: one is the power relations inherent in it. It's not that, you know, capitalism is a bad thing; it's that it inevitably has these power relations, and capitalism inevitably causes ecological destruction unnecessarily because it has to grow. And LETS is more geared to what people need, far more so than the formal economy is. I wouldn't think that LETS would be capable of it on its own [but] . . . I think it's one of the important mechanisms. Taking the wind out of capitalism is how I would best sum it up. (Spencer, Manchester LETS)

Exchanges in LETS must be free and unconstrained, and traders will begin to recognize that cooperation is in their own rational self-interest. Participants joining with no prior knowledge of or commitment to alternatives will gain access to alternatives to full-time employment and will be educated about alternative livelihoods. Cooperative values will be diffused throughout the economy through practice, not protest or agitation:

> By its very nature, as people get involved with it their life does not stay the same. I mean, they still do their shopping at Marks and Spencers but they then take a detour into different people with different ideas, and, you know, have different shopping and eating habits, and way of life. So it diversifies and perhaps undermines the system that we have here at the moment because it involves people taking a bit more of their lives rather than their lives controlling them. (John P, Manchester LETS)

Here LETS is conceived of as a process whereby, as Polanyi would have put it, society aims to gain control of the economic. LETS emerges less as a financial innovation than, in Zelitzean terms, as a way in which emotion, affection, community, and humanity can be

[*89*]

used as ways to regulate, and humanize, economic transactions. The commodity school would argue that this is possible only if this new social money is used to exchange real commodities, while Marx argued that ordinary people own too few resources to enable this process of humanization to go very far unless the fundamental logic of the capitalist system is challenged. These are issues that we will return to after we have examined greening, the twin to humanizing as a micropolitical attack on the way money works to reinforce capitalist domination.

Greening

Greeners, like humanizers, saw LETS as a way of facilitating sustainable patterns of economic development that could widely be used:

> The Green Party . . . were concerned about what they saw as an impending ecological crisis, and people started to think about ways of avoiding environmental disaster and evolving sustainable ways of living. Then it got on to deeper and broader issues that were concerned with politics in a wider sense, and the relationship was drawn between protecting and sustaining the environment, and social justice and the satisfaction of people's lives and relationships between people, and ways communities and societies could be organised in a sustainable and fulfilling way, which was in harmony with one another, and also the environment. (Storm, Manchester LETS)

The "local" of LETS was important to greeners (North 2005). Greeners argued that LETS was a tool for localizing the economy (Hines 2000). Localizers argued that in order to cut down on resource use and the destruction of local difference by globalization, everything that could be produced locally should be in preference to that which is imported. LETS, they argued, facilitated localization by discriminating in favor of local produce and local trading networks within a localized economy, thus reducing transport costs, the burning of fossil fuels, pollution, and the need for road building. Local businesses would be favored over multinationals with no attachment to place, thus strengthening local ownership and control. Just as they believed LETS humanized those who joined for purely rational economic reasons, so they thought it would subtly "green" them.

Greens felt that LETS is designed using certain attributes that they identify as positive from the natural world (Dobson 1990, 24). LETS values *diversity* through a multiplicity of local currencies, views the economy as a collection of *interdependent* actors connected to each other, and through its diversity is *resilient.* These qualities are important, because looming ecological and financial crises can be weathered only if new, resilient systems are constructed that are not, like conventional economies, reliant on a monoculture of money. If one form of money fails, with complementary and alternative currencies another can take its place—something impossible with a money monoculture, as with a crop monoculture. This is an argument we shall return to in our later discussion of a country that did suffer financial crisis, Argentina. LETS was also seen to act as a brake on consumption and thereby on growth and carbon consumption. It was a slower economy: it took time to get someone to perform a task, with the result that participants would question whether the task needed to be done in the first place. It encouraged people to share everyday items such as washing machines, garden equipment, tools, computers, and printing facilities.

Green Anarchism

A political milieu allied to LETS, and one that provided many of its members, was that organized around community, permaculture, organic methods, food co-ops, and conflict resolution circles—all concerned with building oppositional or alternative institutions. The positions of those in this milieu can be called anarchist in view of their antipathy to persuading mainstream economic institutions, small businesses, and the like to join Manchester LETS, which resonates with the politics of Anarchist writers such as Colin Ward (1988), Murray Bookchin (1986, 1995a,b), or Rudolf Bahro (1994). However, a small *a* is used in recognition of the fact that many large-*A* Anarchists did not join LETS in reaction to what they saw as further commodification of the mutual sphere, and also in reaction to the professional image adopted by transformers in their urge to recruit businesses.

The LETS anarchists fell into the nonviolent, Gandhian branch of Anarchism rather than the violent, Bakuninite class-struggle Anarchism associated with newspapers such as *Green Anarchist* or *Class War.* They believed that social change comes from building alternative institutions that enable as much of life as possible to be lived without having to participate in the capitalist system. They argued that LETS increasingly enables members to live outside the mainstream economy in the here and now. According to one proponent: "The great thing about LETS is that you can start to live life outside capitalism, outside mainstream work or on the dole. Being unemployed is very soul-destroying and isolating, but LETS gives you a way to be part of a wider group and sell your skills so unemployment doesn't grind you down" (Andy, Manchester LETS). These LETS anarchists regarded it important to obtain food and other basics within the system to make life outside the mainstream possible. They saw LETS as a scaffold around which a countercultural alternative to the mainstream could be built. They sought to reduce to a minimum their connection with the mainstream economy and the world of work by building an alternative community. Therefore, they sought to deepen LETS rather than widen it, gaining access to food, shelter, and alternative livelihoods, and to withdraw from the mainstream rather than attempting to humanize it by recruiting businesses. They saw LETS as a "lifeboat" enabling participants to shelter from the storm of globalization (Pacione 1997). They saw communal support as growing and growing, so that the use of local currency would become little more than pointkeeping that withered away, and until it did they advocated valuing everyone's work equally, at either six bobbins an hour or at a "bob-a-job"; they wanted to do anything but recreate the inequalities of the mainstream economy.

Green anarchists aimed to recover the self-reliance that, echoing Polanyi, they felt communities had before expropriation from the land under enclosure in the eighteenth century. The anarchists were keen to reconnect in some way to the land they lived on and to live comfortably within a self-supporting framework—that is, to re-embed economic relations that capitalism broke up in the rush to create markets and facilitate factory-based production. The growth of supermarkets, which limits options for buying from local producers, and people's increasing inability to cook basic foods and survive are problems to be addressed if social breakdown is to be avoided. Anarchists saw the "lore of eons"—local knowledge about local plants and foods—as being lost. They argued that if trends toward the development of out-of-town supermarkets continued to erode the business of local shopkeepers, opportunities for self-reliant livelihoods would decline. For the green anarchists, LETS was an attempt to develop sustainable self-reliance while avoiding a full retreat into communes, as advocated by Rudolf Bahro (what Spiro [1970] called the nonwithdrawing commune), or social breakdown.

Here LETS is explicitly conceived of as micropolitical resistance. Elsewhere (North 1995) I have described LETS as a form of postmodern commune within society, not withdrawing physically from it as did the communards of the nineteenth century (Kantor 1972). Rejecting the Marxist claim that social change comes from changing the real economy, with money as a representation of an underlying reality of commodity production, the Green anarchists, following Foucault, saw money as a focus for contestation in its own terms and as a tool for building more liberated social relations in the here and now—as a spatial or temporal heterotopia. Members of LETS, they argued, could use this new libratory tool to create the livelihoods they wanted in the here and now.

The Effectiveness of the Transforming Strategy

Elsewhere (North 1996, 2006) I have examined the transforming strategy in more detail. Because this book focuses on micropolitics, I will not examine it except where completeness so requires. Suffice to say that the effectiveness of the transformational strategy was limited, partly because Manchester LETS remained small, mainly attracting already politically active members with preexisting political views sympathetic to the project. Those who did have more instrumental views found that the number and volume of trades, when compared with those operating in the mainstream economy, were too few for transformation to take place. A very small number of businesses did join—eight according to the April 1995 *Directory*. Three (a cafe, a junk shop, and a beauty parlor) joined LETS because their businesses had been in trouble, in an effort to acquire more customers, but LETS had not made the difference in their eventual business failure. Of the five businesses that survived, one, a car rental firm, left because, based on the other side of the metropolis in Rochdale, it had no trade. Other businesses had happier stories: a law firm, a cycle shop, a recycling company, and a print company formed to print a book. However, these businesses joined for political reasons, out of sympathy with the values of LETS. The law firm was run by one of the founding members of Manchester LETS, who was also a Green Party member. The print company was formed to print a book written by a core group member, and the recycling company joined "as it is something that we want to support which is basically, cooperation." The cycle company joined for political reasons after reading about LETS in the press, but the proprietor also recognized that many of the members of Manchester LETS, as good greens, would be keen cyclists. These four of the eight businesses in Manchester LETS traded fairly successfully, but at such low levels that it is impossible to see LETS as forming anything other than a minor part of their business activities.

Besides, very few members of Manchester LETS supported the transformation strategy, so few resources were put into it; only five of the 550-odd members joined the development arm, LETS Development Agency, which sought to widen participation in LETS by mainstream institutions (see North 2006, 107–37). The inherently transformational nature of the message the activists put out was unattractive both to their fellow LETS members and to those whom the transformers wished to recruit. Far, far more work was put into LETS conceived as a micropolitical alternative to capitalism, and it is to this that we will devote most of our time in this discussion.

The Effectiveness of Micropolitics

The green anarchist heterotopians were generally happy to see the transformers attempting to engage with the mainstream. They did not ask them to stop and wished them well—but they were unconvinced of the likelihood of success. They preferred to build an alternative system that would, eventually, be able to take over many of the state's functions in a peaceable transformation to a decentralized, steady-state, community-based economy. They saw LETS as an observable alternative or a declaration of what one called "other ideas in circulation. They don't necessarily mean that things are going to change, dramatically, and for me that doesn't matter too much. There has to be . . . that struggle and new ideas." A similar comment was this:

To me LETS is mainly about the . . . educative thing. I mean, the kind of capitalist cynicism that goes around, about market forces and about the laws of supply and demand and about people being basically greedy gits that rip people off all the time. I think LETS is a good way of demonstrating, "No—that's not actually true." People are capable of being like that but they are also capable of being different. LETS is a good way of demonstrating to people even if they are not actually involved in it. They can say, well there's a community, a community that's scattered around Manchester. (Spencer, Manchester LETS)

In micropolitical terms, the heterotopians clearly understood the limits of the strategy and how it should relate to other social change strategies:

It'll never undermine [capitalism]. It'll always be a peripheral activity of highly educated, politically conscious folk. For handmade leather shoes and batik prints, for wet Thursdays, etcetera! Middle-class hobbies. (Malcolm, Manchester LETS)

I don't think LETS on its own can create localised economies. . . . If you don't want a telly, and you are prepared to live on an allotment in a bender, that sort of thing, then LETS, no doubt, could do that now . . . provided you were the one growing the food because I don't think anyone else in Manchester is doing it . . . on the LETS system! But if you want a public transport network, if you want to be able to manufacture a bicycle, that sort of thing, then we really need local economies, and that will take political action. (Spencer, Manchester LETS)

Echoing Scott's arguments that micropolitics can be the "weapons of the weak," some heterotopians felt that their life experience consisted of their inability to change life at the macro level:

I am a politically, with a small *p*, motivated person. I believe in the micro rather than the macro. Because in macro terms . . . in my life experience the problems of the larger society are so massive that I can't be arsed with getting my head round them, using my energy, on changing something which in reality, in my experience of life, I've not been able to change at all. For most of my working and adult life I've lived under Margaret Thatcher's Conservative government.

So the big issues are totally beyond my control, and I got fed up with thumping tables and with Politics with a big *P!* But I do feel that what influence I have on the small scale, er . . . is putting my energy into organizations that I give a try to. . . . So I'd still . . . put an enormous amount of energy into anything that calls itself a community. I saw that as one of the ways in which the world can change, as, you know, in my life experience it's almost impossible to try and change the world in a meaningful way for

me by politics, or voting, or standing on street corners and shouting. . . .
I'll concentrate on something I can actually do something about! And a
community like LETS, which does things, shares doing things, is one of
the most hopeful signs that this society might actually be making a [few
steps in the right direction]. (Rose, Manchester LETS)

An interesting interchange between Kos, John P., and Linda took this
a little further. Kos said:

> The thing I'm very worried about, is that the majority, the vast majority,
> are still producing more arms and things like that, the world is arming itself
> against itself. That's still going on every day in factories in the Manchester
> region. . . . The thing that comes to mind, it's that it's a subculture, LETS
> is a subculture. It's how do we get the values out of the subculture, if they
> are good, to a wider group?

John P. replied:

> These are not new ideas, and that alternative is there all the time, and it's
> difficult to suppress it. Happiness is not an unnatural thing. And we are
> living in an artificial environment. It's a struggle for people to live the life
> they are living now. So what I'm saying is, you may be right, something
> may happen that is beyond people's control. . . . But, I think it's the right
> thing to do, to develop that line of thought that makes your life happier,
> basically. If it makes you happier, if you think it's the right thing to do,
> and you think it has an effect on other people, it's got to be the right thing
> to do.

Linda added:

> I really like your ideas. I like to think I do that as well, but . . . the way to
> change based on one to one is quite slow, isn't it? But one of the things I
> like about LETS is that it does speed that process a bit. . . . You've just
> started me thinking about the different ways you can live your life.

We saw from the previous analysis that members of Manchester
LETS were, through micropolitical action, able to create new forms
of money that they agreed to accept from each other and saw this as
a limited social change strategy that was quicker than individual action, but perhaps still a "weapon of the weak," used by those who did
not feel able to make the macroeconomic changes Marx demanded.
This is one side of the coin: they could create money. But could they
spend it? Some could:

> I used it a lot at the beginning because it had a lot of things I wanted, quite
> essential things rather than luxuries, things that others would not see as

essential. And I really wanted those things and I was quite creative about getting them. Sometimes people, I managed to coax people to do things that they weren't necessarily offering in the directory. I knew someone that was quite handy, and they'd done a bit of plumbing and I suggested that they would be able to remove some gas piping. I had this big gas thing in my front room and I wanted a fire there. I coaxed them into removing that, which was really good. Someone changed my toilet for me who . . . who needed a little encouragement a bit, but it was a brilliant job. A guy got my car through the MOT. . . . So I felt like I really needed these things, so I went out to get them. (Katrina, Manchester LETS)

However, Katrina went on to say that although she was able to spend, to create money, she found it harder to earn money from others to balance her commitment. Old ideas of debt from the mainstream money system continued to colonize her mind, and the micropolitics of creating a new money system did not break through. Responding to this, in a focus group Storm commented:

I think people do still think of it as money because why would they have problems . . . [others respond, "Yes, yes") . . . about getting into debt? I know someone who has a balance of minus 300 bobbins, and she's having a great time . . . (others respond, "Yes, yes") . . . because she's just going out and spending more bobbins and that's great because it generates trade within the network, and it means that someone else says suddenly, "Oh, I've got bobbins. What shall I spend it on?" The bobbins are no good just lying under the counter. I think it is a different attitude.

However, evidence for the existence of cultural change comes from the active traders. Only 142 of the 550 members had a turnover of more than 160 bobbins, so they had a limited amount of trading experience. Although turnover is an inappropriate measure of economic activity precisely because use of the bobbin drops off in time as members who get to know each other often stop using them to lubricate the exchange, cultural innovation was restricted by the small scale of trading, even in one of the world's biggest LETS systems. The small scale of trades that took place, when contrasted with the magnitude of economic and social interactions governed by mainstream logic, severely limited the amount of cultural innovation possible. While the active members found it possible to understand and engage in "relationship trading," less active traders found it much more difficult to participate in this cultural innovation, and there were specific barriers to trading. Some were limited in what they could do by a lack of time or being without a telephone (in some cases those with phones but without an answering machine found that people did not call back). Other less active traders were those living some distance away, who found people were unwilling to travel (incurring sterling costs). Others lacked confidence to make the first move and pick up the telephone to commission work from strangers. They were wary of entering a commitment. Others did not have skills that other members wanted.

As a result of low levels of participation, people found it hard to innovate and often fell back on governing their trades by familiar values associated with the capitalist market. They found negotiation difficult, unsure about how much to ask people to do, how much to pay them, what they could or could not be legitimately asked to do. Their ability to socially create their own value systems was also limited by the intrusion of the mainstream economy into the alternative economy. Members complained that others were not accepting bobbins and were trying to charge what they regarded as unreasonable levels of sterling. One member wrote to the core group in January 1995:

> I feel that LETS is becoming rather too money-orientated. More members are asking for Sterling and bobbins for their *labour* as well as for their products/services. We could do with a *general meeting* to discuss our ethos. LETS is, in certain senses, beginning to mirror the money economy and the capitalist class system. Even when bobbins only are charged there is a tendency for those middle class members whose talents and skills are highly valued in the money economy to charge *pro rata* for bobbins. I believed this is wrong and devalues the original LETS ideal which was to subvert the money economy.
>
> Unless we can get back to the notion that an hour of my time is worth an hour of anyone else's, then I fear many whose skills are poorly used/not valued at all in the £ economy will feel disillusioned and will leave.

Here we see less an example of the transformational strategy of relationship trading changing those operating by capitalist logic than the other way around: as Marx suggested, the capitalist economy began to discipline the alternative economy. Worse, the ability of the heterotopians to operate through changed cultural codes around money was limited by the transformers, who professed themselves to be "quite intolerant of this attitude." As one member said, "I want to say to people, 'Get real!' People still have to live and make their way and pay their bills so they would have to charge sterling to pay their bills, and people needed to understand that the self-employed person had a right to a good income as well and to respect that. I'm more and more telling people not to be backward about putting up the sterling component of their charges and not exploit themselves" (Siobhan, Manchester LETS).

While heterotopians could make the jump and revalue fairly easily, transformers ensured that the system was open to all comers and that those with "old" ideas about money were able to join. Transformers insisted that it was for individuals alone to decide what they would use as their definition of value and to wage individual wars against those who had values different from their own. The most active members with heterotopian perspectives were able to create networks that traded using their changed value system. For most members, however, the small volume of transactions through which these individual wars could be fought ensured that attempts to trade often ended with a refusal or made with those who did not accept the acceptable hourly rate rather than with a collective process of redefining cultural concepts around money. Alternatively, members found that cultural codes were not changed and the influence of structural forces in terms of common-sense values about money—that "debt is wrong," that "it is good to have savings," that "you can't spend what you haven't got"—remained to govern the system. Cultural change around money, then, was limited for many, but possible for the active.

Active traders often did manage to redefine work. The LETS economy gave out different price signals and made work—as a healer, a wormery builder, a batik workshop facilitator—viable. Another was brave enough to offer to trade "perished rubber gloves." Members could surf the *New Age* safely without fear of the financial abuse of possibly vulnerable people (one can pay hundreds of pounds for alternative therapies available very inexpensively to LETS members). LETS was a desire-driven economy operating under different rules, with different market signals. However, again there were limits to the ability of members to revalue work. With the volume of trades being so low, many traders found it hard to break through into an understanding that the LETS economy operated under different market signals. They continued to think in terms governed by their life experience within the mainstream economy (as they had with revaluing money). For instance, they found it hard to decide what skills they had, and what was or was not a sellable skill. They found it hard to say what was or was not an acceptable skill level for which they would feel comfortable receiving bobbins without being thought of as a "cowboy" trader:

> I feel that on occasions people do not take responsibility for their product when they advertise it—you know, they advertise it as, you know, being a gardener or being a graphic designer, er—and I know it's up to the individual to negotiate about their skills base when you are forming a contract. . . . It's about honesty and integrity. I wouldn't dream of telling you I could mend a bicycle. Unless I was sure I could mend a bicycle satisfactorily, safely, and that you would be pleased with the product. . . . Because that's one of the rules in which interaction works, you know, we don't have relationships which are open-ended. We have carefully negotiated relationships. It just seems to me that LETS is begging that issue. (Gilli, Manchester LETS)

Some members showed a lack of commitment to trading. Too many mentioned making many calls for someone to provide a service, which meant that for the committed member earning bobbins was not a difficulty, but the loop too easily closed off and the member with a high credit balance found himself unable to spend. One member felt that he was fooling himself by trading and accepting bobbins he could not spend:

> I've accumulated a great pile of bobbins in my bobbin account—which I haven't as yet spent! I don't know where to spend my bobbins! I must say that I'm feeling a smidgen frustrated at this, as I think I'd prefer at the moment to be paid sterling as I could spend that and I'm finding it very difficult to spend bobbins, as when I looked through the list. . . . It's all a bit frustrating. . . . I don't buy very much anyway—I suppose I'm not a very good consumer! . . . of the sort of things LETS offers. I think that what I would like to have done would be to employ a LETS cleaner, but we have a cleaning lady who's been coming for x number of years, and it's impossible to change that relationship. It wouldn't have worked at all. It would have been impossible to keep her. (Malcolm, Manchester LETS)

The same problems observed with the micropolitics of money became observable with work. Work was either successfully redefined—or not—individually rather than collectively and with support. The ethos of keeping administration light left members alone to sink or swim, to decide what to offer alone, with little support in teasing out hidden skills.

Conclusion

This chapter has shown that—within limits set by a lack of owner-ship of the means of production—members of a large network were able to create and use their own form of currency that they agreed to accept from each other, and many who had sellable skills could earn significant amounts of the new local currency. But because the unit of currency was called a bobbin and thus was attractive to the counter-cultural, the market remained small and local, and consequently only eight businesses joined. Thus, what was circulating was goods and services controlled by members, which, although more than dwarfish in amounts, could exist only alongside the mainstream economy. Is that a problem? Not necessarily if we are to value economic diversity rather than trying to impose one agreed-upon form of utopia. Mem-bers of Manchester LETS did create their own forms of money, trade with it, and thus create a micropolitical alternative to capitalism both as resistant practice and as a vision of an alternative. Given that it was small (463 members at its height) and fairly ephemeral (down to 190 members by 2000 and shut down in 2005), a significant challenge to financial domination could not be expected—although by 2001 the total system turnover was 270,305 bobbins, which is the equivalent of 135,152 bobbins-worth or 45,050 hours of work. To see more sig-nificant levels of participation we need to look elsewhere: for trading over longer periods of time, to New Zealand, and for mass usage, to Argentina. But before that we move to postsocialist Hungary.

6

Kaláka and Kör

GREEN MONEY, MUTUAL AID,
AND TRANSITION IN HUNGARY

I N POSTSOCIALIST HUNGARY, ALTERNATIVE CURRENCY SYSTEMS called Talentum (Talents) and Kör (Circles) emerged as part of that country's transition to a market economy. For some, they were institutions through which capitalist markets could be facilitated. For those in the civil society organizations that fought state socialism before 1989, they were part of a wider movement in favor of new, more liberated economic forms. These are very different conceptions of the role of civil society in constructing markets. In this chapter we examine Talentum and Kör in the context of radical politics in transitional countries, organizing our discussion around debates about the role of civil society in facilitating economic alternatives.

Civil society itself is a contested concept (Cohen and Arato 1992; Lewis 1992; Kaviraj and Khilnani 2001; Howell and Pearce 2002; Kaldor 2003). It is generally thought of as the stratum of society between the state and the individual that forms a defense against "tyranny" by providing spaces that the state does not control or in which state-sanctioned ideologies do not necessarily dominate. Neoliberals believe that civil society acts to defend the property rights that provide individuals with resources they can use, if necessary, to escape tyranny (Hayek 1944). Neoliberals also argue that civil society helps establish the rules and norms, or institutions, by which markets work, such as trust and the sanctity of contracts (Fukuyama 1995). These may be in the form of social capital, such as connections of trust, predictability, mutual aid, and cooperation, which, it is argued, make markets work effectively (Putnam 1993, 2001), Civil society–based organizations in market economies help individuals find work or set up small businesses and also help individuals who might feel atomized and alone, struggling in adverse economic situations, to combine to avoid or solve their problems or take advantage of new opportunities. This may be accomplished through establishing new civil society—based agencies that can deliver services, perhaps services formally provided by the state as part of a "modern" three-sector mixed economy of welfare provision (Poznanski 1992; Osborne and Kaposvari 1997). Consequently, civil society organizations can be seen as the "handmaidens of capitalist change," putting a human face on rather inhumane changes that benefit the wealthiest in an economy at the expense of the poorest, destroy local markets, and impose Western and capitalist values throughout society at the expense of nonmonetized mutual aid mechanisms (Kaldor 2003, 92–94).

The opposite conception, from the left, is of civil society as a democratic space counterpoised to the state "socialist" tyrannies of Eastern Europe and the former Soviet Union (Arato 1991, 1999; Cohen and Arato 1992; Kaldor 2003). Here defense against tyranny comes less from individualized exit through control of private property or through a private or family sphere than from collective organization from below. Central to this conception of civil society is self-management in political, and economic, and ecological senses. Rather than seeing civil society as a method of facilitating capitalist market relations based on exploitation, labor discipline, and economic inequality, proponents of this view sought new forms of economic life in which citizens, not capitalists or party bosses, would judge priorities and establish the terms under which economic life was carried out. This counterpower fought centralism as much as it fought for economic self-management; a debate in left politics that goes back to the visions of Edward Bellamy (1888/1946), for whom liberation was citizens' accessing what they needed through centralized workshops and commodity warehouses within a planned economy, as contrasted with William Morris's (1890/1993) decentralized libertarianism. It was also the conception of civil society that inspired the movements of 1989, and it is in that context that we examine green money in Hungary, part of which emerged from Hungary's green movement and its international connections, while part was developed through civil society–based nongovernmental organizations (NGOs) facilitated by development aid–funded East-West links.

Green money developed from Hungary's green movement, one of the strongest in central Europe and one of the key social movements, along with youth and peace movements, in Hungary's transition (Láng-Pickvance et al. 1997; Pickvance 1997, 1998a,b; Szirmai 1997). In the early 1990s, some Hungarian environmentalists learned about experiments with local money through connections with Austrian and German greens. A strong component of Hungarian environmentalism, in the context of resistance to the communist dictatorship they had just left behind and a concern that Western-style capitalism might be another form of tyranny, was a commitment to community support and friendship, mutual aid, and the importance of the local as a place of support and cohesion within which sustainable local economies might offer more liberated and ecologically justifiable alternatives. They were concerned that the transition from communism, which they generally welcomed, was leading not to more economic democracy and freedom but to "wild capitalism" and insecurity, with marketization and urbanization destroying communities and community support mechanisms. The change seemed out of control, and not necessarily leading in the right direction.

The Hungarian greens arranged for the translation of environmental literature on green money, such as the translation of Dauncey's (1988) book *Beyond the Crash: The Emerging Rainbow Economy* into Hungarian. The Austrian NGO Hilfe, which worked with people with disabilities, also promoted the idea in Hungary, and the country's first green money scheme, Talentum building on German and Canadian experiences, was established in Budapest in 1994. Hilfe then organized a conference on ecological issues in Eastern Europe, and the idea was promoted at this and subsequent green conferences in Hungary. Green money therefore emerged as part of the Hungarian green movement's newfound freedom to organize, but also in an environment in which people were concerned that the tyranny of the party was being replaced by the tyranny of money and of the market. It was a new phenomenon, but it was also built on deeper roots that relate to the specifics of the Hungarian experience of communism.

Mutual Aid in the Transition from
State Socialism to the Market in Hungary

For centuries, Hungarians living in villages practiced a form of mutual aid they call *kaláka;* the word is untranslatable into English, but means basically "doing things together" (Hollos and Maday 1983). Houses would be built, new families set out on their life journeys, children looked after, and crops gathered in through complex reciprocal arrangements, often based on blood ties. In a largely rural country, these arrangements were not disrupted by a communist regime that largely left the villages to fend for themselves:

> A pervasive feature of communist Hungary was the "reciprocal exchange of labour," in which households exchanged their labour on a non-market basis. Belying Western notions of the pervasiveness of the communist state, the state largely left villages alone and increasingly abandoned the provision of houses. The reciprocal exchange of labour, always important in Hungary, became an even more important form of network capital, especially in rural towns and villages. Despite modernization and communism, such villages have remained relatively closed because of their physical isolation and fears that external forces will harm them. (Sik and Wellman 1999)

A large "second economy" was also tolerated as a pragmatic so lution to problems of state planning and limited resources. Workers in state-owned companies would work in their own cooperatives on their own time, often using the equipment from their first job, with the toleration of the employers and the state (Hann 1990; Swain 1992). They would also work on their own vegetable plots and would build houses together (Kenedi 1981). As long as the fundamentals, the supremacy of the ruling communists, the position of the Soviet Union, and Hungary's place within COMECON (the Council for Mutual Economic Assistance) were not challenged, economic liberalism, foreign travel, a measure of free speech (but not the right to organize), and levels of consumer consumption above those of their neighbors were possible for Hungarians (Pickvance 1997, 1998b). Levels of freedom and repression can be gauged from statements by an environmental activist from the Danube Circle: "[The state] did have a few house searches executed, in order to keep Moscow assured that we did not tolerate such dissent: meanwhile, towards the West they made a showpiece of their liberalism; one could lecture in the so-called 'free universities,' or write *samizdat* publications, but you could not demonstrate on the street. That was where the line was drawn" (quoted by Pickvance 1998a, 40). Or from the experiences of a member of Green Future, who campaigned against polluting industries in the Budapest suburbs: "At the first [petition] signing sessions people were quite afraid. Many wanted to sign without their neighbours seeing, so I left the forms at the grocer's or the buyer's, so that no one would be seen being visited by me. Later we were not afraid any more" (quoted by Pickvance 1998a, 72).

This "goulash communism" led to Hungary's being known as the "happiest barracks in the camp." *Kaláka* in the villages, cooperative house building, and the "second," entrepreneurial economy released some of the pressure caused by the failing state economic planning system, but Hungarians also lived a schizophrenic existence in a state that was formally committed to state planning while not acknowledging either its shortcomings or the state repression required to keep Hungary in the Soviet orbit. The result of this two-track existence, Swain (1992, 12) argues, was a dual morality and dual society, for Hungarians developed two sets of values: one for public display, indicating conformity with socialist values, and one that was private, used when working in the second economy and with the family, which recognized that it was only through individual or family-based efforts that people would survive, let alone get ahead. The slippage between public ideology and everyday reality led not only to a loss of confidence in the system and a crisis of legitimacy, but to atomization, passivity, a decline in altruism and values of social solidarity, and a perception that violation and evasion of official norms would be rewarded materially through the second economy (Korosenyi 1999, 13). Korosenyi argued that Hungarians built a wall around the family, spending 83 percent of their time with family members. The result, even in the 1990s, was a highly individualized society.

However, these individualized networks began to break down as the disruption of transition led to the contraction of the second economy, and mutual aid relations built around employment suffered as state-owned factories were privatized and then closed. *Kaláka* networks built on kin relations degraded as people increasingly had to travel farther for increasingly hard-to-come-by work. A green money activist put it like this:

A long time ago it was a completely different situation in the countryside, because parents and grandparents all lived together and everybody knew each other, so it was a natural thing that once someone got married they got the presents from the wedding and everybody would build the house for the son and the following one and the following one, and it was going on like that. And nowadays the family members are at a longer distance; they don't have such close connections, and you cannot replace such a close system of relationships and connections that we used to have in olden times in the countryside. (Erika, organizer, Szolnok Kör)

Economic performance did not reach pretransition levels until 1998, and the poor economic conditions in the early and mid-1990s, high levels of unemployment, and a feeling that social solidarity was breaking down in the face of hegemonic neoliberalism led some Hungarians to see a solution in the building of community feeling.

The inheritance was therefore a mixed one. Hungary had both a tradition of mutual aid and, in the "second economy," experience of running cooperatives and microenterprises, especially in the countryside. But the legacy of communism remained in that people were not used to joining civil society organizations such as green money circles; until very recently, this had been a dangerous thing to do. People relied on private networks, families, and close friends, while market capitalism was leading to atomization as these family ties broke down. After 1994, cuts in state welfare provision needed to be made up, especially given the growth of poverty for those who did not prosper under capitalism. The revitalization of mutual aid could be a way of helping those affected by the economic changes, and the new NGO sector might be a vehicle to develop new mutual aid mechanisms. One such mutual aid network might be provided by green money: alternatively, it might better be thought of as part of the wider legacy of 1989, as a micropolitical vehicle for constructing more humane and ecological alternatives to capitalist markets.

Kör and Talentum: Green Money in Hungary

As mentioned earlier, Hungary's first green money scheme, Budapest Talentum, was established in 1994, growing from the first small group of enthusiasts to a network of 102 in 1999, 150 in 203, and 172 in 2006. It met six times a year, with half of the membership active in 2006. Hungary's second scheme was established in 1999 by an ecologist working in a Steiner school in Gödöllő, a small town just outside Budapest. He reports his motivations:

> My start was at political and economical issues. I looked at the political changes. . . . There are great troubles with currency fluctuation, currency movement, and how it circulates between people; there are many obstacles: there is enough money, but not in the right places; money doesn't work. There are different powers in people, different abilities; they can do everything. Other people need things, but they don't meet each other because the currency . . . is not able to circulate. I was so interested in different, alternative currencies, and I didn't feel that it was possible to start a scheme that changes everything at the governmental level, the currency system, so I thought, "OK let's start it at a community level."
> (Gábor, organizer, Gödöllő Talentum)

As civil society institutions began to emerge and were increasingly supported by Western aid agencies, Hungarian NGOs began to explore what ideas might be imported from the West that might help address some of Hungary's problems. In 1998, the Association of Hungarian Nonprofit Services (hereafter AHNHS) was funded by the British Council to develop in Hungary local money schemes that they called "Circles" (in Hungarian, Kör[1]). The British Council funded a study visit to the United Kingdom in 1999 for the Hungarians who would be implementing Kör so they could learn from experience on the ground. On their return to Hungary, they decided to pilot local currency schemes in their hometowns. U.K. training materials were translated and widely disbursed (Szendrö 1999), and the ideas were promoted to a range of civil society organizations. ANHSH developed five pilot projects in towns where they had close links with local NGOs, feeling that they would be able to support development better in places where relations were already strong. Circles were started in the cities of Szolnok and Miskolc in the relatively deprived east of Hungary, in the village of Tizalúc near Miskolc, and in two small towns near Budapest. The Hungarian Telecottage Association[2] circulated the newly translated U.K. materials to its members, and a scheme was established by a telecottage in the small village of Bordány in the south, near the city of Szeged. Conferences were held in 1999 and 2000, and U.K. LETS activists were brought over to share experiences. Green money circles also emerged in the fourteenth district of Budapest and the nearby town of Pomaz. By 2006 new groups were established in Nagykanizsa in western Hungary and in Erdokertes (approximately sixteen miles from Budapest).

Here again we see at work environmentalists, often with much experience of organizing social movements and with strong links abroad. Again, as in the United Kingdom, we see the green movement as the milieu from which green money emerged. In Hungary we see a second, institutional NGO sector able to mobilize resources from international agencies and forge links with local NGOs. For the environmentalists, Talentum was very much a civil society based resistant institution, an alternative, noncapitalist market, while the NGOs saw Kör as a method of facilitating transition to the capitalist market by acting, much as *kaláka* had, as a way of enabling the poorest to get by during transition. This chapter will examine how effectively the two sets of Hungarian green money schemes worked in each environment.

Talentum as Radical Civil Society

The most successful of the Hungarian green money networks, perhaps unsurprisingly, was Talentum in Budapest. While still small, half of its members were active. The main items traded were basic services such as gardening, window cleaning, computer work, teaching English, and babysitting, but more esoteric services such as biofarming were also traded. Growth was not at the spectacular rate achieved by U.K. LETS, which had been fueled by the 1992 recession. Rather, there was a slow start followed by steady but unspectacular growth: "It was not a success at all at first. People did not believe it was possible in Hungary. Only one in twenty believed the idea. People were concerned about the tax implications; they saw it as a way of cheating tax, or [believed] that people would cheat, take and not give" (György, organizer, Budapest Talentum). In a city of over 1 million, a membership of 175, many of whom were inactive, was ineffective as a serious mutual aid mechanism. It was a space for those who wanted to explore economic alternatives. As György said: "Talentum is not big enough to be a real group, a real community. It's an interest group for likeminded people. It does not provide security." Likewise, Gödöllő Talentum had more than a hundred members at its height in 2000 in a city with a population of 25,000. An average month's trading was

November 1999, when 150 transactions were recorded with a turn-over of 15,000 green forint, which is equivalent to 45,000 Hungarian forint ($225). Services traded that month included taxi services, English lessons, a haircut, baking, babysitting, bread making, plumbing, and dentist services, and market items such as clothing, slippers, herbs, honey, and pumpkins were also traded. Gödöllő Talentum provided real services to its members:

> The second group who joined [were] mostly lonely people, in a special situation somehow, for instance a crippled old lady who had a shortage of social contacts . . . divorced, retired people . . . people who had a short-age of social contacts. Immigrants from Transylvania who also looked for social contacts. . . . [They felt,] "OK. This is a nice group of people. I feel good, [there's] good music; maybe we will look what comes from this. Good contacts with people, maybe useful contacts in business or help in getting a job or something like that." (Gábor, organizer, Gödöllő Kör)

However, Gábor, as an environmentalist, was interested in creating an alternative monetary system, not mutual aid. He felt that people would have met each other and helped each other solve their problems anyway. The existence of green money was irrelevant: "I felt it's a very good point and an advantage, a great achievement. It brought together those people who earlier were disconnected and so on. But, you know, it didn't matter whether it was . . . an alternative currency or just a yoga course or vegetarian group. It did not matter." Gábor consequently lost interest in the scheme, which he stopped organizing in 2000. We have no knowledge of the extent to which *kaláka*-like trading continued once the network closed its doors, which is a shame because others could no longer access what had become a closed, hidden network. Similarly, small numbers of Talentum groups emerged and disappeared, but levels of participation and the growth of new groups was both low and slow when compared with those experienced in the United Kingdom, and tiny in comparison with those in New Zealand and Argentina.

A number of problems can be identified to explain the difference. First, the macroeconomic situation affected the extent to which prospective members either felt the need to get involved or, need notwithstanding, felt comfortable in doing so. We must remember that Hungary's transition to markets saw much lower levels of mobilization than were seen in East Germany, Czechoslovakia, or Romania, where citizen mobilization from below was significant in the over-throw of regimes that were not reform minded. Although there were significant levels of organization from below in Hungary in the 1980s, the country's transition in 1989 was very much a top-down affair. The communist party, whose official name was the Hungarian Socialist Workers Party (Magyar Szocialista Munkáspárt) (MSzMP), had lost confidence in the command economy by 1980, and reformers had gained prominence in the party (O'Neil 1998). The MSzMP had con-sequently negotiated pluralism from above in a formal roundtable process with representatives of civil society organizations. There was no Berlin Wall to pull down, no Securitate or Ceaușescu. Hungary's transition was peaceful, but the downside was that activists felt that those they were trying to involve in bottom-up mutual aid organiza-tions were more accustomed to having changes imposed on them:

> One very important feature. The system has changed from the inside here, from the higher level, the highest level of the political power, so the leaders of the party . . . the leadership of the party initiated the changes. . . . We really got used to dependence and feel that political leaders will decide things instead of us. . . . That's why we don't have this approach that we can organize ourselves and help ourselves; that's really lacking. We have tradition; we are just waiting to see when someone will do that instead of us. . . . The communist system, we didn't have to think or make any decisions; we just react to them, to those things, and it as a sort of a security, a secure thing that we had. (Sándor, organizer, Tizalúc Kör)

Second, activists felt that the legacy of dictatorship lingered, espe-cially for those who were politically active or conscious in the com-munist era. Many of the guiding spirits of Budapest Talentum were former environmental or religious activists who had firsthand expe-rience of the communist-era distrust of nonparty organizations and the repression this entailed. They reported a residual fear that join-ing a group was a dangerous thing to do. Hungarians had responded to the repression of civil society organizations and the dysfunctional nature of the command economy by individualization, by putting up a protective wall around the family and immediate friends. Activ-ists therefore found considerable skepticism about groups and their effectiveness:

> It's the historical situation. I was born in 1951, so I have lived most of my life in the socialist period. Then, it was dangerous to join a group and

organize a group. I have experiences of this. So people have not got used
to joining a group. It's also the mentality, the Hungarian mentality. From
the time of the Turks on, Hungarian people had to be used to running
away, or building broad fences to protect ourselves. No independence
until recent years. These experiences are built into your genes, so you
have to take a deep breath before you do anything like join a group. . . .
For six years I had no passport as a penalty for organizing youth camps to
understand the countryside, and ideological camps. (György, organizer,
Budapest Talentum)

While many did not feel confident enough to join, for those with
experience of repression who now felt sufficiently confident to organize or join groups, just being able to freely participate was enough.
Freedom was still novel, and the size of the group was irrelevant. In
the communist era, they were used to small groups of trusted people;
there was a feeling that newcomers might not be what they seemed.
Consequently, the organizers of Budapest Talentum did not feel the
need to actively promote their scheme, feeling that a small group
of like-minded environmentalists was enough. For Tamás, an organizer of Budapest Talentum, while his scheme was small, "it developed naturally; it didn't need to be promoted. The Talentum circle
was small, only about thirty to forty members in the first few years,
but at that time the organizer said, 'That's quite enough what they
have, and they don't want to promote it.' So they don't advertise, or
didn't."

A third problem relates to the "demobilization thesis" (Arato
1999), which holds that social movements in Eastern Europe were
less active after 1989 once the people had "won" and a complex society was emerging to meet needs they had formerly struggled for.
We see some of this in Talentum, which suffered from a lack of key
activists who continued to act as "engines" for the networks, ensuring
that members met, produced a directory, kept accounts, dealt with
problems, and promoted the idea. Activists got jobs, moved to new
towns, or got burnt out, and their schemes did not so much fail as fade
away: "Two years ago we had a leadership group in the Talentum circle. Three or five people were responsible for some kind of task; they
were a kind of formal leadership for each task, and they met prior to
each meeting, and the main effect of this mechanism was that it was
better at getting their creative ideas out and coordinating them. Now,
in these days, we don't have a leadership" (Tamás, organizer, Budapest

Talentum). Demobilization was facilitated by many former activists'
getting jobs with the new political parties and civil society organizations, but also by the fact that, while Hungary's economy had stag-
nated in the late 1980s, the pragmatism that had enabled the second
economy to flourish alongside the so-called command economy continued into the transition. Hungary was relatively wealthy in 1990;
it introduced the market gradually and in a negotiated way, with no
shock therapy until the International Monetary Fund forced cuts in
1994. By 1997, Hungary's gross domestic product was back above that
of 1989, and in 2003 it joined the European Union. This was far from
the rollercoaster ride we will see later in New Zealand or Argentina.
Hungary suffered no shocks or crises, and the future on the current
trajectory seemed bright, even if many Hungarians suffered as a result of transition. Csilla and Otto, members of Budapest Talentum
and recent immigrants from Hungarian-speaking Transylvania in Romania, consequently felt that their new neighbors saw themselves as
being relatively wealthy, not needing help:

> I still speak as an outsider. My experience with Hungarian people is that
> . . . it's not a very high level of life, but they act as if . . . it's a real shame to
> be poor. In Hungary it feels, if something is old, you throw it away; you
> feel ashamed to use it. In Romania people are much poorer than here, and
> they got used to it. I'm poor and you are poor, most of the people. Here
> people think, "I'm not that poor; I don't need that, I don't need to make
> transactions like this." (Csilla)

> I think that the main problem is that what we got from the West, the
> commercialization that we got here, the materialistic point of view, is get-
> ting . . . the money. It's the money at the end that works. People feel that's
> what they can get, reach; they will get more money and then they will be
> able to buy everything for the money. (Otto)

If those who saw their future in terms of European Union membership and Western standards of living did not find economic alternatives attractive, some of those who did felt that green money
represented an unwelcome commodification of pure cooperation.
Gábor set up his scheme in Gödöllő to help make his local commu-
nity-run Steiner school work more efficiently. He felt that, although
the school was a community he was proud to be a member of, it had
been organized using a chaotic and inefficient system of *kaláka*-like
mutual aid. Green money, he felt, would enable contributions to be

better organized and more equally measured. He said his friends at the school did not agree:

> [They] rejected this measurement of their effort and their contribution because... [they felt,] "If I work for money, I don't feel free." They thought that a relaxed system is better than a rigorous contract system. So because people rejected the system, the leaders felt, "Oh, I don't want to work for money." . . . They felt that somehow this was a devaluation of their contribution. . . . They insisted on the old reciprocity, a chaotic system where no one knows who is responsible for doing this or that or the other, who has done enough already, and who is overloaded or disappointed.

Gábor felt that Talentum, green money as part of radical civil society, was caught between two conflicting pressures. On the one hand, post–1989 Hungarians wanted to become part of the world market: "People trust in the national currency, people trust in the world economic system, so [there are] very few of them who feel that something has to be changed." They looked forward to joining the European Union and to a prosperous Western-style livelihood. This shows the extent to which Gábor's fellow citizens, attracted to a Western-style high-consumption lifestyle, did not share his hopes for a humane alternative to capitalism. What attracted Manchester's greens, an alternative to capitalism, was unattractive, perhaps not too surprisingly, in a political environment that had thrown off Soviet domination. In this environment, green money would not meet people's needs. At the other extreme, those already part of *kaláka* mutual aid networks often regarded Kör as an unwelcome commodification of relationships that they felt worked better through reciprocity. Green money seemed either superfluous or an unwelcome alien imposition that disrupted cooperative mechanisms. They did not see green money as a way of facilitating cooperation, as, for example, Zelizer sees money as facilitating household or other affective economies. Rather, they saw money, or more specifically quantification of contribution, as something separate from pure cooperation.

Kör as Mutual Aid to Facilitate Transition

Turning now to the second conception of green money as a civil society–based part of transition, we examine the experiences of the externally generated Kör circles. We recall that after the 1999 study tour to the United Kingdom, Kör circles were established in Szolnok and Miskolc in the relatively deprived east of Hungary and in the villages of Tizalúc near Miskolc, as well as in two small towns near Budapest. The Hungarian Telecottage Association established a small scheme in Bordány in the south.

Szolnok Kör was established in 1999 by members of the Civic Regional Association and quickly grew to forty or fifty members, with five to six hundred wants and offers in their directory of services. They circulated leaflets and organized fairs where people met, but in practice they found that their members preferred to meet face-to-face rather than making contact through a directory. The second thing that they found was that there was little evidence that people needed a new currency, preferring direct barter mainly for the exchange of clothes: "These fairs were very successful, as they were busy and people bought many clothes and there were many trades going on. And they didn't really want to use all of Kör, as they could meet each other at this place. There was no need for the group, for the Kör. They were there at the same place, and they could just trade with each other. Direct barter" (Ferenc, organizer, Szolnok Kör).

A call emerged for a place to store the clothes between fairs, and space was found in an empty flat on a housing estate that then developed into a charity clothes shop. Green forints were used, not for the exchange of services, but to pay members for the clothes they deposited, and members could spend them on new clothes from the shop. By 2003 the clothing exchange program based around the shop had two hundred members, but the exchange of services beyond clothes was minimal (three or four trades a month). The program was still going strong in 2006. The organizers consequently felt that the clothing exchange was a good example of a practical and popular use of the new currency.

Bordány Kör was established by the telecottage organizer, who wanted to reward volunteers working for the village's Association for Cultural and Leisure Services. These volunteers contributed to the social and cultural life of the village by writing articles for the community newsletter and distributing it, running the community cinema, distributing flyers for local businesses, running a youth summer camp, and generally looking after clients at the telecottage. In 2003 there were seventy-six members, all from Bordány and aged ten to thirty. The currency, the Bordány crown, was linked at parity to the Hungarian forint, and accounts were kept on a computer. Individual local money accounts were electronically linked to the telecottage's payment system, enabling fees (for membership and for using the Internet) to be paid automatically in crowns.

From the perspective of the organizer, the scheme was moderately successful in that it involved many of the village's young people, who spent their crowns to obtain discounts for use of the computers in the telecottage. They used the Internet, played computer games, or used services such as photocopying or sending faxes. But older villagers did not join the scheme, because the telecottage was seen as a place for young people and as rather public for carrying out business affairs. Although young people joined, they did not exchange services. While they did help each other out with schoolwork, repairing bikes and motorbikes, working in each other's gardens, and the like, they did not exchange crowns for this. In both Bordány and Szolnok, then, while Kör survived, the extent to which services were being traded was limited. Rather, green money was used to facilitate specific exchanges: the exchange of clothes in Szolnok and of computer services in Bordány.

The mutual aid schemes developed by ANHSH did not last. Miskolc Kör was established on a housing estate in 1999, growing to about forty people, but only ten to fifteen of them were ever active. However, after a year the key activist moved to another part of Miskolc and stopped running the Kör, which then faded away, although attempts were made to revive it in 2006. Tiszalúc Kör was, for a time, more successful. Tiszalúc is a village of about 5,600 people in Miskolc district, in a very rural and deprived part of eastern Hungary. The Kör was set up by an NGO, the Association of Large Families, in early 1999, again by an activist who had participated in the trip to the United Kingdom:

> I moved from Budapest to Tizalúc and did not have local relations. I'm a community person, like organizing, and was there for a year, just saying, "Hello, no relatives." I joined the Association of Large Families . . . and heard about Kör from the association. I decided I wanted to join a group, but there was no group, so we started with four people. The press was useful, and as more people got involved, up to ten. The next six months, six or seven more people [joined], seven or eight more families. (Sándor, organizer, Tizalúc Kör)

By December 2000, there were seventeen members exchanging services in the village with a currency called the Kör point, based on labor time. Members who met in each other's houses twice a month in what they described as a nice, friendly atmosphere involving new members and their children, were mostly newcomers to the village.

Members of Tizalúc Kör who took part in a group discussion in December 2000 included an unemployed man who used to be a police officer. He joined to make friends in the community, and traded services such as repairing cars (which he also did for cash). He traded weekly, seven or eight times a month, with two or three people, and he described himself as one of the most active traders. He felt that the greatest success was getting together a strong, small community who cared about each other and shared and solved problems. The downside was that it could be hard getting new people to join, especially "conservative" people from the village who did not trust what they saw as untested new gimmicks. He wanted ten more people to join in the year, and for the group to be able to trade garden produce, luxuries like a televisions, or expensive goods like winter coats.

Another Tizalúc Kör member was a mother with four small children who had been at home for fourteen years and in the village for eleven. She joined to meet a friendship circle, and offered babysitting and the use of her home for meetings. She used kitchen supplies and household goods, and traded with other families to obtain things that she otherwise would buy. She felt that Kör was like a big family, a good group of friends, and a larger group to call on that still has a family feeling. A strength was that it had a large percentage of people who had moved into the village.

A third member described himself as a full-time "mother" who used to be unemployed and who before that had worked in the library. His wife worked, and he looked after three children at home. The family had moved to Tizalúc from Budapest because his wife's parents lived in the town, but he felt like an outsider. He joined to make friends, and offered agricultural produce such as honey, sour cherries, and paprika because the family produced more food than they needed in their large garden. He also drew pictures and book illustrations. He needed use of a car, and friends to turn to for advice in solving problems. He got things delivered by car. However, although Tizalúc Kör seemed healthy when visited in December 2000, the network did not last. The key activist moved away, and the members gradually decided that in this small village the currency was getting in the way of building friendships and *kaláka*-like mutual aid.

The green money networks facilitated by ANHSH remained small—with three hundred members in Szolnok, seventy in Bordány, forty in Miskolc, and sixteen in Tizalúc—but that does not necessarily mean that they were ineffective as mutual aid mechanisms. Rather, there was varying performance. To some extent, this was due to characteristics of Kör as a mutual aid and problem-solving network in and of itself, while a second set of issues focus on the strategic and political choices made by activists on how they spent their time overcoming the logistical and organizational problems in developing mutual aid organizations in a transitional economy. Sik and Wellman (1999) argue that the insecurity and ever-changing environments of postcommunist societies make networks more important than in the West:

> People and organizations use networks everywhere, but they use them more in communist and post-communist countries than in capitalist countries. One might think that the elaborate bureaucracies of communist countries (made) networks less necessary. In fact, the inherent rigidities and shortages of communist bureaucracies, paradoxically, made the use of networks more necessary. Nor has the end of communism lessened the need to use networks *for the permeability, fluidity and uncertainty of postcommunism have fostered even greater reliance on networks.* (My emphasis)

In their study of house building, academic, and managerial networks in the transition from communism to capitalism, Sik and Wellman argued that under postcommunism "everyone invents, develops, or copies strategies and tactics *to cope* (to protect against threats) or *grab* (to make a fortune)." Networks, then, become fundamentally important for survival in transitional economies. The networks in Szolnok around the clothing shop and in Bordány around the telecottage were built around solving a *specific* problem, but in Szolnok, the center developed into a contact point for solving *broader* problems:

> [I] provide other help to people in the shop, for example, give the name and address of a dentist who is five times cheaper than the others and other good services, and I do that as it's good to do something for people. . . . We have a member who has four children, and she's at home with the youngest, who is two months old and . . . she does sewing for a living, and there is another member, she came to the shop and took her clothes but

there was sort of a problem that needed to be fixed, and I gave the contact of the sewing machinist to that lady. (Erika, organizer, Szolnok Kör)

People don't just come to get clothes here, but also to meet with others, discuss things, and also get other help from the shop. (Ferenc, organizer, Szolnok Kör)

In Tizalúc, Sándor, the organizer argued: "If you worked actively you could get ten percent of your needs through the circle, and it could have stayed like that if we had got new members. Then people could feel the economic benefit. Could see it." Tizalúc was a small village with many members with gardens, and as a result food was available on the network. Unemployed people had time, and people lived close to each other. Other circles did not have such a dense concentration of everyday resources available on the network, with the result that people could not get what they needed, and growing membership was slow.

Why did Kör fail to grow into larger systems, better able to solve problems? A number of problems were raised. There was not a lack of need, given the problems of poverty in postsocialist transition: "There are lots of poor people who could use this type of service. I tried to get them to join, but did not succeed. I could not get them to understand that it was good for them. It's not that it's too abstract, as they do understand *kaláka,* but they do not believe that they will be able to get what they need from it. People have so many active problems that they need help from" (György, organizer, Budapest Talentum). While György did not feel that green money was abstract, intangible, Ferenc from Szolnok Kör found it harder to get prospective members to understand how it could work:

It seems too alternative . . . it seems that Hungarian people also like the things that have a direct value; they give value to those things. We tried to strengthen the approach, including valuable goods and services like a video recorder, things like that, and the price was quite affordable even in points. [We hoped that it would] inspire those who wanted to buy that to get enough points to buy the video recorder, but this was largely conducted among the activists only.

This may have been because the activists were not skilled at either targeting potential supporters or explaining what Kör was in ways that potential supporters would understand. Attempts at widening participation though reference to *kaláka* failed. People who did join found difficulties in using green money. A major issue, perhaps unsurprisingly for students of mutual aid, was lack of time given work commitments, especially for those working long hours, perhaps with two jobs, for low pay. Ferenc from Szolnok Kör found that "people were working very, very hard for low salaries, so they did not get too much income, and they didn't really have the time and energy to meet and contribute given all the other things in their life.... Newly retired people have to continue to find a job here, and those who are able to work, they can find one, so they don't have energy and time." Sándor from Tizalúc found that people working long hours did not have the energy for mutual aid: "In Hungary, people do not have as much time as people in the West; we work much harder and don't have time to take care of each other, relatives and the human side of things . . . or watch television, try to escape from reality. They don't see the hope, don't fill their life with real things."

The other side of lack of time, for those without work, was lack of money and isolation. It takes a minimum amount of money to participate in mutual aid, because materials might need to be bought, one might need tools or work clothes, fuel or a bus fare to travel to trade, and this might be beyond the means of the very poorest. This was a particular issue in Szolnok for a scheme based on a relatively isolated outlying housing estate: "Those who are on low income can't really afford the ticket for the bus; they won't go by bus to the garden area and do work; they stay here. There are people who don't even go to the city for months, two or three months" (Erika, organizer, Szolnok Kör). Lack of money also caused residents who had bought their homes to be evicted when they were unable to pay their utility bills, leading to a disruption of the network for all and exclusion from it for those directly affected:

> In this estate, at least 50 percent of these families are lone parents, and they are members of the shop. They have a long relationship with families, and if the couple get divorced . . . they can come in, the lone parents, and this relationship continues and they can have services from the shop, or they can buy clothes here. The problem only comes when they don't even have enough money to pay their bills, and after a while they have to move out from the estate and then the relationship just stops. (Erika, organizer, Szolnok Kör)

The networks remained small because, although some came up against barriers to participation such as lack of time or money or dis-

tance, others were unconvinced that an appropriate solution to their
problems was a re-creation of the traditions of *kaláka*. The unconvinced saw green money as a romantic throwback to a mythical happy
past that could not work in the new conditions of transitional economies, in a complex society like that of modern Hungary where such
relationships were breaking down:

> I explained that when people help each other in the villages, that's *kaláka*
> and it's similar to that. . . . They knew about it, but they are not using it;
> only neighbors and relatives are helping each other out, lending things
> to the others, and the difficult thing was for them to think about how
> it could work in a wider circle, and how they could get their investment
> back. . . . In towns . . . people don't have those close relationships anymore.
> Everyone is just watching TV; they don't have strong contacts with each
> other anymore. It's an atomized society, so neighborhood was another
> thing in the town that was not very, sort of, developed. (László, organizer
> of Miskolc Kör)

> Traditionally we have, we have traditions of self-help or helping each
> other, like the *kaláka* and people say that that's a good thing, it worked . . .
> [but] they don't really feel that the circle could replace *kaláka*. (Ferenc,
> organizer, Szolnok Kör)

Given an orientation toward achieving Western-style consumption
levels, the alternative currency was incomprehensible, not a serious
alternative:

> [They] misunderstood the whole thing. They found it strange. They
> found the system complicated at first. They didn't really trust in this
> other currency, and they didn't really see the currency that they would
> get back if they provided some work. "Money is the way, and if we haven't
> got the money, what have we got? Money is the value that I can buy things
> in shops, but now I haven't got the money, so how can I buy things?" So
> they didn't really understand it. . . . It wasn't about taking it seriously;
> they didn't understand it at all. I had to introduce a completely new world
> here, a completely new concept; I had to break through a wall. (László,
> organizer of Miskolc Kör)

While the organic blood relationships between family members
that did not connect outside small isolated villages were breaking
down, they were being replaced by new connections. These were Sik
and Wellman's "grab" networks: more diffuse, private, invisible networks that allow those that have them to get ahead. To make them visible, to codify them, as is the case (and a claimed advantage) of green

money networks, is to remove the specific advantage members of the network have over their economic competitors in an ever-changing, unpredictable environment.

> Under goulash communism we had this blood relation. It was quite a strong relationship among people. I think that the situation is different as after the changes; those people who have got some talents, have entrepreneurial skills, they started to build relationships with those who are above them . . . with those who are in higher positions than they are, and they didn't really care about their previous relationships. They just acted according to their interests and tried to . . . build relationships according to their career. (László, organizer, Miskolc Kör)

Networks were required, but not networks like Kör, fueled by green, localizing agendas. The services Hungarians wanted—access to jobs, contacts, business support—were not available in a network of post-materialists. Kör seemed backward. Activists consequently commented on the way Kör did not resonate in Hungary's materialist postcommunist environment, a condition they bemoaned, if they understood it.

At the other end of the scale, the members of the small, close group in Tizalúc felt that "really good friends help each other anyway, so why charge? Why calculate? . . . People start as traders, become friends, and stop using points" (Sándor, Tizalúc Kör). They felt a formal scheme was too bureaucratic, another state socialist holdover. In Szolnok, the lone parents came to the shop to meet each other, and then solved problems through mutual reciprocity: "Those young mothers who know each other from school, or from other places, it works without the system because they are just helping each other out without the system" (Erika, Szolnok Kör.). There, Kör successfully created a trading network through which people could solve their problems, but they discontinued use of the local currency.

Green money projects set up by the nonprofit services project were aimed at building communities and mutual aid in places with real social problems. But green money proved to be not up to the task. Although small networks were constructed that did act in ways their enthusiasts hoped—that is, provided a way of *formalizing* hidden networks and making them available to those outside them— the Simmellian functions of money were rejected in favor of currencyless mutual exchange invisible to outsiders and, outside strong bonds of kin, vulnerable to a breakdown of reciprocity from imbalances of usage.

It consequently proved difficult to build mutual aid from the outside. One legacy of communism was that vulnerable people found it hard to negotiate, to ask for help, to work the network. They were used to Hungary's paternalist system, which had offered a kind of safety in return for political conformity. Working the new networks required skills that those on the sharp end of transition did not have, and Kör did not build them:

> Within the group, when they made trades, they couldn't really discuss and argue about the value of it. Negotiating skills, but not just the price but also the services that I need that you can provide me with ... they couldn't really use it, they didn't have practice.... In the Communist era, they got used to [the idea] that there is one opinion provided by the party and they couldn't have their own opinion, their own ideas, act according to their own ideas, so they just didn't have the skills to deal with it. . . . The new system requires new skills, but they don't have it. Everybody had a job under the socialist era, and loyalty to the ... ideology of the government. People were told where they have to go to satisfy their needs, for example, if they didn't get a job they knew where they are supposed to go ... but now it's very different; now you have to look for the opportunities, and now you don't have these skills. (László, Miskolc LETS)

Staff appointed by the nonprofit services association to manage the program moved to new jobs once funding ceased, and there was little follow-up of the projects started. A national network or organization was not established, something the Hungarian green movement also resisted, feeling that the country was small enough for this to be unnecessary, but this meant that an institutional support structure for green money was lacking. External support did not make up for local deficiencies or a lack of experience in running and developing sustainable civil society organizations.

Conclusion

The experience of Kör was limited but does point to some of the problems of building mutual aid projects in transitional economies. Some of the problems were similar to those in the United Kingdom and, as we shall see later, in New Zealand (as well as elsewhere). These included the low level of trades, the lack of resources accessible by already poor people, and the difficulty in getting those outside green networks to understand what can seem rather strange and esoteric. Other problems were characteristic of transitional economies generally, such as the breakup of networks under a restructuring economy, insecurity, a feeling of runaway change, and great unmet need. A third group of problems were specific to Hungary, such as the top-down nature of the transition, the existence of poverty but not a severe economic crisis, an individualistic political culture, a fear of outsiders, and a trust in family-based solutions.

Yet it is still early: Budapest Talentum is only twelve years old, and the activists are still enjoying their freedom to organize, connecting a new group of postmaterialist greens who have no wish to return to communism (which was not for them the rosy milieu of the post-hoc reconceptualization of a mythical communist past seen in the hit film *Goodbye Lenin*), but neither do they buy into the new market-oriented, Westernized, consumerist Hungary. In the rush to build markets, it is worth remembering that in 1989 another future was the aim of many involved in fighting for transition—another, more human, world, closer perhaps to that fought for by the anticapitalist movement. Hungarians in Talentum wanted to build another, perhaps more inclusive, supportive economy, make a generational turn that will create something new and as yet unknown:

> I think we are another generation. Not the one they expected, but another one. They are expecting a generation that would agree to this tradition, and I don't think we are that generation that they expect—we are something else.... We are trying to find our way, *our* way.... We don't want to be something that we are expected to be. We want to be, we are trying to get our way of expressing things, to be ourselves, without the limitations put down by others. . . . Now is the time for another kind of community, less limiting. I don't think it's a time to go back to the oldfashioned communities; this is a time for new communities. (Csilla, Budapest)

This analysis would suggest that friendship and community are very important to members of Kör, and the networks do seem to have been effective at building communities, albeit small ones, at a time when the market was seen to be destroying them. Csilla seems to be getting her wish fulfilled, to some extent.

Dahrendorf (1990, 1997) argued that it takes ten years to build civil society, while Putnam's (1993) study of Italy suggests it can take centuries. In 2006, sixteen years after Hungary's transition and twelve after Budapest Talentum was founded, the group continues to function as a space within radical civil society for those who want to experiment with alternatives. It has built connections with other groups aiming to build economic alternatives in the city: anticapitalists, anarchists, squatters. But green money's ability to help large numbers of people through transition, through mutual aid, has been limited. Perhaps the Hungarians were very experienced at surviving communism and in developing civil society organizations from below, but a short-term, externally funded project aiming to build competency to manage change from the outside will fall short if activists move on to other projects when funding ceases. If Kör had been more widespread during the early days of transition, could it have provided more support during the transition? Might Kör be called upon anew as it becomes clearer that those Hungarians who hoped for a high-consumption Western European lifestyle may not get their wish anytime soon? Those with such desires got a rude awakening when in September 2006 Prime Minister Ferenc Gyurcsany was forced to admit that there were fundamental problems with the Hungarian economy. A leaked report of an internal meeting of the ruling Socialist Party reported that Gyurcsany told party members how it was (expletives have been deleted):

> We have screwed up. Not a little but a lot. No country in Europe has screwed up as much as we have. We have obviously lied throughout the past 18 to 24 months. It was perfectly clear that what we were saying was not true. . . . In the meantime we did not actually do anything for four years. Nothing. . . . The thing is, in the short run there is no choice. . . . We can muck around for a bit longer, but not much. The moment of truth has come swiftly. . . . Reform or failure, there's nothing else. And when I'm talking about failure, I'm talking about Hungary.

The Hungarian economy could be in for a rocky ride, and more people might be forced to rely on mutual aid, as they had to in New Zealand and Argentina. Could alternative currencies be up to the task? To examine this question in another economy undergoing widespread restructuring, we move from postsocialist Hungary to neoliberal New Zealand twelve thousand miles away.

7

The Longevity of
Alternative Economic Practices
GREEN DOLLARS
IN AOTEAROA/NEW ZEALAND

NEW ZEALAND HAS ALWAYS BEEN AN EARLY ADOPTER. From the Treaty of Waitangi, the 1840 experiment in a partnership between new Pakeha[1] colonists and indigenous Maori to votes for women through the foundation of the welfare state, New Zealand (Aotearoa) has been in the forefront of social reform and innovation, so that in the nineteenth century New Zealand's liberal elite believed that

> New Zealand . . . offered an example to humankind as a whole. . . . With votes for women, old age pensions and labour legislation in particular, New Zealand was showing the way to the rest of the world. . . . "God's own country" was . . . a social laboratory which other countries could study with envy and profit. Indeed a whole procession of luminaries—Mark Twain, Beatrice and Sidney Webb, Keir Hardie, Tom Mann, Benn Tillet and Michael Davitt among them—all came to study the country and its institutions. (King 2003, 282)

New Zealanders themselves, living as they do in a small, isolated South Pacific island nation, were used to looking out for new developments that would secure their economic prosperity. Thus New Zealanders moved from early innovation related to the welfare state to early adoption of neoliberalization and to the identification of responses to neoliberalization, such as alternative currencies. New Zealand, therefore, offers us an opportunity to examine the micropolitics of alternative currencies over a period of nearly twenty years of break-neck economic change.

Neoliberalizing New Zealand

Green dollars were introduced to New Zealand at a time when the country was undergoing the fundamental processes of economic change that we now associate with neoliberalization. The Labour governments of the 1940s had introduced a comprehensive welfare state, while even the conservative National Premier Robert Muldoon, in power in the 1970s and early 1980s, regarded as his highest priority the protection of the "ordinary bloke" from the ravages of the Great Depression he had experienced as a child. Muldoon consequently regulated the New Zealand economy to such an extent that it was colloquially called the "Albania of the South Pacific." Like Hungarians under state socialism, ordinary Kiwis expected the state to look after them in a "land of plenty," in which high prices for wool and dairy produce and imperial preference ensured that New Zealand was one of the world's richest countries in terms of per capita wealth.

This protected Eden ran into trouble by the late 1970s, when, as a result of a long-term decline in wool and dairy prices, the double shocks of the hike in oil prices and the United Kingdom's joining the then Common Market, and the industrial unrest and high inflation experienced throughout the Organization for Economic Cooperation and Development (OECD) nations, New Zealand began a fifteen-year experiment with neoliberal-inspired structural adjustment. The New Zealand dollar was floated, a mass deregulation and privatization program was instigated, a prejudice in favor of market solutions to policy goals took hold, and financial probity was entrenched in the Fiscal Responsibility Act of 1990. New Zealand would need to be disciplined so it could compete with other Asia-Pacific nations. Meanwhile, New Zealand politics was captured by a tight coalition of neoliberal advocates, including Labour politicians, Treasury officials with strong connections to the Chicago School, and the private-sector pressure group Business Round Table, which pushed through its "reforms" at breakneck speed (Douglas 1993; Kelsey 1995; Jesson 1999; Sheppard 1999).

The two-term Labour administration was replaced in 1990, first by the National Party and then, with the introduction of proportional representation in 1994, by a series of coalitions built by the National Party and the populist center-right New Zealand First Party. National rekindled the neoliberal revolution with the Employment Contracts Act, which replaced New Zealand's system of compulsory labor arbitration to set wage rates at a national level with individualized employment contracts. Wages immediately declined, and hours of work went up (Easton 1997). Benefit cuts of up to 30 percent and a significant tightening of eligibility criteria in April 2001 meant that welfare beneficiaries faced real hardship, with an immediate rise in applications for food and clothing parcels and for help with mortgage payments (Stephens 1999, 238). For example, Department of Social Welfare figures showed that 365 food banks were operating in 1994, giving out some 40,000 parcels a month at a cost of NZ$25 million. The Salvation Army gave out 1,226 food parcels in the first quarter of 1990 and 14,906 in the same quarter of 1994 (Stephens 1999, 251). Inequality and destitution grew to levels that critics argued were unacceptable in an OECD nation. From 1996, National moved toward "active welfare" in a way that mirrored contemporaneous moves in Australia, the United Kingdom, and the United States (Castles and Pierson 1996; Burgess et al. 1998). "Active welfare" involved state intervention to discipline beneficiaries into work through tightened benefit eligibility criteria and work testing for the long-term unemployed (Higgins 1999). In October 1998, unemployment benefits were replaced with a Wisconsin-inspired "hard" workfare program (Jones 1996), the "community wage," which required all beneficiaries to do up to twenty hours of work per week, with the rest of their time spent in training, education, or job searching.

New Zealand became an exemplar of the neoliberalized residual state, a "world model for Structural Adjustment" (Kelsey 1995). The savage welfare cuts came to be known, after the treasurer (finance minister) of the time, Ruth Richardson, as "Ruthenasia," a form of social euthanasia.

The coalition lost power in 1999 with the election of another coalition consisting of a reformed Labour Party and the left-of-center Alliance. After a short period of excitement in which it looked as if neoliberalism would be rolled back, Labour kept the bulk of the reforms in place but, in contrast with the National Party's conception of a residual state (where government action was seen inevitably as a burden on private business), their policies were founded on a conception of an activist state. The state could add value through effective policy making, they argued (Kelsey 2002). The community wage was abolished, as were cuts in housing benefits, and the whole climate of "beneficiary dobbing," stigmatizing the sick and unemployed, changed. New Zealand's unemployment rate fell from one of the highest to the lowest in the OECD (3.4 percent in September 2005), although wage levels did not recover from the reductions associated with the Employment Contracts Act of 1990.

Green dollars emerged as a response to this rollercoaster ride, surviving to the time of writing (January 2006). Although many examples of local exchange trading schemes (LETS) in the United Kingdom, such as Manchester LETS, were healthy for only about five years before closing after ten, and many of the Hungarian Kör did not become established at all, some green dollar exchanges have had eighteen years' experience. This chapter will therefore concentrate more on experiences of trading using green dollars over long periods of time to examine the validity of the critique of alternative economic practices as ephemeral, unable to resist the pressures of the capitalist economy for any length of time. The final chapter, on Argentina, will examine alternative currencies as mass phenomena operating over a wide geographical space.

New Zealand's Green Dollar Exchanges

Two New Zealanders heard a presentation by Michael Linton, designer of the LETSystem, at an environmental conference in the United Kingdom in 1984. On their return to New Zealand, LETS was promoted around the country at green "Festivals of Cooperation," receiving much interest from many within the green or left countercultural milieu who were engaged in developing more positive, community-based economic alternatives to Rogernomics, such as the green social enterprise network CELT (the Community Enterprise Loans Trust). As we saw in chapter 4, Social Credit was riding high as a possible third party in New Zealand, and many of its adherents saw green dollars as an example of their politics at a grassroots level. The first two exchanges were established in 1986–87—the height of the dislocations associated with Rogernomics—in the North Island cities of Whangarei and New Plymouth. A TVNZ broadcast on the Whangarei scheme spread the idea across the country, and then exchanges sprang up across the country. New Zealand's green dollar exchanges are like U.K. LETS or Hungarian Kör or Talentum in that they are built around a small network of people trading with each other through a directory, recording their balances on a computer. Two differences are that the unit of currency is the green dollar, linked roughly in value to the kiwi dollar (rather than time), and that although the exchanges are local (focused around a town or city), New Zealanders can also trade nationwide using a system of exchange between their local currencies called Green Dollar Connections.

The first national conference was held in 1991, involving thirty-eight exchanges. By 1993, Jackson contacted some fifty-five exchanges in various stages of development (Jackson 1995), and in 1995 Williams surveyed 30 percent of the fifty-seven exchanges identified by *Green Dollar Quarterly,* from which he extrapolated a membership of some 5,900 in a country with a total population of 3.9 million people (Williams 1996a). Kitco (1998) found forty-five schemes in 1997. By 1999, *Green Dollar Quarterly* listed forty exchanges, while representatives of only seventeen attended the 1999 conference. Conferences held annually after 2000 involved a hard core of ten to twelve exchanges that seemed to have achieved some sort of sustainability. Williams's research (1996a) suggested an average of 104 members each, but this hides considerable diversity. Auckland Green Dollar Exchange had 2,040 members in 1997, which made it the world's largest network then. This membership was so high because 78 percent of the members held automatic membership in the Green Dollar Exchange through Auckland's People's Centre, a campaigning organization that also provided a range of welfare and community services (crucially, a doctor and dentist) to people suffering from the savage welfare cuts of 1991. The center also hosted a shop where members sold second-hand goods, jams, produce, and craft items for green dollars (G$).

Wellington Green Dollar Exchange had 207 members (in October 1998) across the Wellington metropolitan area, collectively trading between G$32 and G$266 a month, a mean of G$141. Over its five-year history the Wellington Exchange had attracted a total of 508 members, with an average of 50 members joining a year. Perhaps

New Zealand's most successful exchange was Golden Bay's HANDs Exchange,[2] established in 1989. In 2005 HANDs had just over 260 members and had just introduced a paper currency. A typical example of a successful exchange was New Plymouth's Taranaki LETS, established in 1988, with 130 members in April 1999. The most active member's turnover was G$9,941, with a mean cumulative turnover of G$750. Similarly, Wairarappa Green Dollars had 130 members and a turnover of G$51,732. An average annual turnover of G$487 in the Wairarappa agrees with Williams's research, which suggested a mean annual turnover of G$448 (Williams 1996a, 323). Williams' (1996a) survey found that 60 percent of members were women, 50 percent "greens/alternatives," 38 percent people on a low income.

Building Resilient Alternative Economic Spaces

In 2005, concerned that the experiences I had observed in the United Kingdom and Hungary were of rather ephemeral economic alternatives that seemed to provide evidence in favor of the Marxist critique of the possibility of building alternatives to capitalism, I visited ten of the thirteen surviving schemes, some of which had been trading since the late 1980s. I held interviews and group discussions with longstanding members of Wellington, New Plymouth, Wairarappa, Blenheim, Nelson, Motueka, Golden Bay, Christchurch, and Timaru Exchanges to discuss the extent to which they had been able to participate in alternative economic activities and live more liberated lives for significant periods of time. Many had traded for over ten years, some for as many as sixteen or seventeen years. Although no one I spoke to could say that they had been able to live the sort of economic life they wanted entirely through green dollars (in contrast, as we shall see in the next chapter, with the experience in Argentina), many members found that green dollars did provide a real help at crucial points when what was needed was available from the network. This is a typical experience:

> It was really good for me on lots of levels. And at the markets I bought things which strongly supported me setting up a new home; it was perfect for me. Occasionally it would be furniture, but occasionally there'd be hanging baskets or a woman joined who was making homemade beeswax candles, absolutely incredible. So I gave beeswax candles as presents for

two, three, four years after that. And if anyone had greetings cards, secondhand clothes. Not much fruit, because I was eating totally organic
then, so the hot dogs and that which were served, I couldn't go for that.
But some food, and of course everyone would dash for lovely organic
food, pickles and things. (Amrita, Plains Exchange and Barter System
[PLEBS], Christchurch)

Neoliberal policy makers would have thought Amrita should have
been "disciplined" into finding paid work to enable her to buy bees-
wax candles and hanging baskets. State welfare benefits were deliber-
ately set at a level below what was necessary to adequately feed and
clothe oneself; otherwise, the neoliberals argued, they would act as a
market-distorting disincentive to independence through paid work.
For Amrita, green dollars emerged as a tool of resistance and a way of
mitigating this effect.

Neoliberal disciplining similarly failed when others used green
dollars as a way to escape from jobs they no longer enjoyed and become more independent:

> I actually run a small one-person business. . . . So, yes. It has helped. The
> fact that my business is going ahead and I'm turning it to a kiwi (dollar)
> business is [due to green dollars]. . . . I started off doing bits and pieces for
> people on green dollars. . . . I don't think I would have had the courage to
> go out on alone. . . . To me it's a case of green dollars' showing me a way
> that I can beat the system by working by myself to do things. . . . Green
> dollars actually gives me security, because I know if I go out there and
> do the extra, I'm going to get what I want. . . . It depends on a person's
> mental attitude often to work. If you enjoy your work nine-to-five, that's
> fine. If you don't enjoy it, it's a killer. But the green dollars, I can do what
> I want, when I want to do it. I enjoy this more [than a nine-to-five job].
> I've got freedom. If I wanted to work from two o'clock until five o'clock
> in the morning, fine, I can go and do it, and I often do. (Jan, Wellington
> Green Dollars)

Green dollars worked for those who actively and creatively sought
out opportunities to trade, looking at green dollars as the first point
of call for their consumption choices. They stressed knowing who
their fellow members were, and what they could do:

> I've been by far the most active trader in our group. Probably something
> to the order of twice the next highest trader. . . . I would, right from the
> start, spend time on looking for opportunities to trade with the mem-
> bers, and it may be that I needed something for our own household, or I
> might have seen that here's an opportunity to get something for a gift for

my family or my friends or whatever, as the first option rather than going to town. And so I would look for all sorts of opportunities—I'm pretty lateral in my thinking at times—to do some trading. (Helen, Wairarappa Green Dollars)

Active members understood the need for "relationship trading," recognizing that green dollar trading is unconstrained and that it works best when the social and the economic are mixed to provide an enjoyable trading experience for both giver and receiver. They understood the relationship between the social and the economic in this liberated, noncapitalist marketplace:

> At that time I was pretty active in the growing of the plants, and so I would employ people here to help me produce them. And it was wonderful because it was social as well, because we would work side by side, we'd be potting away and chatting away, and talk about getting paid twice or three times for one job. I mean, here I am making things grow, which I love to do, and there's the satisfaction in that . . . I've made it grow, and then I had company and get to know somebody, and we'd get to know each other in that process. And then I take [the plants] to the market and I can sell them, and I can get paid again! So I mean—wow! I like it! Yes. (Helen, Wairarappa Green Dollars)

Successful traders understood the micropolitics of how the green dollar worked, how the implications of credit and debit were different from those of the kiwi dollar and capitalist markets:

> It's one of the few accounts where I don't mind being in minus, versus the [situation at the] EFTPOS [electronic funds transfer point of sale; ATM] machine, when you have negative dollars! . . . And it gives you more incentive to trade when you are in negative. (Nicky, Blenheim Green Dollars)

> Much as I regard [a green dollar as a] credit card, it's only worth what you can spend, or trade it for. And you can only trade it for what's available. And once I got myself round to that way of thinking, it's easier then to find things which you can treat yourself to. (Linda, Nelson Green Dollars)

Finally, members took green dollars—or, more clearly, their commitment to their fellow members—seriously:

> I think you owe it to the rest of the group. You've got to give it value, because if it's not valuable to you, it is to somebody else. It's an intrinsic value. It's a moral obligation to me. . . . It's an obligation that you know you owe it. . . . If I'm in credit, I think that's fine. If I'm hugely in credit, I think, "Hey, I've got to disperse this back amongst the people. What can I do to help them?" So it's a social obligation as well as a semifinancial obligation. (Jan, Wellington Green Dollars)

Others seemed to be Adam Smith's natural traders, wheeler-dealers. Green dollars fitted with the natural rhythm of their household economies, providing new opportunities to do what they did anyway as an alternative to engaging in paid work for an employer:

> I've been trading most of my life. When Neville came round, he decided that as I was always trading anyway I could be a good member of the club, and yes we do trading every so often, me and my partner, and we do all sorts with the veggies, caregiving, babysitting, catering, all sorts of weird and wonderful things. Been in a couple of years, and I think we do at least two or three trades a month. My other half does gardens and steps for someone at the moment, for a member, and we've done wood. . . . Fruit and vegetables, plants, housework. Not part of a system, but we've always traded something for something. For example, we did housekeeping for a fireplace. Did stuff and got wood for the fire. My daughter is three, and 90 percent of the children's clothes are traded for other clothes. We only spend money when we sorta have to spend money. But New Zealand is one of the richest countries for trading, because somebody always needs something that you might have, like baby stuff and baby knitting. . . . Most people don't know what's under their noses for trading. You've just got to open your eyes a wee bit for trading purposes. For example, one person came to our club, and she said I haven't got anything to trade, so I said, "What's in your garden?" (Lynn, Blenheim Green Dollars)

Trading worked for other people who wanted to develop a lifestyle outside full-time paid work: people, for example, with young families, limited resources, time to combine trading with child care, and many needs that could be met by trading with a network of other young families with similar needs, worldviews, and resources who all lived near enough to each other for trading to be practicable:

> It seems to work for [for example] young people with young families who are thrilled to have the occasional babysitter or to be able to do trading toys or trading clothes, whatever. . . . There are a couple of them with children. . . . With their family [they] would happily trade three hundred green [dollars] each way every month. Because they were imaginative. They would find things that they wanted or needed. [Name] is a jeweler, so she would allocate so many pieces per month which she would sell for green, and that would get her lawn cut and her repairs done and things done. You know, she could buy some bread, and she could have babysitters if she wanted. (Linda, Nelson Green Dollars)

Others had a philosophical preference for a low-consumption lifestyle. They found that a mixture of kiwi use and green dollar self-

THE LONGEVITY OF ALTERNATIVE ECONOMIC PRACTICES

employment enabled them to meet their needs and have the sort of livelihood they wanted:

> Some of us think a bit different, too, because I eke out our living between a few companies, and I only charge about twenty bucks an hour going around to do factory maintenance, and people say to me, "That's too cheap. You can't get a tradesman for that price." I said, "Yeah, but I only want five hours of work at twenty bucks an hour; that's all I need." A hundred bucks a day is enough for me to live on, because I hate being a tax collector for the government! The more I earn, the more I'm gonna pay tax. I've got to ask for GST [goods and service tax, a value-added or sales tax] and everything else, and I don't wanna do that. So I keep my earnings to a minimum, so I'm not paying them a whopping great amount. Doesn't matter that I'm not earning a lot. I only want to earn my living, not make my fortune. (Neville, Blenheim Green Dollars)

Those who combined green dollars with casual self-employment, informal mutual aid and trading, and home production of food on their section (smallholding)[3] could, at times, meet many of their needs outside of formal employment patterns:

> From the end of summer up to the good growing season we could proudly look at our plates and say, "Oh, we've got ten different vegetables that we've grown from our own garden, and the meat's from our own sheep," and so forth. So there were rare occasions when we did feed ourselves, yes, but it does take a lot of effort, and you might be saving money. But, you know, the efficiency is always being out earning money; buying the goods is a more efficient way of doing it, because it does take a lot of time to grow a small plot of vegetables in many ways. . . . It was all very hit and miss. Markets were usually monthly, sometimes a little more frequent than that, and sometimes people would grow vegetables here, and other times they wouldn't. And I think during that time we got involved in a couple of food co-ops too, so that was another aspect, but they weren't related to the green dollar currency; that was New Zealand money. . . . And [green dollars] supplemented a lot of these things. (Hayden, Wairarappa Green Dollars)

Green dollars seemed noticeably more successful in some places than others: for example, the north of South Island (with the Blenheim, Nelson, Motueka, and Golden Bay Exchanges), the Wairarappa (a rural area north of Wellington), New Plymouth, Timaru, and Thames (towns acting as service centers to a rural hinterland). That the northern part of South Island became a center for successful green dollar trading is interesting in that it is a relatively isolated part of New Zealand characterized by low wages but a very benign climate and beautiful scenery. It consequently had a strong downshifting flavor, with (for New Zealand) a large number of people who would find green dollars attractive. HANDs, for example, seemed to capture the ethos of Golden Bay:

> It was kind of an icon, I suppose. [Laughs.] And philosophically it's what a lot of people believe in. . . . It's been around for a while; it's something that we can identify with, you know; it feels good, you know; people say, "Oh yes, I've been a part of that for so long." Yes. I don't know if *icon* is the right word, but . . . ["Emblematic?" the interviewer suggests.] . . . Yes, yes. . . . We tend to want to do things a little bit different here, yes. . . . I suppose part of it is the isolation, and having something that's unique to itself, although there's other [exchanges] around. It's something that people say, "Yes, this is something that's unique to Golden Bay; this is part of one of the things that's Golden Bay." [Golden Bay attracts] a lot of artists, a lot of natural healers, probably a lot of people who would like to try to get by without having a large income. People who like rural environments. The climate's pretty good, the rivers, the ocean. The town, going through the town, it's a pretty interesting town, all the different types of shops. It's not a typical New Zealand town. I would say people are probably not in such a hurry as in other places. There's a lot of artists who work here. The natural environment is very beautiful. And it's probably, the people who are tired of the rat race, let's say. (Murray, HANDs, Golden Bay)

Another center for green dollars, the Wairarappa, is in some ways quite a conservative rural community. But it is also well connected to Wellington by train, elected a transsexual Member of Parliament (MP), has a large lesbian community, and has a biker as a local mayor. It attracts those interested in alternative ways of living and in the diverse.

Green dollar schemes that worked had strong commitment-building mechanisms that helped enforce norms of trust and obligation and provided penalties for defection. They threatened to take members to court to enforce payment on negative balances in kiwi dollars (a member in Blenheim agreed to pay G\$10 a week to reduce a G\$250 debt). Or they reminded members of their obligations to their fellow traders. The Wairarappa Exchange newsletter put it baldly:

> In the case of bad debt: don't try to get away with it. The committee has no wish to take people to court. Remember, the green dollar is a unit of trust. Again, the answer is simple: trade until your account is at zero, and if you want you can pay the debt in kiwi dollars. The committee is keen to maintain a good image and will take appropriate action when members are not conducting themselves properly. Members should be able to trust

each other and have faith that the system won't let them down either. Members should be aware that the Wairarappa Green Dollar scheme is small and word soon gets around who can be trusted and who can't.

The usual regulatory mechanism for complementary currency schemes is to publish the names and balances of members, so policing can be done by the membership collectively. Anyone taking and not giving will be named and shamed. However, in New Zealand a cultural concern for privacy and the individualistic ethos of the Kiwi with his "section," compounded by the neoliberal onslaught against those who did not contribute, militated against the use of this regulatory approach. Balances generally were not made public, and green dollar exchanges were more likely to set a credit limit and attempt to enforce it—if needs be through the courts. Some would print names of people who needed help trading to address their commitment.

Other commitment-building mechanisms were more positive. Schemes in which members were able to trade with each other over long periods of time were characterized by strong bonds of solidarity and community feeling as evidenced by the way people spoke positively about each other, demonstrably helped and encouraged each other, and valued green dollars for the community feeling the scheme engendered. This came out strongly in group discussions with long-term members; their regard and affection for each other was palpable. Others schemes had activists at their heart who had put in years of hard work to ensure that the networks worked well. They often had strong green, Social Credit, or religious backgrounds. Their fellow members often described the green dollar networks as a testament to their hard work and commitment, and when these key activists moved on, the schemes often died.

To summarize, members of ten of the thirteen long-lasting green dollar exchanges found that they worked for them in terms of providing (though not all the time) observable material and psychic benefits over up to (in the case of the oldest member interviewed) eighteen years. Green dollar exchanges worked for those who understood their rhythms; whose livelihood strategy or philosophical, political, or moral orientation was strengthened through membership of the network; and who were surrounded by a similar group of people who lived close enough for trading to take place, preferably in a place that attracted like-minded people. This could be a small group, five or six, who formed the core of a wider, less active membership. But we are not here addressing how widespread membership was, but how it could work for activists.

Green Dollars under "Ruthenasia"

While green dollars did work for the committed, trading levels in even the largest schemes were too small, twenty years after their introduction to New Zealand, to make a huge difference to large numbers of New Zealanders. Although by 2000 Wairarappa Green Dollars had turned over G$51,737, the mean annual trading turnover of G$488 is boosted by the coordinator's turnover of G$5,991 and includes both income and expenditures. If the coordinator's turnover is removed, and the remaining turnover divided by half to give an average income, the figure shows an income of approximately G$173 a year to militate against benefit cuts in 1991 of $25 a week. Besides, the range of goods and services to be accessed with these green dollars was limited to home-produced goods such as crafts and jams, alternative therapies, help with odd jobs, and the like, so even the Wairarappa coordinator described its narrowly economic impact as "not on the radar" (although some lucky members were briefly able to buy beef in bulk). Although the goods and services available were valuable and worthwhile, they did not meet the basic needs of those for whom welfare had been reduced to the extent that it had been in New Zealand. Rather, in the times of extreme need under Ruthenasia the slack was taken up with the food parcel program.

Often things sounded desperate, as people tried to make ends meet. For example, an item in the Wairarappa Green Dollar Exchange newsletter argued:

> No formal complaints have been received by the committee, but the following incidents have been brought to our attention, and we feel strongly that the practices must stop! Unsupervised children attempting to steal sales goods and otherwise causing damage to private property during trading days; members entering houses and helping themselves to food and petrol without prior arrangement; and items being bought for green dollars and then sold (often at a profit) for kiwi dollars.

Again from the Wairarappa exchange:

> It has been noticeable that some of the trading has been very greedy. Many members, especially new members, were missing out because goods were being swooped on by bargain hunters who are buying in bulk anything they can get their hands on. . . . First in, first out, grabbing all they can get, demanding purchases before the start time. . . . The trading meetings have been turning ugly.

Green dollar exchanges found it hard to meet needs where long distances between members meant that they never got to know each other well or understand how the new currency worked. Isolation and the traditional robust New Zealand independence epitomized by the "number nine wire" mentality[4] meant that the exchanges were unable to do much to counter the high levels of mental illness and extreme loneliness experienced by many rural New Zealanders when formerly subsidized rural industries closed. The big cities, in particular, failed to develop sufficiently dense trading networks. Those who joined to develop alternative forms of livelihood found, as the 1990s progressed, that green dollars became less alternative and more of a poor people's movement in which people with few resources struggled to get by. Some started requesting kiwi dollars for services, which meant that the poorest could not afford those services, and those with green dollars could not necessarily spend them:

> It's been very hard in Nelson to get anybody to do anything for you. Even though they were listed on the skills thing, they'd say, "Oh well, you know, I'm too busy," or, "I don't need it right now; I don't need the extra." And a lot of them in Nelson, too, got to the point where they were wanting a cash content. . . . And a lot of people like myself were on low income, and we couldn't afford to pay hard cash, because that was defeating the object. . . . I don't know that I could call it an income, because I couldn't; I found I wasn't able to use it. And when I left I actually gave it back to the system. (Linda, Nelson Green Dollars)

A small, limited network could not meet people's needs or requests:

> It's really hard to get people active in the group, trading things, because people want things that are not inside the group. They have unrealistic expectations about what can be provided. At one stage we had a real bout of people wanting to join the group and saying, "Who can do my garden for me?" "Who can provide me with firewood?" "Who can do something for me?" without realizing it was actually a reciprocating thing. It wasn't about providing free stuff to people; you have to do something back. (Mike, Blenheim Green Dollars)

There's a lot of "wanters" out there. We could have a lot of members, but there are always the wanters that want without giving. I think that's half the problem these days. (Lynn, Blenheim Green Dollars)

As in Manchester, not everyone took green dollars seriously: "People don't quite take it as seriously as those who run it would like them to, and to be specific, it's people leaving the area without paying their debits, and it's much higher than people leaving who have a credit" (Murray, HANDs, Golden Bay). By and large, Maori and Pacific Islanders did not participate. Although many rural Maori had their own *Whanau, Iwi,* or *Mana whenau*-based mutual aid mechanisms,[5] urban Maori and Pacific Islanders, many with the greatest problems, did not participate in the exchanges in proportionate numbers.

Others feared debt, which suggests that they did not reformulate cultural codes they had developed around money. Their problems were so great that green dollars was not an answer:

I would have had to earn money as well as spend it, and I didn't have energy for doing anything. I could barely, barely get through my days. I was looking for neighbors to help me vacuum and things like that. I was pretty low energywise. . . . I knew you could go to [a debt of] five hundred or something before somebody yelled at you. But I went into a lot fear, too. I went into fear that my energy would never come back. . . . It was quite a difficult time, so I would not have wanted to go into debt, because, oh dear, I won't have the energy to balance out, ever. . . . If they had told me they'd wipe [the debt], I would've asked for help, because I would've had people cleaning the house or something. But it was the fear of not having the energy in the future to balance it. I mean, we're all different with different attitudes and that, and for me it's important, yeah, I don't like any kind of debt. (Amrita, PLEBS, Christchurch)

[What] people don't understand is that because our society works strongly on the basis that you have to have credit before you can have anything, they don't understand a system where some of our most successful traders have started off by getting into debt for several hundred dollars and then later on working their way out of it and then going into debt [again]. People in the green dollars, that I've experienced, some of them have real problems about going into debt. They want to keep credits up all the time, and yeah, I think you have to go above and below that zero, back and forwards all the time, to be most successful. (Mike, Blenheim Green Dollars)

A structural problem emerged in many green dollar schemes when a small number of active members developed fairly large positive balances that they did not want to increase. They then stopped providing services, arguing that they wanted to spend what they had earned. However, they found this difficult for the reasons discussed earlier. In addition, some of the political activists who in the early days had developed green dollars as an alternative to Rogernomics found in practice that they themselves, poor consumers with few needs and a commitment to a low-impact lifestyle, were able to meet their own needs themselves or through other forms of mutual aid. They were committed to the ethos of green dollars and wanted the network to be available to others, but did not find it practically useful themselves:

> The first members and coordinator . . . I wouldn't necessarily call them alternative lifestylers, but they were certainly our Greenies in Blenheim. People outside the conventions of the usual morals of conservative lives. They've all dropped away over the years. [Green dollars] didn't meet their needs. . . . They had a lot of self-sufficiency skills; they grew plants and vegetables and traded skills, carpentry and the like, and one of the things you tend to get a lot of in green dollars is people joining that are very confident and have lots of skills. They join to do work for others, not to get stuff for themselves, because they don't have a lot of needs. . . . I think they didn't stay in because they probably found that most of the things they could probably do themselves, and they weren't getting satisfied, and in any organisation you join, there has to be something that you want to give, and something you want to get out of it, and for them, I think they spent a lot of time giving, and there wasn't what they wanted to get out of it. (Mike, Blenheim Green Dollars)

The system consequently jammed up. This could be a major problem when, for example, as in Nelson, a large number of traders with small negative balances left, leaving an exchange composed mainly of the ten people who had all the money issued in their accounts and no one to spend it on because no new members were issuing any more currency. Further, Nelson's administrators had wiped out the debits of departing members, so the number of credits and debits did not balance. Finally, the administrators paid themselves for running the system, but did not raise the required revenue in membership fees. In Blenheim, the administrators tried to overcome the problem of a small number of people holding all the currency by unilaterally providing everyone with a grant of a thousand green dollars, hoping this would spark spending. But it did not: everyone had an unspendable balance, everyone wanted to earn and not spend, and the system seized up. The thousand green dollars was promptly taken back. A third response to that of an unspendable high balance was inflation. In Christchurch, people began to spend their credits at auctions, happily paying high prices for goods on offer, realizing that something was better than nothing. In all three examples, the elegance of the LETS scheme from which trust and integrity sprang, in that all credits and debits balanced, was breached.

Some urban green dollar exchanges developed links with the People's Centres, activist organizations working for the new poor that also provided an element of mutual aid: as we saw earlier, Auckland People's Centre members had automatic membership in Auckland Green Dollar Exchange. Problems emerged when it became clear that many of the 2,040 members were unclear about how the scheme worked, what they could offer, or how to get their needs met. Many had joined the center only for medical reasons, were unwilling to provide services, or did not take the currency seriously. Others found it difficult to provide a quality service or took more than they gave either because they saw green dollars as a soft touch or through desperation. The computer system could not handle the volume of membership, and as a consequence directories and accounts were not produced. Auckland Green Dollars was thus swamped with need, was unable to cope, and crashed, even when supported by one of the larger organizations established to meet the new demands. It is not possible to say how many Aucklanders in real need suffered when the state threw them onto inadequate voluntary provision.

At the other end of the scale, the Whangerai Exchange and Barter System—New Zealand's first scheme—was self-described as "moribund" when visited in April 1999. Although the listings included the names of the 450 or so people who had passed through the scheme since 1986, only four members attended the last trading day. The coordinator, who had recently taken over the scheme and was attempting to resuscitate it, had no information on trading levels. The membership of Nelson Green Dollars was around 600 in 1995–96 but by 2001 down to about 200. The litigious actions of one member caused the scheme to close in 2005 and relaunch with a small membership who knew and trusted each other. Rotorua Green Dollars was damaged when the treasurer stole money and leased expensive equip-

ment the exchange could not afford. In a note to the 2001 conference, members discussed the effect this had on them:

> Over a four month period the committee spent all its energies on this
> problem, to the almost total exclusion of other in-group matters. At one
> stage the committee was meeting almost weekly as the various twists and
> turns came to light. Group activity slowed right down to less than a quar-
> ter of what it might otherwise have been as members lost faith in the idea
> of green dollar trading. No longer were we a group of friendly, caring and
> helpful people, ready to offer our time and energies to help others. Mem-
> bership of the group has also declined, although this has mostly been
> those who were not particularly active anyway and may not be entirely
> the direct result of our Treasurer's activities. (Duxfield 2001)

Waiheke Island, another center for countercultural life just a short
ferry ride from Auckland, suffered from the large number of Auckland green dollar traders in geographical proximity, but with few resources flocked over to the island. Before long, the scheme was dis-
torted, because everyone had a healthy green dollar surplus they could
not spend. It died in 2001:

> Unfortunately I write to post a bereavement notice. After a varied life the
> Waiheke Green Dollar Exchange is currently in its last death throes. We
> had a small but reasonably active exchange but unfortunately no one with
> the time and energy to run it any more. When no one came forward at the
> last AGM [Annual General Meeting] to man the committee we had no
> choice but to go through the process of winding up the exchange as per
> our constitution. (Duxfield 2001).

PLEBS in Christchurch struggled, too: "When we were at our peak
and had four or five hundred members, we had a computer system
that was definitely struggling, and the whole administration . . . struggled. We had a newsletter that was sixteen pages long, and a quarter
of it was old things which had been there the last six months and we
couldn't weed them out, and couldn't get the computer to get reports
on a regular basis. We got so big our computer systems couldn't keep
up with it." (Group discussion participant, PLEBS, Christchurch)

Some schemes were attacked by the employment department,
Work and Income New Zealand (WINZ). WINZ decided locally
how to relate to exchanges in their area, and some offices were more
aggressive in their treatment of green dollar earnings than others. For
example, concerns about possible loss of New Zealand kiwi dollar
benefits from the treatment of green dollar earnings led to the demise

of the Hamilton system in 1998. In Taranaki, the second most active trader was subject to a high-profile newspaper series, investigated as a benefit "bludger" (welfare queen), which led to a perception in the town that green dollars were some kind of benefit fraud. WINZ promptly demanded the trading records of the entire scheme. An angry ex-partner reported another Taranaki member to the self-titled "Benefit Crime Team" for earning green dollars. WINZ was perceived by green dollar members as interested only in scaring beneficiaries so that they would leave the benefit register rather than in actively facilitating their well-being through access to services payable with green dollars. Such an atmosphere is, to put it mildly, not conducive to building community and trust among people:

> At several conferences we heard from other areas where the office was not as enlightened. They said, "If you are doing green dollar trading, we want to know, as we want to deduct that value off your benefit," and one year we had a ring from Inland Revenue actually saying, "How many of your members have traded? We'd like to know how much your members have traded in the year." And I said, "I'm not telling you," and they said they wanted to know if any members had traded more than two thousand dollars, 'cos that's taxable earnings sort of thing, and I said, "To away. I don't know if anyone is in that category, and I wouldn't tell you anyway if I did," and they never came back again. (Mike, Blenheim Green Dollars)

The negative climate encouraged by the beneficiary scapegoating campaign raised the costs of participation for poor people in a movement that offered an explanation for economic crisis and a possible solution, but a solution it could not deliver in more than a prefigurative form. Membership was overwhelmingly composed of those with a political interest in alternative forms of money, work, and livelihood or for whom part-time work was beneficial rather than relied on.

Post-Neoliberal New Zealand?

Things could have changed in 1999 with the election of the Labour-Alliance coalition, a government that declared: "The free market experiences of the last century failed." A Labour MP spoke at the 2000 green dollar conference, arguing that the new government wanted to recognize the work being done by green dollar exchanges and to encourage their development as a social tool to empower people at the grassroots level. Green dollars, he argued, had positive spin-offs, such as helping people to become work ready and to develop skills and networks. Another spin-off, he argued, was that people felt better about what they were doing and about themselves, resulting in better general community health. However, he did little more than encourage green dollars to make their case for a more favorable benefit regime as a contribution to Labour's focus on paid work: opening up alternatives to paid work was no more attractive to Labour than it had been to National.

Worse, in 2001 National's Revenue Spokesperson Annabel Young put out a press release arguing that green dollars were part of a "NZ$9 billion 'Black Market' Tax Dodge." In a series of press releases that implicitly recognized that green dollars could provide alternatives to paid work for an employer, she argued:

> The Inland Revenue Department isn't policing the green market. . . . The Green Party actively promotes bartering and "people-to-people" activity which is a clear invitation to cut the taxman out of their business loop. They are a partner to the Labour-Alliance Government yet they are encouraging participation in this tax dodge. When transactions move from "the odd pot of honey sold over the fence" to fencing and roofing you are entering a different scale of things. Honest taxpayers end up footing the bill when the Minister of Revenue doesn't treat this problem seriously and the Green Party encourages people to partake in what is effectively tax evasion. Greens are very pious about the environment but where do they stand when it comes to making sure that proper taxes are collected on regular, systematic work?

Young's attack was small-minded—and plain wrong. Black market, tax-dodging activities are difficult in a system that records every trade on a computer available for tax authorities to inspect, where traders are encouraged to declare their earnings. The British Inland Revenue goes as far as seeing LETS as a way of accounting for informal earnings, and this is one reason why LETS has been unattractive to those used to meeting their needs through illicit ends (North 1996). What Young failed to identify, from a neoliberal perspective, is that a combination of state benefits and unreported green dollar trading *could* provide an alternative to independence through paid work. But even here, active welfare programs would make life difficult for anyone who did see this as a livelihood strategy (as some did). Even neoliberals could not object to what is a Smithian utopia, a very entrepreneurial livelihood strategy based on self-employed work for a mix of green and kiwi dollars, as long as all taxes are paid and regulations adhered to. That such a livelihood strategy is not governed by capitalist rhythms should be irrelevant to a liberal.

Green dollars could have continued to be relevant after 2000 not only by providing alternatives to paid work but also by providing other types of help to the poor at a time when unemployment was replaced by working poverty in the still neoliberalized New Zealand (Laugesen 2004). Although the headline unemployment rate was down to 3.8 percent in December 2004 and food bank usage fell by two-thirds between 2001 and 2004, this disguised the fact that 23 percent of the population were still in working poverty below the poverty line (60 percent of median income), down from only 28 percent in the early 1990s. Some 20 percent had "somewhat restricted," "restricted," or "very restricted" livelihoods, with the 4 percent classified as "very restricted" missing out on one-third of nineteen basics such as a telephone, washing machine, heating, fresh vegetables, and access to a doctor (Laugesen 2004). Most likely to be poor would be families on low wages or benefits, especially single parents. Those on benefits, especially with children, did not benefit from Labour's focus on work (St. John and Craig 2004).

The fact that unemployment was down sharply meant that those who could find work did so. But with pay low and hours long, they had little time for other things in their leisure time:

> "I can look back over the last fourteen years and think how the circumstances of each individual have changed drastically over the time." . . . "Work commitments—suddenly a person would get a job, and so they would be far too busy. The majority of people have to work weekends. So therefore the whole of society has changed." . . . "Nobody is interested at the moment because of the economy of the country, I think." . . . "It seems to be the economy, but also I think just recently young families are having to work longer to survive. The wages haven't gone up in comparison with the costs, and a lot of families are working six days a week and more just to survive." . . . "It's getting harder. The cost of housing is getting much more expensive for young families. . . . There's a lot more money around, but people are having to work harder to pay their mortgages and so on." (Discussion comments by members, Timaru Alternative Trading System)

Green MP Sue Bradford, founder of the Auckland People's Centre, said that with their focus on paid work, Labour governments are always "toxic for the voluntary and community sector." Certainly, after the very real poverty of the 1990s, by 2005 members in the surviving exchanges saw, with hindsight, the rise and fall of usage of green dollars in the context of restructuring and the welfare cuts of the 1990s. New Zealand now had fuller employment, so green dollars had less immediacy as a way of helping address issues of poverty. Full employment to some extent meant less need, although the prevalence of working poverty meant that unmet needs remained. Green dollars did not, however, fill the gap, because the "time poor" are consequently also "time-money poor."

Those who remained in exchanges were not those who saw such membership as a survival mechanism. They were people who rejected full-time employment for various reasons and who were critical of market economies that focused on growth. By 2005, climate change and the end of the era of cheap oil as drivers for the need to move to localized, steady-state, participatory economies had replaced fear of financial crisis. That is not to say that financial crisis was no longer an issue. It was:

> People's perceptions will change, because at the moment, we are pretty affluent . . . look at all of this [points to the house, food, etc.] . . . like we don't need to worry about where our next meal is coming from. So, once that changes—which it is bound to; it always does—people's . . . way of seeing the world will become a lot more real again. . . . That sort of thing goes in waves, I think, . . . and . . . it's easy to lose heart when it's in trough, but we just need to make sure [the exchange] stays there for when we need it. (Eva, Motueka Skills Swap)

Thus a political commitment to participatory, noncapitalist economic diversity meant that the long-term agenda of no-growth localized economies was still vital to human development, irrespective of the effectiveness of neoliberal restructuring.

Conclusion

The experience of green dollars shows that, in contrast with the more ephemeral experiences of the nineteenth and twentieth centuries, green dollars worked for some for long periods of time. Activists were able to build long-lasting alternative livelihood strategies where they were creative in sourcing their needs from the network first, knew their fellow traders and their skills, understood the way the network operated, and had the confidence and skill to make the network work. Where they had access to food from their section, a part-time job, and a wider network of mutual aid outside green dollars, they often were able to provide for themselves the alternative, freer form of economy they wanted—as long as they were not materialistic. Natural wheeler-dealers and those with young families found the network worked well if they took it seriously, that is, valued the currency and their commitments to their fellow traders. They found a network that promoted security, friendship, and support, and perhaps a little vision of a good life. They helped build a better future, carried on the fight against marketization, and showed that something else was possible. In their own words:

> All over the world new economic subsystems are being created, in an effort to take back the initiative from neoliberal globalisation strategies. TINA—there is no alternative—is still being loudly proclaimed. However, it is becoming increasingly more urgent that new alternatives are being realised, where human dignity is being realised, solidarity between people is strengthened and resources used responsibly. LETS in New Zealand is one such alternative. (Hensch 2004)

Green dollar exchanges performed better in some places than in others. They were effective over the long term where a large enough number of people with a commitment to alternatives provided a fairly geographically dense network of people with skills to share. They worked where there was (at least one) respected, rooted activist committed to building the network over the long term, usually an activist with a vision of an alternative future. They worked where members had commitment-building mechanisms and an ethos of taking green dollars seriously, whether these were bureaucratic (taking defectors to court) or more solidaristic (a shared ethos).

New Zealand provides experience of alternative currencies over some time. We now move to the country that found itself disciplined far more severely than was New Zealand, and where as a result alternative currencies evolved into mass resistance to neoliberalism—Argentina.

8

Surviving Financial Meltdown
ARGENTINA'S BARTER NETWORKS

THE PREVIOUS CHAPTER SHOWS THAT IN NEW ZEALAND committed participants were able to create and use alternative forms of money for long periods, although the numbers involved were small and the economic benefits still not great. The complementary currency movement that emerged in the late 1990s and the first three years of the twenty-first century in Argentina, the *redes de trueque,* seems to be different in scale, with levels of mobilization previously achieved perhaps only by the Populists: literally millions of users. The literal translation of *redes de trueque* is "barter networks." In Argentina, "barter" is not used in the sense of one-to-one exchange without use of money; it refers to exchange using nonstate forms of currency generated by community groups, nongovernmental organizations (NGOs), communities, and private businesspeople. We call it "barter," as Argentines do, but technically it is not barter.

In this chapter we investigate Argentina's barter networks to uncover the extent to which they formed a significant part of the livelihood strategies of millions from 2000 to 2003. If so, can they best be thought of as a way of surviving through a financial crisis or as a fundamental micropolitical challenge to neoliberal financial stability that involved millions in a collective repudiation of capitalist disciplining? Alternatively, as Hayek suggested, is usage of alternative currencies on a mass scale part of the problem? Does *trueque* entail the overissuance of money as a shortcut, as an alternative to the more difficult job of getting the economic fundamentals right?

Argentina in Crisis

In the wake of the 1987 stock market crash in the United Kingdom, Guy Dauncey (1988) published what became for many an inspirational book called *Beyond the Crash: The Emergence of the Rainbow Economy*. In a populist and accessible style, it pointed to the potential of community-created local currency networks to help people survive a perceived imminent financial crash. Dauncey wrote:

> The LETSystem seems to be an idea whose time has come. Global crash or no global crash, local communities have much to gain by establishing their own systems. It offers a return to the values of community in which we care for each other and support each other. It enables local people to develop their skills, make new local contacts and to get on with their lives without necessarily having to depend on a "proper job." It provides a boost to the vitality of local economies hard hit by unemployment or recession. And it provides a secure basis for local economic self-reliance and sustainability. In the event of a crash, a thriving local LETSystem would enable a community to keep trading through the storm. The LETSystem is an important component of the economics of love, which can be the only kind of economics for a fragile and much loved planet. (Dauncey 1988, 69)

Although the 1987 U.K. stock market crash did not portend financial collapse, a series of crashes and crises across East Asia, Russia, and Latin America caused misery for millions. Throughout the 1990s, Argentina underwent a process of privatization and deregulation such that it moved from one of the most regulated economies in the world to the poster child of the International Monetary Fund's (IMF's) approach to structural adjustment. The reforms were not without cost. Restructuring a large public sector led to high unemployment, while the gross domestic product (GDP) fell 7.6 percent in the period from 1994 to 1996 and the debt grew to finance a peso "pegged" unrealistically to the U.S. dollar. Although the economy rallied again in the late 1990s, the U.S. economy entered a recession in April 2000, and Argentina suffered huge capital flight because it was assumed that the "peg" meant that problems in the United States would be transmitted south. By 2001 the economy was in a deep crisis.

The Argentine people responded to the crisis and to a growing disillusionment with what was increasingly seen as a corrupt and incompetent government by casting four million blank ballots in the

October 2001 midterm elections. Things came to a head over three days in December 2001. A mass mobilization of an alliance of savers, pensioners, and unemployed and underemployed people converged on the Plaza de Mayo in Central Buenos Aires, banging pots and pans, revving motorcycles, and setting off fireworks. The immediate cause of their anger was the freezing of their bank accounts by the government—the *coralito*—in an attempt to use their savings in a desperate attempt to avoid defaulting on a debt repayment to the IMF, which the state could not otherwise make.

Argentina entered economic meltdown when the peg was unceremoniously abandoned and savers who thought they had savings in currency at parity with the U.S. dollar found they were worth a quarter of their former value (Halevi 2002; Rock 2002). As a result of the *coralito*, people literally could not withdraw more than three hundred pesos a month from their bank accounts, not enough to live on. The Argentine GDP sank by 16.3 percent in the first three months of 2002, while manufacturing output was down by 20 percent. Some 20 percent of Argentines were reported to be living in "severe" poverty, which in the provinces included starvation; 52 percent, or 19 million people, lived in poverty; 20 percent were unemployed, while 23 percent were underemployed. Throughout 2002, the economy endured a slow, painful recovery on the back of a newly competitive devalued peso, but millions had to get through the crisis and find new ways to make a living.

For some this was just another of the financial crises to which capitalism was prone, and from which it would recover. For others it was the opportunity to develop a new form of economy on the bones of the failed capitalist system (Harman 2002; "IM" 2002; Aufheben 2003; López Levy 2004; North and Huber 2004). Argentines occupied closed businesses, picketed roads (Dinerstein 2001; Petras 2002), formed neighborhood assemblies (Dinerstein 2002, 2003), and took to bartering by the millions to such an extent that for a time it looked as if they were actually building an economy based on the noncapitalist, liberated forms of economic relations others only dreamed about. They did not try to change the big system or take power themselves, but instead opted out of a failed capitalism. As Gibson-Graham suggested, Argentines did not wait for the revolution; they made it, but not by storming the Casa Rosada (Holloway

2002). If this is the case, it suggests that Marx was wrong to see such movements as private withdrawal from collective action, and that the right have some justification in seeing complementary currencies as fundamentally opposed to their neoliberal economic agenda. Argentina is our case study of the large-scale usage of alternative currencies. How did it fare?

Argentina's Barter Networks

Argentina's barter networks emerged in 1997 in Bernal, part of Buenos Aires's industrial rust belt, during the period when many thousands suffered from an overrestrictive fiscal policy and the loss of their jobs to restructuring (De Meulinaire 1999; Pearson 2003; Powell 2002). An environmental NGO, Programma de Autosuficiencia Regional (PAR) (the Regional Self-sufficiency Program) wanted to explore environmental solutions to the growing poverty and unemployment that surrounded restructuring to see if it might also provide better livelihoods than the market (Primavera et al. 1998). The original project involved twenty neighbors, and in relying on the issuance of "credit notes" to facilitate trade was modeled on the Ithaca Hours program in upstate New York (Glover 1995). The founder's aims were summarized thus:

> Our main stand is that barter networks are able to reinvent the market and not only reinclude people that have been excluded by globalization, but—even beyond that—can include people never included before. We believe that we need not oppose this new market to the formal market, but we need rather to develop our ability to join them [sic], in different rhythms and forms, if we choose to do it. We also believe we need not oppose government but rather developed our ability to act with government in order to build democratic life with equity and solidarity instead of competition and exclusion. Finally we believe that barter networks are able to reshuffle cards to build a new social game. (Primavera et al. 1998)

Between 1997 and 2000, barter spread across Argentina as quickly as did the crisis. The barter networks worked through what Ramada (2001) called a "chaordic" or trusslike structure made up of "nodes" organized geographically, but not vertically. The nodes were markets where traders (called *prosumidores*—"prosumers"—after Alvin Tofler's consumers and producers) met, typically in a church hall, an unused factory, a car park, or a baseball field at a set time each week.

Prosumers came and traded with each other using *créditos,* or credits—essentially coupons.

Nodes boasted honey, empanadas (turnovers), pancakes, pizzas, green vegetables and fruit, jams, wine, vinegar, breads, biscuits, shoes, shampoos, jumpers, nightgowns, haircuts and manicures, a café, a samba band, a notice board—and always, heated debate and haggling. Some had stalls in the tens and visitors in the hundreds, while some had visitors in the thousands. By 2001, the organizers claimed that 1,500 markets were used by half a million people spending 600 million credits across Argentina (Norman 2002). The real figure is unknowable.

Using public transportation, Argentines would travel across the city, into the informal settlements in the suburbs, to the countryside, and on to another city to attend as many nodes as possible. No one with access to credits would starve, which was not the case for many in the more remote, indigenous, and impoverished parts of Argentina close to the border with Bolivia. Consequently, people would line up for hours to get into the markets, and would travel some distance. People might establish their own node with their neighbors or through their church, print their own currency, and get their neighboring nodes to accept them. Some nodes were tightly governed, and only members could trade, while others were more open, less formal. Some nodes accepted each other's credits, while others did not. But there was no central control or administration, and nothing to stop people from the other side of a very large country from trading if the individual they wanted to buy from felt their credits were good.

The cultural and social geographies and relations within which the economic life of *trueque* took place mattered. To impose some order on what was considerable diversity, four types of barter network can be observed with very different attitudes to the micropolitics of alternative forms of money. First, the Red Global de Trueque (RGT) (Global Barter Network), established by PAR, operated across Argentina using a franchising system controlled from Bernal and centrally produced notes, the *arbolitos.* Second, the Red de Trueque Solidario (RTS) (Solidarity Barter Network), centered mainly around the federal capital (but with supporters across the country), used their own locally produced notes, which sometimes could and other times could not be exchanged for notes from other approved nodes.

The RTS took a more militantly localist and bottom-up approach that they vehemently contrasted with that of the RGT. Third was Zona Oeste (Western Zone) in the periurban informal settlements of Greater Buenos Aires. Zona Oeste was run in a robustly autocratic manner by a businessman, Fernando Sampayo, who issued his own currency backed by his own reputation for straight playing. Sampayo was Hayek's "businessman of a conservative temperament" embodied. Fourth were barter networks in other urban centers, especially Mar del Plata and Mondoza, which were separated geographically from the center and had their own local characteristics. They were broadly sympathetic to RTS, but wished to avoid the internecine wars that, as we shall see later, broke out in 2001 between RGT and RTS.

When the *coralito* was in place between December 2001 and April 2002 and Argentines were physically unable to get their money out of their bank accounts, the economy literally ground to a halt and millions faced acute hardship, if not starvation. PAR responded to this crisis by printing enough barter currency to meet the demand of millions of users, arguing that the inflationary consequences should be disregarded in the short term in what was essentially a "Keynesianism from below." They supplied thousands of "start-up kits," including a number of credits, paid for in pesos. Critics in RTS did not see this as legitimate or responsible. To put it bluntly, RTS accused RGT of printing and selling credits for pesos, thereby evolving into a "get-rich-quick" outfit, the latest snake oil salesmen, disconnected from its base. PAR's view was simply that it was responding to a crisis of an unforeseen magnitude and at worst was guilty of a lack of transparency in its dealings. In any case, they believed that as the developers of the world's largest alternative currency system they had the right to use their innovation as they saw fit, and critics were small-minded, interfering, jealous busybodies.

RTS argued that the best response to the crisis was the development of small, localized networks from below. The market would be reinvented through money socially constructed by whoever was using it, not created for them by a benevolent or otherwise NGO or businessperson: "The social currency [is] necessarily local because the construction of the currency is not the decision of a group of people, nor is it a private decision, but it has to be a process of social construction of the currency—where all the participants of this ... social construction, are the real actors, who control it, . . . who give the value to this money" (Alberto, organizer, Mendoza). RTS was concerned that PAR's actions were inflationary and opened the networks up to abuse, and that consequently the value of the currency should be maintained through community regulation to ensure limited issuance and to prevent forgery. They argued that strong community-building mechanisms should be used at the weekly node meetings to ensure that a reflexive economy was created in which traders would share and reproduce the values of mutual aid that inspire barter and would be on the lookout for shysters and abusers. These values were summarized in the March 2002 edition of the Buenos Aires *trueque* magazine, which has the following advice on the front (given by the cartoon character Jose Solidario):

- *Don't buy credits.* All this does is fatten the pockets of the unscrupulous people who are selling them.
- *Produce with solidarity.* Take what you can produce and what you know others will need to the node.
- *Distribute with solidarity.* Don't trade all of your products with one prosumer. Let many prosumers obtain your products.
- *Consume with solidarity.* Only consume what is necessary, and give other prosumers the opportunity to consume the same as you.

RTS therefore insisted on members' actively signing on to the "prosumer" values of the network in an induction meeting and contributing produce (something they have made themselves) before receiving credits, on a management structure to ensure that markets were well and fairly run, and on an active decision by all groups about whether to accept a new node into the network and about how much currency to print. This commitment to collective decision making meant that in 2002 the RTS nodes met monthly, at a national level, to coordinate their work. For example, the April 2002 meeting in the Entre Rios town of Gualiguachu had representatives from fourteen regions, including some who travelled from as far as Mar Del Plata, Salta, Cordoba, Rosario, and Chaco. Unanimity and inclusion were insisted on in all decision making. PAR countered that this response was too small-scale given the depth of the crisis and that the organizers were imposing their left-wing political ideals on what should be an apolitical economic or mutual aid activity. Zona Oeste argued for large-scale usage of barter to meet the great need and agreed that

RTS's commitment to direct democracy was too slow, too political. But they also agreed that PAR's lack of transparency and aggressive promotion opened them up to the challenge that they were taking advantage. Zona Oeste ran itself as a business, insisting on full and open record keeping.

The year 2002 saw both sides of the argument borne out. RGT were right that RTS's small, LETS-like approach was too slow given the millions that flooded to the nodes in that awful year, and their commitment-building mechanisms were overwhelmed. As we shall discuss in more detail later, many of the nodes became wild, anarchic spaces in which impoverished people struggled with each other, often physically, to get into the market and to purchase the best goods. The embarrassed RTS organizers, unable to induct the millions flowing into the nodes, felt they had created a "monster." But RTS was also right: printing millions of credits was inflationary. The chaotic nature of PAR's central structure was a problem, because PAR's franchisees were not always perfect. Peronist Party machines would incorporate barter networks by purchasing PAR's starter kit, setting up a node for their clients, and at times, violently closing down "rival" RTS nodes. One RGT franchisee was secretly filmed selling stolen shoes, then jailed.

Then, seemingly overnight, barter catastrophically lost credibility. In November 2002, a prime time television show on Canal 9 "exposed" what it called the "great barter scam," claiming that stolen goods were being sold, that credits were forgeries, and that the food on sale was of poor quality. This was seen by RGT activists as a political attack by a Peronist government concerned that barter was giving Argentina a bad name internationally[1] and undermining the clientelist networks on which the Peronist Party was based (for details of clientelistic practices, see Auyero 2000). They argued that the television station concerned was a Peronist mouthpiece, that criminal gangs were forging *arbolitos* en masse and giving them out from the backs of unmarked vans, and that the Buenos Aires police had raided PAR's headquarters and stolen 100,000 pesos. RTS said that this was nonsense—PAR had caused the inflation and worked with many nonethical franchisers, and the television program had been right to point this out. But the result of this dispute was that the use of barter—from all four networks—plummeted across Argentina to

SURVIVING FINANCIAL MELTDOWN

a fraction of its former level (activists claimed to between 10 and 40 percent). Hundreds of nodes closed.

To some extent, the spectacular decline of barter in Argentina shows that the localist concerns for an ecological diversity of currencies that characterized just about all of the contemporary alternative currency movement, with the exception of RGT, make sense. Those RTS nodes that were relatively isolated from the *arbolito* by geography or by a refusal to accept it did prove themselves better able to withstand the shock, and after November 2002 attempts were made to rebuild the networks with a wider diversity of local currencies that operated closed nodes (did not accept anyone else's currency). But PAR's approach also meant that usage of nonlocal alternative currencies did rise to an economic level that dwarfed all other models since the 1930s, kept many people alive during a devastating financial collapse, and perhaps prevented revolution by bouncing Argentines through the worst of their financial travails (an ironic result for a noncapitalist program). This was due partly to the efficiency of PAR's franchising approach. PAR provided people with a ready-made currency program, the node provided an accessible space to facilitate trading (compared with a telephone-based directory), and the concept of alternative forms of money was readily accepted in a country where previous experiences of inflation and political instability meant that people were used to the form of money changing. As Ingham (2004, 165–74) argues, Argentina was a country where the state's monopoly over the right to issue currency was not well established, and Argentines were used to getting by during periods of hyperinflation by unorthodox means. But there is also an issue of scale. The success of barter in Argentina was partly due to the ability to spend credits across a region and a willingness to travel, which created a much larger market (North 2005). This suggests that a larger scale facilitates greater levels of trade, albeit still largely based on an extension of household provisioning to a greater group in a period of extreme crisis. The market was so large, and the capitalist market in such disarray, that factories would sell goods unsellable on the open market at barter nodes that, open to anyone, provided a significant market. Thus, at the height of the crisis the barter economy significantly accessed the realm of production for the first time in the history of alternative currencies.

Barter Networks as Mass Livelihood Strategies

The other case studies in this book have examined the micropolitics of alternative forms of money. We saw that in the United Kingdom, Hungary, and New Zealand they were too small to provide welfare and livelihoods in any serious sense. This was not the case in Argentina, where barter was more than a struggle for new forms of money: it was also a livelihood strategy for millions that was able to include those that were unable to make their livelihoods any other way.

Monica is a typical *trueque* prosumer. In her early forties, she first started going to *trueque* nodes after she lost her job and became depressed. In the beginning she went around selling watch straps and other similar produce left over from the shop she used to have. In 2002 she was able to support herself completely through the three different nodes she visited each day. Another couple of prosumers were a mother and daughter who made doughnuts that were sold out within twenty to thirty minutes at nodos. The doughnuts sold for 15 *créditos* a dozen, with all the ingredients bought at the *trueque* market in 2002. A third prosumer made chocolate pancakes, with the ingredients all from the formal market; only the chocolate, the most expensive thing, came from the *trueque*. At the market where we met the pancake maker, she took home enough vegetables for three days, along with a shaver, a flashlight, garlic, twelve little pizzas (enough for one family meal), juice, a packet of biscuits, toilet paper, and four lemons (enough for a week), and she still had some *créditos* left over. Before the crash, just visiting nodes on Saturdays and Sundays, she could get enough to eat for the whole week, even too much for the week: "For me it was like a job. . . . That year I could live off the *trueque,* more or less." But it was not an easy life; meat was scarce. She had to budget carefully, and with a friend she set up a system for searching out specific items from the myriad nodes. Without careful planning, she said, "if you are not a realist, you're lost. . . . It worked very well for me, but you did have to be going around."

Other prosumers said that they could get 90 percent of their food needs met before the crash of 2002: "I could get all I wanted." "My freezer was always full, and there was always enough to eat for the six of us." "I would not miss it even once." "I don't know what I would do without it." "[The *trueque*] supplements and helps me as I work; but it is a complete help for others." Prosumers could obtain professional services—those of dentists, doctors, and psychologists—at cheap rates. As the middle classes sold their unwanted clothes, household goods, and other possessions to survive through use of the *coralito,* the poor gained access to things that had previously been out of reach and were still unaffordable for pesos. ("I bought lots of things that I had never been able to buy: a raincoat, shoes with brand names; it gave me a lot of well-being.") Not only did people meet their needs; for many, the experience was enjoyable. In Buenos Aires, *trueque* was "almost fashionable" at first; it was enjoyable to visit and browse the stalls, meet friends, and buy a snack.

Trueque was especially an economy that women controlled and enjoyed. This was partly because, given the depth of the crisis, household provisioning was best achieved through barter, and this was work overwhelmingly carried out by women. Alternatively, men might be working on and off and barter supplemented the household economy. But more than that was involved. Women argued that they kept the family together and that, although Argentina was outwardly patriarchal, in reality women were in charge of the home: "We women are entrepreneurial; men are shyer." Others said, "It's like reconstruction after a war": men were panicking or protesting; women got on with making sure that the family ate and was adequately clothed. Node coordinators were usually women, often strong coordinators about whom prosumers would make comments such as "The girl is a good organizer" or "They don't run around screaming at people here." Coordinators made sure people produced as well as consumed, and in the better nodes supervised food allocation, ran the nodes transparently (especially accounting for where the money went), or organized a queuing system so everyone got equal shares. Management was crucial to the effective running of a node, and "La chica sabe coordinar muy bien" (She knows how to run things) was praise indeed. Women excelled in running these markets, something patriarchal Argentina would not normally allow.

Many markets were supportive, cooperative environments. They were small and cozy or well run and effectively organized. Some had prices on blackboards, others a group of coordinators to help people and dissuade inflationary pricing. Induction programs taught people how to negotiate (especially over price and quality), say what they needed, and be aware of what others would need. As a community, prosumers learned not to buy goods at inflated prices and to either confront those overcharging or get a coordinator to say a word. People generally did trade ethically, as part of a community: "We are all friends." "They are like a family." "I like the way the people are." "We are like a large solidaristic family." "Yes, it is wonderful: we talk and talk; ideas are exchanged, and friendships are made." And best: "Charly, antes que vos viniste nos saludabamos; ahora nos conocemos" (Charly, before you came we used to greet each other; now we know each other).

Even those who did not use the markets to meet their livelihood needs stressed their cooperative nature—"Al nivel sociologico: funciona; al nivel economico: ayuda" (In the sociological sphere [the *trueque*] works; in the economic sphere, it helps)—while others stressed the equality of their nodes: "We all have the same opportunity to get things." Prosumers felt, "I have lived solidarity. . . . Here you choose what you consume; the encounter with things is different; I'm taking [home] things made with love." Going to the markets was a release from the crisis: "It was like a way out; instead of therapy I came here." "A distraction—a way to take my mind off of things." "It is therapeutic." "We are all in the same situation." "If we had money, we wouldn't come here." "Here there are no differences between different social classes." Seemingly, then, in Argentina the hopes of advocates of alternative currencies were being realized: here a better form of economy was being created out of the wreckage of neoliberalism.

A Micropolitical Response to Crisis

Barter provided a way of surviving the crisis and—the organizers argued—a way, along with microcredit, small business formation, cooperative development, and participatory budgeting, to develop indigenous production focused not on export, but on meeting local needs as a way out of the crisis. This is a strategy that found some sympathy from Buenos Aires's leftist city council (North and Huber 2004).

As a development strategy, a focus on economic life based on self-provisioning through presuming, forming a base for the development of new microenterprises that will in turn grow into new larger businesses, is a well-known process of formalization of informal ways of making a living. By strengthening informal employment opportunities, many livelihoods can be generated quite quickly and cheaply to satisfy and stimulate local demand. New opportunities can be generated in tourism and handicrafts, taking advantage of local customs and artwork, as well as incubating new small businesses and subcontractors. Informal enterprises reuse and recycle resources, thereby meeting local demand, reducing the need for imports, and helping with the balance of payments (Bromley 1990, 338).

There are two approaches to development through formalization. The Peruvian development economist Hernando de Soto and his Institute for Liberty and Democracy sought to make capitalism "work" for the poorest by removing, streamlining, or simplifying of ten unreasonable or overly bureaucratic barriers (commonly regis tration and regulation) to new small business formation by what de Soto argues are often pompous and corrupt vested interests. Central to his vision is the regularization of existing black market and informal activities such as street trading, informal buses and taxis, and informal settlements, for he sees those behind them not as tax-dodging criminals or marginal petty capitalists but as plucky entrepreneurs who will be the wealth generators of the future (de Soto 1989, 2000). Focusing on markets, entrepreneurship, and getting the state off the backs of wealth producers are, simplistically, classic right-wing positions, and de Soto was attacked by the left on that basis. However, as Bromley (1990) argued, a focus on squatters and those struggling to cope with capitalist change is far from a right-wing position; the right would prefer to have squatters and street traders cleared out of the way. Bromley contrasted de Soto's approach with that of the International Labour Organization, which supported a focus on the importance of the informal sector, arguing that de Soto was wrong to conflate economic success with a lack of regulation and support. While it is right to challenge overregulation and red tape, successful economies are those in which a development state works effectively to facilitate economic development rather than getting out of the way, and therefore the state should look to work with that sector to strengthen and develop it.

Barter in many ways resonates with de Soto's ideas. While Powell (2002) saw barter (before the crisis of 2002) as petty capitalism, some prosumers did move on to trade at the many craft fairs—*ferias arte-sanal*—that sprung up around Buenos Aires after the financial crash, focusing on the flood of tourists who took advantage of the now devalued peso. Another *trueque* had a baker happy to teach anybody to bake and other classes for new microenterprises, which were seen as "an exit into the formal market."

However, although many used *trueque* to meet their needs and found the experience enjoyable and solidaristic, many traders saw *trueque* only as a way of getting through an awful financial, social, and political crisis. In 2002, the overwhelming number of prosumers and node organizers alike saw *trueque* as driven by acute financial need, not political conviction:

> [We] never got involved in politics. . . . The *trueque* has done nothing like the large protest of the *piqueteros,* or the CTA, or the Madres de Plaza de Mayo, or anything like that.[2] . . . This organization never got involved in politics, and the politicians understand this very well, because the number of people which are involved in the Zona Oeste is very large, and if the *trueque* wanted to organize some kind of demonstration [it could]. . . . I in particular never got involved with any of those movements. (Fernando, organizer, Zona Oeste, Buenos Aires)

Given the depth of the crisis, key activists saw it less as an alternative to capitalism than a way to help the middle classes, not used to fending for themselves, to survive the crisis and generate new forms of livelihood. Barter was almost a game, a trial run for a market-based economy of microtraders, but one that focused on need, not on capital accumulation:

> It's a matter of changing people's way of thinking . . . from that of an employee to that of a businessperson who runs a microenterprise, a producer. All this means changing people's ways of thinking. They say: "There are no jobs." I respond: "There is no employment, but there is work." . . . And there is work, because there are needs to be met; and some of these we can cover with work, no? . . . The charismatic aspect—to lift the spirit of a population which was left without work, and . . . and [the] thought that there was no alternative—worked. . . . Lift the spirits; stimulate production, services; the added value of recycled goods. . . . To see abundance where another sees poverty or nothing at all. . . . It is mainly people from the impoverished middle class in the *trueque;* unlike the conventional poor, who are used to look for other resources. The impoverished middle class is struggling in a flat with phone bills, gas bills, etc. (Charly, organizer RTS, Capital Federal, Buenos Aires)

With a more radical perspective, Alberto, from the nonaligned network in Mendoza, saw barter as a way to generate new forms of production:

> We saw, very clearly ... social exclusion ... this new phenomenon [that] we had to solve through creating new productive systems. . . . Employment had already been declining more and more ... and has recently been continuing to decline. In other words, ... what's happening is a structural problem. So we aimed to generate productive development, which generates work, which organizes people, in a new way.

Alberto argued that the Argentine left had traditionally counterpoised the state to the market and looked to the state to provide solutions. Post–1989, he argued, this was an inadequate solution, and what was needed was community-controlled and -regulated markets based on reciprocity, not competition. Similarly, Carlos from Mar-y-Sierras *trueque* in Mendoza was known colloquially as *"El Orga"* in a reference to the leftist guerrillas of the 1970s. His politics and methods of organization were closer to those of the disciplined left-wing party man. For Carlos, barter was a means to an end: if people's values did not change through trading, barter would have no value. Traders in Mar-y-Sierras were called *"socios"*—partners. Carlos argued that although it was easy to find examples of cooperation and livelihoods being made, it was harder to find examples of real *reciprocity*. The partners required strong management and organization from above, where Carlos would have preferred self-organization based on deeply held feelings of reciprocity:

> In the *trueque*, capacity building is there from the beginning. Our way of going about the *trueque* is not just to have a marketplace where you just have a different type of money to a capitalist market, and call it social money ... but to have a node, with a real social money; but despite capacity-building efforts it is very difficult to get people to understand—the success is very limited. . . . People go along with it, but there is no deep commitment; there is no militancy, which means not just being conscious of the ideas, but also passing them on. . . . It is difficult to have them understand that it's not just about luxury and economic well-being, but about solidarity; and it's especially difficult under these circumstances of economic necessity.

The reference to extreme economic necessity is important.

Overwhelmed by Crisis

As the crisis bit, the ability of the coordinators and prosumers who wanted a cooperative or solidaristic economy to regulate the nodes they had established declined. As millions flooded to the networks, new members were not inducted. They found it hard to negotiate prices, and did not understand how barter works. Unregulated or underregulated nodes with thousands of impoverished, desperate visitors (they were no longer prosumers; they did not produce) searched tables full of bric-a-brac and other poor-quality produce because the middle classes' "spare" capacity, piles of old clothes and the like, was exhausted. People arriving late found a long line and nothing of value to be had once they got inside the hall, so they would line up for hours before markets. If inside, those with good-quality produce found themselves disadvantaged because they could not scour the market for good-quality produce at the same time as selling, while those who did not bring anything to the market were free to search. Many people were never prosumers; they had forgotten how to produce, did not have the wherewithal, or had to buy ingredients for food on the open market at prices they could not afford. There were few courses or training opportunities to enable people to raise their skill levels or acquire new ones. Or they just bought *créditos*. The markets seemed out of control; people got crushed in the line through 400 people cramming into a room that took 150. Nodes were described thus: "It upset me — dark, airless, poorly presented" or "A bad environment, very expensive." One commented, "I got scared; there were so many people; you couldn't walk, and you couldn't breathe," while another said, "People used to fight; they killed each other for a rag or for food."

The street-smart "*vivos*" went from node to node buying low from the inexperienced and reselling high (sometimes right in front of those just taken advantage of). They sold merchandise on the streets outside the markets. People were "grabbing"; it was no longer a "nice environment." The organizers felt ashamed, believing, "Poor people taking advantage of poor people is the worst of crimes" or "There are people without shame. We try to be solidaristic, but there are always infiltrators." Barter turned from a solidarity economy into a commercial relationship: "I do not make friends, just say 'Hello' and respect the people there. It's just one hour and 'Bye.'"

For many, especially the fallen middle class, and most especially men, participation in *trueque* was anything but enjoyable. The "new poor"—middle-class people—tended to be ashamed to have to go to a node, seeing it as the last resort, equivalent to admitting how far they had fallen. Men were characterized by the women who made up the overwhelming majority of participants as ashamed, proud, shy, slow to change, and more likely to abuse *trueque:* "Es mas dur por el hombre—tienen verguenza" (It is harder for the men—they are ashamed). Middle-class professionals missed their former status. For example, Susanna was a psychiatrist and her husband a painter. She was frustrated with the nodes. For a long time both of them were producing what was required—food—but they got fed up with a sub-sistence lifestyle. They wanted to practice the work they loved and had trained for. Susanna then offered English lessons, psychiatry sessions, and tango lessons, but hardly anybody ever wanted those; they needed the bare necessities. We asked if she could offer her services in lots of nodes, to have a greater chance of attracting clients. She responded that she did not have the time; she needed to earn money. Another commented, speaking for many professionals: "El trueque es toda una fantasia, una obligacion, no para salvarme. Es para el dia; vendo para comer" (The *trueque* is all an illusion, a necessity, not for salvation. It's for the day; I sell and I eat).

The markets were, then, often far from liberated economies. They were second-rate survival mechanisms for many (although providing community and social support in hard times when well organized), or anarchic free-for-alls at worst. RGT's decision to franchise credits was disastrous, compounding the number of poorly organized nodes. Either they themselves, or politicians, or criminal gangs (or all three) printed 50-credit notes in abundance, and, unsurprisingly, a wave of inflation hit barter between April and November 2002. A bag of flour, which had cost 1 or 2 credits when *créditos* were at parity with the dol-lar-linked peso, moved from 500 to 800 to 1,000 credits. A bolt of cloth selling for 40 credits in April went to 5,000 in November. One woman said her friend had bought 10,000 *créditos* for 10 pesos, just to see what she could find in the nodes. Those are extremes. Even after the market stabilized in 2003 and the old, inflationary notes were no longer honored, prices remained high. Dried pasta had been 2 *créditos;* after inflation it was 25. Flour had been 50 centavos; after the inflation it was 40 *créditos*. At that time, in the market economy, it cost two pesos. People felt conned, ripped off. They did not bring quality goods to nodes. One respondent said, "After the crash, I had enough credits to wallpaper a room."

In a fluid environment where problems seem to be emerging more quickly than solutions, some form of organization, regulation, and control is necessary, but finding this became all but impossible during the crisis of December 2001 through September 2002. Some nodes fared better than others: they were strongly managed, typically with some form of control at the door to ensure that only those who were bringing produce were admitted and coordinators walking around the markets solving problems, talking to prosumers, and providing oversight against poor-quality produce or inappropriate pricing mechanisms. The Mar-y-Sierras network in Mar del Plata was exceptionally well and democratically managed, while the strong business hand at the top of Zona Oeste kept a steady, if caudillolike paternalistic hand on the till. These markets suffered less from the crisis of confidence than those without strong management. Many nodes, though, were vulnerable to poor management. Coordinators were sometimes ineffective, sometimes corrupt, and were accused of a multitude of crimes. Veronica from Nodo Nikkai, an RTS node, said:

> There were lots of privileges created. Normally coordinators ask people at the door what they've brought, and many coordinators took advantage of this and took the best stuff for themselves. The system was corrupt: you would have to pay 50 centavos to get in, which was supposedly meant for the coordinators to run the place and for primary products for people to cook with, but the system sucked, because you then wouldn't be given any primary products, and would have to pay for the cooked stuff; also, many coordinators kept the money for themselves. It made a good business with so many people having joined.

A prosumer at one RGT node, angry faced, interrupted a conversation to exclaim:

> A lot of people came to make money; they are all street-smarts who want to earn money; this is how it fell apart. . . . One of them is in prison [he points at the area where the coordinators hang out]. The Argentines think that they are street-smart. These people aren't capable of building our capacity; they want to earn money; they are not interested; they want to earn money—that's it. They charge money for people to enter; nobody

else can sell for money; it's a cheat. They did not learn how to make things better, but they learned a lot of ways to make things worse. . . . I'm sorry that I'm talking a lot; it's just that I'm really fed up; they cheated on me.

A third said, "The business is for the coordinators; today there are five hundred people [here], which means [they would have paid] 750 pesos; the rent of this place per month must be something like 3,000 pesos."

Whether the coordinators under fire were corrupt, inefficient, or just not transparent is impossible to say. There was no evidence to show anyone obviously living the high life from coordinating a *trueque* node (which is not the case with some new religions), although critics would say that that they would not be so stupid as to parade what is salted away in foreign bank accounts. Corrupt, overwhelmed, or inefficient, markets were usually dependent on a good coordinator or group of coordinators, rarely self-managed. Sometimes coordinators found that "the best way to solve problems is to shout," while at others "they are very strict: that's the only way to be," meaning that prosumers were likely to defer to a good coordinator. In their place, coordinators got exasperated that what they were running was not the liberated economy they had dreamed of, but a replication of the pathologies of capitalism (and in this case, capitalism in crisis). One coordinator put it this way:

> In the beginning 90 percent of the node rules were accepted. Prosumers who came every Sunday would make sure that they would be enforced; then it got out of hand, just too many people. The coordinators lost control. We couldn't even get the prosumers to keep the place tidy. In the end, the coordinators had an evaluation session, and decided that we just didn't want to go on giving our free, unpaid time for something ugly that wasn't working. We had to do all the cleaning and organizing and weren't compensated, and just didn't believe in it being a worthwhile project anymore. There are good and bad coordinators; the role of the coordinator is very important. Everybody has to participate, but they also have to be directed well. I got upset to see how, when the economic situation was getting really bad, people were fighting over a bag of flour.

At another poorly attended and stocked market in an occupied factory in Buenos Aires, the coordinator, rather offhand when we introduced ourselves, evoked Marx's comment about poor people attempting their own salvation in a private fashion:

> You have come on a bad day. I am in a bad mood with the prosumers, as they aren't producing and are not bringing any products, but simply coming to the market with any old rubbish from their houses, like empty coffee jars. Everybody wants to take things home from the *trueque,* but no one wants to bring anything. . . . They should all bring either flour, sugar, or eggs, to stimulate production.

From the prosumers' point of view, coordination could be haphazard, illogical, or capricious. They resented heavy-handed control by what they saw as a self-appointed elite, and were confused by inconsistency of modes of regulation between markets. A couple of prosumers at an RGT node commented on an RTS node that they had found too managed:

> They treated us badly; they put a stop on us entering; they did not let us enter in the Calle Urquiza; they had their rules, and they had to be listened to; it was so inconvenient that we ended up leaving. . . . We went to many *trueques* in the time when they were shutting down, and we encountered closed doors. . . . There is a lot of variability [in the way nodes are run]; there is anything you can imagine.

After the crash, coordinators did seem to be able to regain control of the now much smaller markets: "They are the same people with a different way of thinking. . . . It went out of their hands; now there is a little bit more control." In a process of re-regulation, nodes put a new emphasis on induction and regular problem solving meetings of prosumers, and reinforced the need either for democracy (Mar-y-Sierras) or for strong management (Zone Oeste). A chastened RGT stopped franchising and refloated their original Bernal node with more group-building mechanisms. RTS moved to small, LETS-like closed nodes of twenty to thirty traders, spending a considerable amount of time in group discussion about how to deal with the crisis in the economy.

Conclusion

Barter, then, was a mass-based grassroots micropolitical response to growing unemployment, social distress, and what the founders referred to as the burial of their welfare state by neoliberalism. New livelihoods were created for millions that helped them survive the crisis. For many, until the markets were overwhelmed when Argentina hit economic meltdown in 2002, the experience was pleasant: they found cooperation, friendship, and support. Mass usage meant that in 2002 people lived from barter.

Thinking of barter as a better, freer economy begs the question—for whom? For those who had done well in the Menem years, the 1990s, barter was a short-term, second-rate survival mechanism of variable adequacy that involved humiliation and standing in line for access to secondhand or inferior goods for too many—a way of surviving the near-collapse of capitalism, but not one that could be a substitute for the Gucci and Prada to which many middle-class Argentines had become accustomed. It survived for as long as it did because the Argentine middle classes were able to recycle and reuse the goods they had accumulated, but provided few opportunities for pursuing middle-class occupations or for developing new microenterprises.

The poorest were able to gain access to these goods being recycled by the new poor, and many benefited from barter. In the well-organized markets they got the food, clothes, and provisions they needed, communally. But, as in New Zealand, this rather left a bad taste in the mouth. Argentina is not one of the poorest countries. It had a well-developed welfare state and a highly organized workforce until this was dismantled by Menem in the 1990s. Celebrating barter without recognizing the context of extreme crisis would be perverse. It can legitimate the exclusion of large numbers of people from the economic mainstream: need governments help those who are helping themselves? And given the large amounts of money that, it is claimed, the rich were able to move out of the country as a result of neoliberalization (Klein 2003), was it not perverse to spend so much time on this "funny money"? Was it not taking one's eye off the ball of change in the mainstream economy, where real power and money lie? Barter did help those participating in it to survive the crisis and learn to be entrepreneurial, perhaps thus stabilizing capitalism rather than changing it into what the founders hoped would be new rhythms that would include those previously excluded. This was celebrated by some coordinators:

> I think politically the *trueque* generated a very large social containment; if a politician is intelligent, he will see this, and he has to be grateful that this social movement has existed which stopped a large civil war or a large social problem; unfortunately we have politicians which are not intelligent. . . . If the politician was intelligent and collaborated with the *trueque*

organizations, he would create a large movement of work without cost for the state. (Fernando, Zona Oeste, Buenos Aires)

Unfortunately, barter did not "reinvent the social or economic game." Marx seems to have been right. Prosumers had few resources with which to produce the solidarity economy they hoped for, and, as I show elsewhere (North and Huber 2004), there were few attempts to build a wider solidarity economy through connection to the other elements of the Argentine crisis—pickets, neighborhood assemblies, or recovered factories.

This was partly due to the extremity of the crisis, something that barter was not set up to handle and was not welcomed. Coordinators who were committed to the solidarity economy recognized that prosumers came out of economic necessity, but once they were there, it was the coordinators' job to help them understand the ethics behind it, to help them understand the solidarity side, and to help them run parallel lives: one in the consumer economy and one in the solidarity economy. It was not their fault that need was such that their commitment-building mechanisms were overwhelmed and they could not build the levels of internal solidarity they had hoped for. As we saw in chapter 3, Galbraith argued that revolutions and wars can often be financed by unorthodox means when money must be subservient to need. Millions were bounced through the extreme crisis caused by the complete collapse of the Argentine economy and the *coralito,* then out the other side when the Argentine economy began to recover on the back of the newly competitive peso, achieving a growth rate of 7 to 10 percent in 2003–5. Without *trueque,* the alternative could have been truly awful, with a modern economy completely breaking down and mass hunger leading to a war of all against all for survival. The crisis was that serious. However, the organizers did not agree; they wanted a new economy, not a survival system:

> No, no, no. The result is that it has not helped people. . . . Not only did it not help people, but it corrupted people . . . and it hurt people a lot, so that today it is very difficult to start believing again that this might have any value. . . . It was the result of the interests of the salesman of the *créditos*, who made a large amount of money with this. . . . What's more, in this process a lot of people lost a lot of things; . . . it was not something that helped them, but something that harmed them. (Alberto, Mendoza)

[*170*]

Rather than creating a new economy, many felt that "the rhetoric was of solidarity, but the reality was one of cheating."

Given the ruined livelihoods left in the wake of barter's collapse, it is possible to be harder—to see the widespread use of barter in Argentina as part of the problem, not part of the solution. A major element in barter's runaway success was the decision to use notes, not computerized records. This is obviously quicker; notes can go in and out of people's wallets much more quickly than they can write checks. Any accountant dealing with the levels of economic activity in Argentina would have been overwhelmed, as was Auckland Green Dollars with just two thousand members. LETS would have been too slow. But notes are vulnerable to forgery and to overissuance unless control is taken by Hayek's people of "conservative temperament" and issuance is controlled. It was in RTS nodes, but they were overwhelmed either by RGT's extravagance or by the state (depending on whom one believes).

It is possible to see the mass printing of notes as "part of the problem," an attempt at a quick economic fix rather than attending to the economic fundamentals, be these sound money and efficient enterprises or productive, liberated livelihood options. For a short period, *trueque* filled a gap, as an Argentine economist argued in 2002:

> Right now, *trueque* fills an important role as a social safety net. It offers flexibility in prices and wages, and allows all idle resources to be used. In the midst of record high unemployment, depression, and a lack of cash, the development of *trueque* is logical, since it provides an alternative way of supporting oneself . . . [but] . . . with no regulation, there is always a risk of printing too much of the currency. As the market keeps growing, no one will notice this. But if the market sinks, the result will be massive inflation. (Daniel Ocks, UADE [Argentine Business University])

Barter also took off because Argentines have a flexible view of what constitutes "money," having seen numerous changes in the national currency as it has been devalued, abolished, or subject to hyperinflation (Powell 2002, 7). During the peg, pesos and dollars were used interchangeably. During the 1990s, the peg caused a liquidity shortage in the provinces, which provincial governments responded to by printing their own parallel currency, *patacones*. By 1996, for example, Pilling (1996) estimated that in Tucuman province there were $53 million bonds in circulation, about a third of the state's paper money circulation (although local economists felt that economic statistics were so poor that "nobody here really has any idea"). This contributed to the financing of a state payroll that consumed four-fifths of the state's income. In Jujuy province, Pilling reported that overissue caused the bonds to become worthless, while many bonds were printed on poor-quality paper that disintegrated through wear and tear. In what was thought to be a crafty move, the debt vanished with the destroyed *patacone* notes. From the perspective of the Washington Consensus, this very laxity has been part of Argentina's problem, because "corrupt governments let the printing presses run to pay their employees." Barter, then, can be seen from the perspective of neoliberalism as "part of the problem" in that again profligate Argentines were printing money rather than attending to the economic fundamentals, attempting another get-rich-quick scheme rather than working their way out of the crisis. There is some limited validity to this argument, particularly in terms of the actions of RGT. But these were undertaken only in response to an extreme financial crisis caused by a crisis of capitalism after millions of livelihoods had been sacrificed at the altar of financial orthodoxy. Many nodes—just about all save PAR—did not overissue, and did their best to fight this over-issuance, and PAR may have been subverted rather than being the bad guys themselves.

The example of Argentina shows that individuals, social movements, and NGOs can create credit money to meet necessary volumes of exchange in the real economy, provided that those issuing it are subject to some discipline so that its quality is maintained. The guarantee of a state or a bank's good name is usually enough. When the guarantor is an NGO, it is more difficult, especially when that NGO acts in an undisciplined manner or is taken advantage of. Second, the experience shows that despite micropolitical challenges, monetary institutions form a hierarchy, with those with good names and acting in a disciplined manner at the top. Subaltern groups can attempt to disrupt this hierarchy, especially where the state is acting in quixotic or overdisciplined ways. Here, individual choices of what money to use—with preference usually given to hard, usually state-sanctioned currency—are disrupted along with the normal reproduction of the hierarchy of financial institutions on which capitalist reproduction rests. Third, the experience underlines Harvey's

SURVIVING FINANCIAL MELTDOWN

(1982, 246–50) argument that money and credit can be used to discipline economies through restricting credit, but cannot control what individuals choose to do. Banks can discipline, but they cannot create. The IMF disciplines countries, central banks discipline banks, and banks discipline individuals. They can loosen credit and create economic activity, but they cannot stop the creation of credit by individuals. The power to discipline ends at the bank's doors if individuals have access to other forms of credit produced from below. The underlying message of *trueque*, therefore, is still valid: although Argentina did recover from the extreme crisis in 2003–4 through an export boom on the back of the now competitive peso, there is still a need for the generation of production and livelihoods based on reciprocity and through the internal market to balance export-led growth, which is susceptible to the next crisis to hit Argentina. When governments failed to produce money that fulfilled this requirement, social movements, supported by millions, stepped in.

Conclusion

THE GHOSTS OF MARX AND SIMMEL?

———

One can almost hear Simmel's ghost whispering: "So you found a few ripples. The current is still running strongly in my direction. Just wait, and money will disenchant the world. Haven't you noticed the way electronic transfers of money are converting all moneys into a single, global, invisible, megabyte money? Haven't you heard [about the Euro] replac[ing] all national currencies? Money is becoming increasingly homogenous but also unstoppable. Simply look around you. Money is turning all aspects of social life into marketable commodities—blood, babies, organs, courtship, funerals."

—V. Zelizer, *The Social Meaning of Money*

NOW IS THE TIME TO CONCLUDE OUR DISCUSSION. RECALL that the argument is that the best way to examine the contemporary effervescence of alternative forms of currency is within the wider claim that Morris has won out over Bellamy in the debate about the extent to which markets rather than state planning are the best economic allocation system, but that it is inadequate to assume, a priori, that markets are always capitalist and that market-based economic activity is always capitalist activity. However, advocates of alternative economic practices ignore the extent to which such practices have been tried before, always ending in shipwreck. The pressures of the capitalist system are too great to be resisted for too long. They also claim that advocates are conflating second-rate, constrained informal coping strategies with freely chosen economic alternatives. In this book it has been argued that this should be a question for further research. Just because economic alternatives have been tried before and found wanting, that does not mean that they will always be wanting. It could be that they did not work under conditions prevailing at the time and could work in the future, not that they could never work. Alternative currency systems should be examined using this question: are they still the utopianism critiques by Marx—remember, Owen and Proudhon were Marx and Engels's targets in their critique of utopianism—or have conditions changed?

Similarly, there are debates about the contestability of money. Quantity theorists, the commodity school, and Chartalists all argue that money is in some way related to the "real" economy out there or legitimated by states. Subaltern groups cannot—or, in the opinion of the monetarists, should not—create alternative forms of money if the intention is to try to cut corners and print money rather than attending to the real economy. Keynesians say that it might be possible to create money, but it might not be spent. Theorists of capitalist credit money believe that because money is no longer directly linked to existing commodities, but represents a claim on future commodities, trusted institutions can create it, while the evolutionary school sees money as an innovation, a financial tool that evolves over time. The quantity school argues that if there is too little money in the economy, it may be that the issuance of more money will facilitate real economic activity previously limited by an overly tight monetary issuance policy. Simmel thinks that modern all-purpose money rationalizes and acts as a tool for freedom, while others argue that money commodifies, and commodification should be resisted. Zelizer believes that people earmark money for special purposes and that money does not automatically commodify: it can lubricate transactions driven primarily by emotion, family loyalty, or solidarity and comradeship. Poststructuralists say that money has become a disciplining or structuring discourse, but it remains a discourse none the less. Taking a Foucauldian approach to money enables the way that money disciplines and regulates to be unpacked and fought by creating micropolitical alternatives; local money schemes can be thought of in such a way.

The nineteenth-century legacy seems to bear out the views of the Marxist pessimists. Owenism seems poorly planned on weak ground, with problems valuing goods in time given different levels of skill. Owen promoted it as an apolitical bridge to a better society, yet it was attacked and ridiculed by middlemen, the churches, and other political opponents. The poorest could not participate, because they had no capital and could not get food or other basic goods. Proudhon's plans never got off the ground. Populism was a mass movement that did provide a real micropolitical alternative to the local system of domination prevailing in the American South—the lien system—and used creative micropolitics to organize many of the weak. But again, it could not help the very poorest, those whose land was mortgaged, and poor people could not raise the capital they needed to buy their comrades out. Calls for government aid or help from the banks predictably fell on deaf ears, to say nothing of attacks from Democrat night riders and the employing class after 1896.

Early twentieth-century experience seems little better. The swap movement rose and fell quickly in response to the Depression once Keynesianism superseded it, while Social Credit, billed as an apolitical change to the nation's accounts, was utopianism to the core. Rebuffed, Douglas descended into anti-Semitism, while Social Credit in Canada and New Zealand limped on in small business and farmers' parties. The Green Shirts, though small, did engage in creative micropolitical action and benefit their members by providing security, comradeship, and a sense of purpose during the Depression (as did the communists and the British Union of Fascists), but could not implement their plans.

Alternative Economic Spaces: Still Utopian?

Turning to the current movement, we must ask: do the critiques still hold? We saw in U.K. LETS a claim that better, more ecological, and more community-minded economies could be created from below through "relationship trading," which will slowly structure participants into better ways of trading. We also saw debates between those who saw relationship trading and the use of alternative currencies as an unproblematic new financial innovation, but also a lack of interest in the new currency by business or mainstream organizations. We further observed the claims of greens and anarchists that LETS could be best thought of as a resistant alternative space and as a declaration that alternatives are possible, but that these spaces remained small and transitory. Cooperation was more than dwarfish and did work for the most active, but it was still ephemeral. Roger Lee and his collaborators argued that U.K. LETS are less significant for their material effectiveness than for their demonstrable potential to offer alternatives in the face of what is generally thought to be homogenization, that alternative currencies help us to illuminate the complex social and economic relations behind economies, and that economies are constructed by those who work and make their livelihoods in them (Lee et al. 2004, 497)

Talentum and Kör emerged in resistance to the introduction of capitalist markets in Hungary and as a way to smooth their introduction, respectively. They seemed to work better as alternatives to capitalist markets, but the legacy of dictatorship and a relatively benign economic environment, where transition was smooth and the economy did revive, meant that the attractiveness of green money was limited. In contrast, the environment in New Zealand was more benign. Transition was fast and ruthless, and the state withdrew from providing adequate levels of welfare. New Zealanders were used to looking after themselves and sorting out problems together, and the green movement and Social Credit provided a wider core of activists and support. So although the alternative groups did not last in the cities when the economy revived after the election of the Labour government in 2000, some had built networks that lasted. In Argentina, the collapse of the economy and an environment where monetary evolution was accepted and normal, millions used alternative currencies before overissuance or political attack led to their decline.

So what are the lessons? Alternative currencies can work in terms of providing enjoyable or valued political activism, feelings of solidarity and community, and real material benefits for large numbers of people and for long periods of time. At least they worked when the political environment was conducive to large-scale mobilization: the recession of 1992 in the United Kingdom, Rogernomics and Ruthenasia in New Zealand, and the Argentinazo. Hungary's negotiated transition, New Labour in the United Kingdom and New Zealand, and the post-2002 Kirchner administration in Argentina caused the economy to revive, and millions no longer needed alternative currencies. Nevertheless, some preferred alternative economic networks as a positive choice. They understood their rhythms; their livelihood strategy or philosophical, political, or moral orientation was strengthened through membership in the network; and they were surrounded by a group of similar people who lived close enough for trading to take place, preferably in a place that attracted like-minded people. This could be a small group, say five or six, who formed the core of a wider, less active membership.

Where participants had access to food from their local area, a part-time job, and a wider network of mutual aid, they often were able to provide for themselves the alternative, freer form of economy they wanted—as long as they were not materialistic. Natural wheeler-dealers and those with young families found the network worked well if they took it seriously: if they valued the currency and their commitments to their fellow traders. They found a network that promoted security, friendship and support, and perhaps a little vision of the good life. They helped build a better future, carried on the fight against marketization, and showed that something else was possible.

New Zealand green dollars did better in some places than others. The scheme worked and lasted where a large number of people with a commitment to alternatives provided a fairly geographically dense network of people with skills to share and there was at least one respected, rooted activist committed to building the network, usually an activist with a vision of an alternative future. Members had commitment-building mechanisms and an ethos of taking green dollars seriously, whether these were bureaucratic (taking defectors to court) or more solidaristic (a shared ethos). The levels of livelihood achieved by green dollars alone were not great, but when participants were connected to a wider alternative network these livelihoods were satisfying and were freely chosen as an alternative to paid work. Money was not counterposed to community or solidarity, but was seen as a way to lubricate transactions within an economic community, as suggested by Zelizer.

The lessons seem to be that subaltern groups can create money, but when they create it out of proportion to or outside of real economic activity the monetarist critique seems to have validity: they create unspendable paper or worthless entries on a computer. Subaltern groups can create money, agree to exchange it among themselves, and give it value, but it can be exchanged only for resources that group controls. This is more than low-level cooperation: when an economy imploded and no one had state-issued money, many lived for two years off of the networks and could get everything they needed, within reason. The International Monetary Fund (IMF) and banks can discipline individuals through restricting access to credit, but they can also be subverted—and millions of Argentines put a collective thumb up to the IMF. The postmaterialist greens in New Zealand often had access to food grown from their own areas; to help, affection, and solidarity from their co-members; and to a part-time job, and they could make their living, if not their fortune.

Marx's critique of utopianism seems accurate for the nineteenth century, but less so now. So-called poor people can be those who actively choose nonmonetized and resource-poor livelihoods and have access to far, far more resources than did the poor of industrializing England, the postbellum American South, or the Great Depression. Living standards in the global North are immeasurably higher for the great majority, even if the poorest and those outside the basic standards of modern complex society, homeless people, and asylum seekers suffer levels of real hardship. In places where the state withdraws further, alternative currency schemes do not fill the gap, as experiences in Hungary and New Zealand show. Nor can alternative currencies alone go beyond capitalism and allow those who wish to delink from the system do so in the here and now. But in certain spaces people with access to land to grow food and time to provide services for their co-members, in spaces wealthy enough for unwanted goods that cannot be produced in households or small-scale economies to circulate (Argentina) or be recycled, the collective wealth of society is great enough for those who choose to mix a part-time job for cash or a microbusiness with home production and green dollars. EBay, Freecycle, Loot, and other ways of recycling secondhand goods enable participants to access goods not produced locally, and fashion and other consumption choices mean that often perfectly serviceable goods with years of reliable service ahead of them are discarded. Our postmaterialist utopians, not wishing to engage with the fetishization of the new, of fashion or of designer brands, can access and use them. But we can go further. If we add other elements of a localized or social economy, such as the credit unions that are in many ways the modern equivalents of Proudhon's Bank of the People or the subtreasuries and other local finance vehicles, local food production schemes like food boxes, community-supported agriculture and farmer's markets, local business networks and community businesses, as well as cooperatives and social enterprises, we can perhaps begin to envisage actually existing localized economies (see Dauncey 1988; Imbroscio 1997; Amin et al. 2002; DeFilippis 2002).

None of this was available to Owen's artisans, struggling to resist proletarianization in the post–Napoleonic War period when capitalism was being constructed and its benefits—higher wages and living standards, technological advantages such as gas, electricity, railways, and the like—had not yet flowed through to working people. When they did, after the 1850s, the people stopped resisting capitalist encroachment, but regulated it, aimed to gain a fair share of the benefits through trade unions or political action, or aimed to go past capitalism to socialism through revolution.

If we no longer accept the teleological argument that capitalism must be replaced by state-planned socialism and explore decentralized socialism and noncapitalist markets, it is possible to see these alternative economic spaces as precursors of something different that at present is unattractive to most (except when capitalism collapses), small scale, and often ephemeral. But Molineux is also wrong: capitalist rationales for economic action can be resisted for long periods of time by those who choose to. The resource levels accessible are high enough, and if we start producing more of our more complex goods though cooperatives, nonprofit enterprises, or community businesses, as the Argentines started to do, the sector could grow. The services provided by a complex state—hospitals, schools, infrastructure, and the like—would need to be provided, but by a democratic state. And perhaps there would be more local provision of schools and hospitals. State-run is not necessarily better than locally run as long as there is some form of regulation regarding minimum provision and redistribution from richer to poorer areas.

A second reason why alternative economic spaces could grow now is that, in contrast to previous periods, repression is less prevalent now. Owen faced the forceful imposition of capitalism; the Populists faced organized capital, Democratic mobs, and night riders; while in the 1930s the European scrip movement faced Nazism. True, Argentina's barter network was attacked and destroyed, but no one brought the same degree of repression to bear on the small-scale alternative currencies in our three other case studies. It could be objected that, unlike in Argentina, they were no threat and could be safely ignored while levels of repression changed, but against that capitalism in the global North often results in jobless growth or in growth in certain high-tech or knowledge economy sectors. It no longer needs to force independent self-provisioning peasants into the factories: the factories have closed, capital has no interest in unskilled labor, and the problem is now how surplus proletarians are to gain economic independence (we might say, again). As long as our new utopians are not claiming state benefits, the state cares little how they choose to live their economic lives. Repression is no longer in the form of armed bodies of men, but is found in structuring discourses of the need for financial stability, the war on terror, and technologies of surveillance and categorization. This can still seem overwhelming, if in a different form from that of the past. But as Deleuze and Guattari argued (1987, 217), power can also be defined in relation to what escapes it or by its impotence, and in the interstices of capitalism or in geographical fringes such as the north of South Island, the west of Britain, or parts of the United States such as Ithaca, spaces outside this surveillance can offer alternatives. Our modern utopians may be ridiculed, but they were not—outside Argentina—attacked by the same forces that were the utopians of the nineteenth century, presumably because arrogant neoliberalization sees itself as the only real game in town.

Were alternative economic spaces growing to such an extent that, for example, capitalist firms that need labor could no longer attract employees or worker-owned businesses were building forms of cheap public transport that threatened the automobile industry, things could be different and, perhaps, dreams of slow, evolutionary change might begin to be replaced with strategies based on fundamental change. Remember, Marx and Engels's critique of utopianism was not a critique of building alternative economic forms: when they showed that alternatives to capitalism were possible, Marx and Engels were fans. They raised their objection when these alternatives were presented, *pace* Proudhon, as a panacea to be implemented through persuasion. When Owen combined labor exchanges with building trade unions and other forms of mass politics, Marx and Engels had no complaint.

A second way in which repression is less is paradoxically a result of neoliberalization. The Achilles heel of much work on alternative economic spaces, squatting, and the like in the 1960s and 1970s was that its adherents professed economic independence and freedom, but relied on welfare payments for the cash element of their livelihoods. We need not be moralistic or censorious here: welfare payments are small compared with corporate welfare or the money wasted on wars, and they do something to make recompense for cuts in other forms of social provision. And what is so moral about working for a wage in an inherently exploitative relationship anyway? Too often we see the radical agent as the factory worker thrown together with his or her comrades in exploitation, forging a collective identity through struggle, or we see the employed as tamed and disciplined through work. We pay less attention to the marginal championed by Foucault, especially those who refuse or resist participation in capitalism. But there is an inherent flaw in a strategy of building independence from capitalism while relying on it or, worse, being dependent on it. Neo-liberalization has in many ways closed off these interstices. For example, welfare recipients are no longer able to move to Golden Bay and other low-income spaces in New Zealand and claim benefits. In the United Kingdom, active welfare means that no one under age twenty-five can claim benefits without becoming involved in a welfare program, while older people are actively encouraged to engage in work or entrepreneurial activity. This could mean setting up the sort of businesses we discuss here. Neoliberalization has also emphasized local provision of services and welfare, for it believes that it will be less expensive, will encourage self-reliance, and deter abuse. This can lead to both more local control and responsiveness to local conditions and privatized services on the cheap. Not seeing local provision in totalizing ways helps unpack how this might contribute to more liberated economic spaces.

While this form of economic life is not for everyone, and perhaps cannot exist as a large-scale alternative for millions without more thoroughgoing political change, who is to say whether it is any more or less valid than any other choice? We now know better than to claim one form of liberation will be attractive to all, be this liberal democracy or socialism: the future must be diverse if it is to be truly democratic. And a low-impact, ecological lifestyle might provide a vision of a new way of living or a real alternative if climate change and the end of the carbon economy mean that we will have little option but to live in less greedy and ecologically destructive ways.

NOTES

Introduction

1. In response to Tony Blair's argument that the poor need the same choices in schools and hospitals that the rich already have (by being able to buy a house near a good school or hospital) and that markets in education and health will enable the poor to choose, critics argue that we do not need choice about which school or hospital to use; we just want a well-funded and -organized one at the end of the road. Markets help us choose between a red or a blue coat, not between schools and hospitals.

2. See http://www.communityeconomies.org.

3. Utopians, Anarchists, and Populists: The Politics of Money in the Nineteenth Century

1. For a review of the myriad proposals for monetary reform generated from time to time, see Boyle (2002).

2. Note that *The Wizard of Oz* has been analyzed as a fable based on the 1896 election. The Wizard is any U.S. president, a trickster who is at heart a common man, while the Cowardly Lion is Bryan. The Scarecrow and the Tin Man represent the natural alliance between farmer and worker, while Dorothy is hope. The Wicked Witch of the East is finance (Dorothy's house lands on her and kills her, reversing the "natural order" of repossession), while the Witch of the West is drought. Dorothy's slippers are silver, not ruby as in the MGM movie. See Littlefield (1964).

4. Twentieth-Century Utopians: Gesell and Douglas

1. Kibbo Kift's small size contrasts with the much larger German outdoor youth movement, a precursor of National Socialism as a mass move-

ment. The Woodcraft Folk survives to this day as a socialist alternative to the scouting movement.

2. The crossed-keys logo obviously performed the same functions as the Nazi swastika or the BUF's lightning bolt symbol, conceived by Moseley as "a flash of action in a circle of unity" (or as a "flash in the pan" by opponents).

3. The residence of the chancellor of the exchequer, the finance minister.

4. Drakeford (1997) found that, looking back on their experiences, some Social Crediters regarded the welfare state as the legacy of their movement, for it provided a guaranteed income to all and boosted purchasing power. In this way, they had "won," but in a way different from that which they had expected.

5. Any Web search using keywords such as *Illuminati* or *Reptilian Conspiracy* will provide a wealth of data. For example, look at http://www.David-Icke.net.

6. See http://www.democrats.org.nz.

5. New Money, New Work? LETS in the United Kingdom

1. A "dating agency" for members.
2. Markets at which traders would exchange goods and services.
3. For a full discussion, see North 2006.
4. Many quotes in this chapter are from fieldwork respondents in Manchester. For a fuller discussion of methods, see North 1998b, 2006, 75–96.

6. *Kaláka* and Kör: Green Money, Mutual Aid, and Transition in Hungary

1. KÖR is an acronym for Közösségi Önsegítő Rendszer, Community Self-Help Scheme/System.
2. Telecottages are information technology centers in rural areas. Typically they provide Internet connection, computers, scanners, fax services, and the like to those likely to be excluded from the "knowledge economy."

7. The Longevity of Alternative Economic Practices: Green Dollars in Aotearoa/New Zealand

1. Europeans.
2. HANDs stands for How About a No-Dollar scheme?
3. The plot of land on which Kiwis build a home and grow their own vegetables.

4. An old saw in New Zealand is "There isn't anything that can't be fixed with a bit of ingenuity—and a length of number nine wire!"

5. An *Iwi* is a confederation of extended families, or *Whanau*. A *Mana whenau* is an area or territory, the resources of which can be used to meet the needs of an *Iwi* or *Whanau*.

8. Surviving Financial Meltdown: Argentina's Barter Networks

1. Argentine elites see themselves as residents of a European outpost on an otherwise "uncivilized" continent. Headlines such as "Barter Nation" (Norman 2002) did national pride no good.

2. The CTA is the Central de Trabajores Argentinos (Argentine Workers Congress), a leftist trade union federation that also organized unemployed workers and worked closely with the pickets *(piqueteros)*. The Mothers of the Plaza de Mayo campaigned first to find out what had happened to their children "disappeared" by the 1976–1984 military dictatorship. By 2002, as a memorial to their lost children, they had become the de facto conscience of the Argentine nation, campaigning against what they saw as injustice and human rights abuse.

BIBLIOGRAPHY

Aldridge, T., and A. Patterson. 2002. "LETS Get Real: Constraints on the Development of Local Exchange Trading Schemes." *Area* 34, no. 4: 370–81.

Amin, A., A. Cameron, and R. Hudson. 2002. *Placing the Social Economy*. London: Routledge.

Amin, A., and N. Thrift. 2000. "What Kind of Economic Theory for What Kind of Economic Geography?" *Antipode* 31, no. 4: 4–9.

Arato, A. 1991. "Revolution, Civil Society, and Democracy." In *The Reemergence of Civil Society in Eastern Europe and the Soviet Union*, ed. Z. Rau, 161–82. Boulder, Colo.: Westview.

———. 1999. "Civil Society, Transition, and the Consolidation of Democracy." In *Dilemmas of Transition: The Hungarian Experience*, ed. A. Braun and Z. Barany, 225–52. Oxford: Rowman and Littlefield.

Åslund, A. 2002. *Building Capitalism: The Transformation of the Former Soviet Bloc*. Cambridge: Cambridge University Press.

Aufheben. 2003. "Picket and Pot-Banger Together: Class Recomposition in Argentina?" *Aufheben* 11: 1–23.

Auyero, J. 2000. *Poor People's Politics: Peronist Survival Networks and the Legacy of Evita*. London: Duke University Press.

Bahro, R. 1994. *Avoiding Social and Ecological Disaster*. Bath, England: Gateway Books.

Beecher, J., and R. Bienvenu. 1970. *The Utopian Vision of Charles Fourier*. London: Jonathan Cape.

Bellamy, E. 1888/1946. *Looking Backward, 1887–2000*. New York: World.

Bello, W., N. Bullard, and K. Malhotra, eds. 2000. *Global Finance*. London: Zed.

Berman, M. 1982. *All That Is Solid Melts into Air*. London: Verso.

Best, S., and D. Kellner. 1991. *Postmodern Theory: Critical Interrogations.* London: Macmillan.

Bey, H. 1991. *TAZ: The Temporary Autonomous Zone, Ontological Anarchy, Poetic Terrorism.* Brooklyn, N.Y.: AK Press.

Blanc, L. 1840/1975. "Organisation of Work." In *Self-Governing Socialism—A Reader,* ed. B. Horvat, M. Markovic, and R. Supec, 73–77. White Plains, N.Y.: International Arts and Science Press.

Bonefield, W., and J. Holloway, eds. 1996. *Global Capital, National State, and the Politics of Money.* London: Macmillan.

Bookchin, M. 1986. *Post-Scarcity Anarchism.* Montreal: Black Rose.

———. 1995a. *From Urbanisation to Cities: Towards a New Politics of Citizenship.* London: Cassel.

———. 1995b. *Social Anarchism or Lifestyle Anarchism: An Unbreachable Chasm.* Edinburgh: AK Press.

Boyle, D. 1999. *Funny Money: In Search of Alternative Cash.* London: HarperCollins.

———. *The Money Changers: Currency Reform from Aristotle to E-Cash.* London: Earthscan, 2002.

Boyne, R., and A. Rattansi. 1990. *Postmodernity and Society.* London: Macmillan.

Brechter, J., T. Costello, and B. Smith. 2000. *Globalisation from Below: The Power of Solidarity.* Cambridge, Mass.: South End Press.

Bromley, R. 1990. "A New Path to Development? The Significance and Impact of Hernando de Soto's Ideas on Underdevelopment, Production, and Reproduction." *Economic Geography* 66, no. 4: 328–48.

Buber, M. 1949. *Paths in Utopia.* London: Routledge and Kegan Paul.

Burgess, J., W. Mitchell, and M. J. Watts. 1998. "Workfare in Australia and New Zealand: A Critical Assessment." Paper presented at the 5th National Conference on Unemployment, Royal Melbourne Institute of Technology, Melbourne. Available from the author at ecmjw@cc.newcastle.edu.au.

Callinicos, A. 1989. *Against Postmodernism: A Marxist Critique.* Cambridge, England: Polity.

———. 2003. *An Anti-Capitalist Manifesto.* Cambridge, England: Polity.

Cameron, J., and K. Gibson. 2005. "Alternative Pathways to Community and Economic Development: The Latrobe Valley Community Partnering Project." *Geographical Research* 43, no. 3: 274–85.

Carter, J., and D. Moreland, eds. 2004. *Anti-Capitalist Britain.* Cheltenham, England: New Clarion.

Castles, F., and C. Pierson. 1996. "A New Convergence? Recent Policy Developments in the United Kingdom, Australia, and New Zealand." *Policy and Politics* 24, no. 3: 233–45.

Castree, N. 1999. "Envisioning Capitalism: Geography and the Renewal of Marxian Political Economy." *Transactions of the Institute of British Geographers* 24, no. 1: 137–58.

CEC (Community Economies Collective). 2001. "Imagining and Enacting Noncapitalist Futures." *Socialist Review* 3 and 4: 93–135.

Cockburn, A., J. St. Clair, and A. Sekula. 2000. *Five Days That Shook the World: Seattle and Beyond.* London: Verso.

Cohen, B. 1998. *The Geography of Money.* Ithaca, N.Y.: Cornell University Press.

Cohen, J., and A. Arato. 1992. *Civil Society and Political Theory.* Cambridge, Mass.: MIT Press.

Cole, G. 1925/1965. *Robert Owen.* London: Benn.

Coleman, D. 1994. *Eco-Politics: Building a Green Society.* Brunswick, N.J.: Rutgers University Press.

Croall, J. 1997. *LETS Act Locally: The Growth of Local Exchange Trading Systems.* London: Calouste Gulbenkian Foundation.

Crooke, B. 1990. "The End of Radical Social Theory: Notes on Radicalism, Modernism, and Postmodernism." In *Postmodernity and Society,* ed. R. Boyne and A. Rattansi, 46–75. London: Macmillan.

Dahrendorf, R. 1990. *Reflections on the Revolution in Europe.* London: Chatto and Windus.

———. 1997. *After 1989: Morals, Revolution, and Civil Society.* Basingstoke, England: Macmillan.

Dana, C. 1896. *Proudhon and His Bank of the People.* New York: Benjamin R. Tucker.

Dauncey, G. 1988. *Beyond the Crash: The Emerging Rainbow Economy.* London: Greenprint.

de Brunhoff, S. 1976. *Marx on Money.* New York: Urizen.

DeFilippis, J. 2004. *Unmaking Goliath: Community Control in the Face of Global Capital.* London: Routledge.

De Goede, M. 2005. *Virtue, Fortune, and Faith: A Genealogy of Finance.* Minneapolis: University of Minnesota Press.

Deleuze, G., and F. Guattari. 1987. *A Thousand Plateaus.* Minneapolis: University of Minnesota Press.

De Meulinaire, S. 1999. "Reinventing the Market: Alternative Currencies and Community Development in Argentina." *International Journal of Community Currency Research* 4. http://www.geog.lc.ac.uk/ijccr/volume4/4no3.htm.

de Soto, H. 1989. *The Other Path: The Invisible Revolution in the Third World*. New York: Harper and Row.

———. 2000. *The Mystery of Capital: Why Capitalism Triumphs in the West and Fails Everywhere Else*. Boston: Basic.

Dinerstein, A. 2001. "Roadblocks in Argentina: Against the Violence of Stability." *Capital and Class* 74: 1–7.

———. 2002. "The Battle of Buenos Aires: Crisis, Insurrection, and the Reinvention of Politics in Argentina." *Historical Materialism* 10, no. 4: 5–38.

———. 2003. "Que se Vayan Todos! Popular Insurrection and the Asambleas Barriales in Argentina." *Bulletin of Latin American Research* 22, no. 2: 187–200.

Dobson, A. 1990. *Green Political Thought*. London: HarperCollins Academic.

Dobson, R. 1993. *Bringing the Economy Home from the Market*. Montreal: Black Rose.

Dodd, N. 1994. *The Sociology of Money*. New York: Continuum.

Donnachie, I. 2000. *Robert Owen: Owen of New Lanark and New Harmony*. Phantassie, England: Tuckwell.

Douglas, C. H. 1937. *Social Credit*. London: Eyre and Spottiswoode.

Douglas, R. 1993. *Unfinished Business*. Auckland: Random House New Zealand.

Douthwaite, R. 1996. *Short Circuit: Strengthening Local Economies for Security in an Uncertain World*. Totnes, England: Green.

———. 1999. *The Ecology of Money*. Totnes, England: Green Books.

Drakeford, M. 1997. *Social Movements and Their Supporters: The Green Shirts in England*. Basingstoke, England: Macmillan.

Drakulić, S. 1987. *How We Survived Communism and Even Laughed*. London: Vintage.

Duxfield, B. 2001. *New Zealand National G$ Conference 2001: Report*. New Plymouth: New Zealand Green Dollars.

Easton, B. 1997. *The Commercialisation of New Zealand*. Auckland, New Zealand: Auckland University Press.

Eckersley, R. 1992. *Environmentalism and Political Theory: Towards an Ecocentric Approach*. London: University College London Press.

Elkins, P., ed. 1986. *The Living Economy: A New Economics in the Making*. London, Routledge and Kegan Paul.

Engels, F. 1968. *Socialism: Utopian and Scientific*. London: Lawrence and Wishart.

Feffer, J., ed. 2002. *Living in Hope: People Challenging Globalisation*. London: Zed.

Fernbach, D., ed. 1974. *Karl Marx: The First International and After.* London: New Left Review.

Findlay, J. L. 1972. *Social Credit: The English Origins.* Montreal: McGill-Queens University Press.

Fine, B. 2000. "Neither the Washington nor the Post-Washington Consensus." In *Development Policy in the Twenty-First Century,* ed. B. Fine, C. Lapavitsas, and J. Pincus, 1–27. London: Routledge.

Fine, B., and C. Lapavitsas. 2000. "Markets and Money in Social Theory: What Role for Economics?" *Economy and Society* 29, no. 3: 357–82.

Fisher, I. 1933. *Stamp Scrip.* New York: Adelphi.

———. 1934. *The Crisis.* New York: Pantheon.

Foner, P. S. 1955. *A History of the American Labor Movement IV: From the Founding of the American Federation of Labor to the Emergence of American Imperialism.* New York: International Publications.

Foucault, M. 1980. *Power/Knowledge.* London: Harvester Wheatsheaf.

———. 1982. "Afterword: The Subject and Power." In *Michel Foucault, Beyond Structuralism and Hermeneutics,* ed. H. Dreyfus and P. Rabinow. Brighton, England: Harvester.

———. 1984. "Truth and Power." In *The Foucault Reader,* ed. P. Rabinow, 51–75. Harmondsworth, England: Penguin.

———. 1998. *The History of Sexuality 1: The Will to Knowledge.* Harmondsworth, England: Penguin.

Fourier, C. 1971. *Design for Utopia: Selected Writings of Charles Fourier.* New York: Schoken.

Frank, T. 2002. *One Market under God: Extreme Capitalism, Market Populism, and the End of Economic Democracy.* London: Verso.

Frankel, B. 1987. *The Post-Industrial Utopians.* Cambridge, England: Polity.

Freeland, C. 2001. *Sale of the Century: The Inside Story of the Second Russian Revolution.* London: Little, Brown.

Friedman, M. 1962. *Capitalism and Freedom.* Chicago: University of Chicago Press.

———. 1963. *A Monetary History of the United States, 1867–1960.* Princeton, N.J.: Princeton University Press.

Fukuyama, F. 1992. *The End of History and the Last Man.* Harmondsworth, England: Penguin.

———. 1995. *Trust.* London: Simon and Schuster.

Galbraith, J. 1975. *Money: Whence It Came, Where It Went.* London: Andre Deutsch.

Geras, N. 1990. *Discourses of Extremity.* London: Verso.

Gesell, S. 1958. *The Natural Economic Order.* London: Owen.

Gibson-Graham, J. 1996. *The End of Capitalism (As We Knew It): A Feminist Critique of Political Economy.* Oxford: Blackwell.

———. 2002. "Beyond Global vs. Local: Economic Politics beyond the Binary Frame." In *Geographies of Power: Placing Scale,* ed. A. Herod and M. W. Wright. Oxford: Blackwell, 25–60.

———. 2006. *A Postcapitalist Politics.* Minneapolis: University of Minnesota Press.

Gilbert, E. 1999. "Forging a National Currency: Money, State Making, and Nation Building in Canada." In *Nation-States and Money: The Past, Present, and Future of National Currencies,* ed. E. Gilbert and E. Helleiner, 25–46. London: Routledge.

Gilbert, E., and E. Helleiner, eds. 1999. *Nation-States and Money: The Past, Present, and Future of National Currencies.* London: Routledge.

Gledhill, J. 1994. *Power and Its Disguises: Anthropological Perspectives on Politics.* London: Pluto.

Glover, P. 1995. "Ithaca Hours." In *Invested in the Common Good,* ed. S. Meeker Lowry, 72–80. New York: New Society Publishers.

Godschalk, H. 1985. "The Moneyless Economy: From Temple Exchange to Barter Club." *German Yearbook on Business History 1985.* Cologne: German Society for Business History.

Goodwyn, L. 1976. *Democratic Promise: The Populist Moment in America.* Oxford: Oxford University Press.

Gordon, C. 2002. Introduction to *Power,* by M. Foucault. Harmondsworth, England: Penguin, xi–xli.

Gore, C. 2000. "The Rise and Fall of the Washington Consensus as a Paradigm for Developing Countries." *World Development* 28, no. 5: 789–804.

Greco, T. H. 1994. *New Money for Healthy Communities.* Tucson, Ariz.: Self-published.

———. 2001. *Money: Understanding and Creating Alternatives to Legal Tender.* White River Junction, Vt.: Chelsea Green.

Gwynne, R., T. Klak, and D. J. B. Shaw. 2003. *Alternative Capitalisms.* London: Arnold.

Halevi, J. 2002. "The Argentine Crisis." *Monthly Review* 53, no. 11: 15–23.

Hammersley, M., and P. Atkinson. 1983. *Ethnography: Principles in Practice.* London: Tavistock.

Hann, C. 1990. "Second Economy and Civil Society." In *Market Economy and Civil Society in Hungary,* ed. C. Hann, 21–44. London: Frank Cass.

Harman, C. 2002. "Argentina: Rebellion at the Sharp End of the World Crisis." *International Socialism* 94: 3–48.

Hart, K. 2001. *Money in an Unequal World.* London: Texere.

Harvey, D. 1982. *The Limits to Capital.* Oxford, England: Blackwell.

————. 1992. *The Condition of Postmodernity.* Oxford, England: Blackwell.

————. 1993. "Class Relations and the Politics of Difference." In *Place and the Politics of Identity,* ed. M. Keith and S. Pile, 41–66. London: Routledge.

————. 2001. "Militant Particularism and Global Ambition: The Conceptual Politics of Place, Space, and Environment in the Work of Raymond Williams' Social Text." In *Spaces of Capital,* 158–87. Edinburgh: Edinburgh University Press.

Hayek, F. 1944. *The Road to Serfdom.* London: Routledge.

———— 1990 *Denationalisation of Money: The Argument Refined.* London: Institute of Economic Affairs.

Hensch, C. 2004. "Complementary Currencies." *LETS Community News* 9, no. 4: 1.

Higgins, J. 1999. "From Welfare to Workfare." In *Redesigning the Welfare State in New Zealand,* ed. J. Boston, P. Dalziel, and S. St. John, 260–77. Auckland, New Zealand: Oxford University Press.

Hines, C. 2000. *Localisation: A Global Manifesto.* London: Earthscan.

Hollos, M., and B. C. Maday, eds. 1983. *New Hungarian Peasants: An Eastern European Experience with Collectivization.* New York: Social Science Monographs, Brooklyn College Press.

Holloway, J. 2002. *Change the World without Taking Power: The Meaning of Revolution Today.* London: Pluto.

Houtart, F., and F. Polet, eds. 2001. *The Other Davos: The Globalisation of Resistance to the World Economic Systems.* London: Zed Books.

Howell, J., and J. Pearce. 2002. *Civil Society and Development: A Critical Exploration.* London: Lynne Ryner.

Hurst, P. 1995. *Associational Democracy: New Forms of Economic and Social Governance.* Cambridge, England: Polity.

Hutchinson, F., M. Mellor, and W. Olsen. 2002. *The Politics of Money: Towards Sustainability and Economic Democracy.* London: Pluto.

"IM." 2002. "From Riot to Revolution: An Anarchist Analysis of Recent Events in Argentina." http://thesaloniki.indymedia.org (accessed 27 March).

Imbroscio, D. 1997. *Reconstructing City Politics: Alternative Economic Development and Urban Regimes.* London: Sage.

Ingham, G. 1999. "Capitalism, Money, and Banking: A Critique of Recent Historical Sociology." *British Journal of Sociology* 50, no. 1: 76–96.

————. 2001. "Fundamentals of a Theory of Money: Untangling Fine, Lapavitsas, and Zelizer." *Economy and Society* 30, no. 3: 304–23.

————. 2004. *The Nature of Money.* Cambridge, England: Polity.

Jackson, M. 1995. "Helping Ourselves: New Zealand's Green Dollar

Exchanges." Available from the author at markj@redgum.bendigo. latrobe.edu.au.

Jesson, B. 1999. *Only Their Purpose Is Mad: The Money Men Take Over New Zealand*. Palmerston North, New Zealand: Dunmore.

Jones, L. 1890. *The Life, Times, and Labours of Robert Owen*. London: Swan Sonneschein.

Jones, M. 1996. "Full Steam Ahead to the Workfare State? Analysing the U.K. Employment Department's Abolition." *Policy and Politics* 24, no. 2: 137–57.

Kaldor, M. 2003. *Global Civil Society: An Answer to War*. Cambridge, England: Polity.

Kantor, R. 1972. *Commitment and Community: Communes and Utopia in Sociological Perspective*. Cambridge, Mass.: Harvard University Press.

Kaviraj, S., and S. Khilnani, eds. 2001. *Civil Society: History and Possibilities*. Cambridge: Cambridge University Press.

Kelly, P. 2005. "Scale, Power, and the Limits to Possibilities: A Commentary on J. K. Gibson-Graham's 'Surplus Possibilities: Postdevelopment and Community Economies.'" *Singapore Journal of Tropical Geography* 26, no. 1: 39–43.

Kelsey, J. 1995. *The New Zealand Experiment: A World Model for Structural Adjustment?* Auckland, New Zealand: University of Auckland Press.

———. 1999. *Reclaiming the Future: New Zealand and the Global Economy*. Wellington, New Zealand: Bridget Williams.

———. 2002. *At the Crossroads*. Wellington, New Zealand: Bridget Williams.

Kenedi, J. 1981. *Do It Yourself: Hungary's Hidden Economy*. London: Pluto.

King, M. 2003. *A History of New Zealand*. Auckland: Penguin New Zealand.

Kitco, P. 1998. "From Pro-Motion to Co-Motion: An Examination of the Potential of LETS in Pursuit of a Viable Contribution to the Future of Community in New Zealand." Available from the author at auwrc@ ihuyg.co.nz.

Klein, N. 2003. "Argentina: A New Kind of Revolution." *Guardian Weekend*, 25 January, 14–22.

Korosenyi, A. 1999. *Government and Politics in Hungary*. Budapest: Central European University Press.

Kuti, É. 1997. "The Hungarian Non-profit Sector: Institutional Answers to Social Challenges." In *A New Dialogue between Central Europe and Japan*, ed. V. Gáthy and M. Yamanji, 165–72. Budapest: Institute for Social Conflict Research.

Laidler, D. 1990. *Taking Money Seriously*. London: Philip Allan.

Lang, P. 1994. *LETS Work: Revitalising the Local Economy*. Bristol, England: Grover.

Láng-Pickvance, K., N. Manning, and C. Pickvance, eds. 1997. *Environmental and Housing Movements: Grassroots Experience in Hungary, Russia and Estonia*. Aldershot, England: Avebury.

Lapavitsas, C. 2003. *Social Foundations of Markets, Money, and Credit*. London: Routledge.

———. 2005. "The Social Relations of Money as a Universal Equivalent: A Reply to Ingham." *Economy and Society* 34, no. 3: 389–403.

Laugesen, R. 2004. "In a Land of Plenty: Special Report; Poverty in New Zealand." *Sunday Star Times,* 5 December, c1–c3.

Lee, R. 2002. "'Nice Maps, Shame about the Theory'? Thinking Geographically about the Economic." *Progress in Human Geography* 26, no. 3: 333–55.

Lee, R., A. Leyshon, T. Aldridge, J. Tooke, C. C. Williams, and N. Thrift. 2004. "Making Geographies and Histories? Constructing Local Circuits of Value." *Environment and Planning D: Society and Space* 22: 595–617.

Le Grand, J., and S. Estrin. 1989. *Market Socialism*. Oxford, England: Clarendon.

Levitas, R. 1990. *The Concept of Utopia*. London: Philip Allan.

Lewis, P. G., ed. 1992. *Democracy and Civil Society in Eastern Europe*. London: St. Martin's Press.

Leyshon, A. 2004. "The *Limits to Capital* and the Geographies of Money." *Antipode* 36, no. 3: 462–69.

Leyshon, A., R. Lee, and C. C. Williams, eds. 2003. *Alternative Economic Spaces*. London: Sage.

Leyshon, A., and N. Thrift. 1997. *Money Space: Geographies of Monetary Transformation*. London: Routledge.

Lietaer, B. 2001. *The Future of Money*. London: Random House.

Littlefield, H. M. 1964. "The Wizard of Oz, Parable on Populism." *American Quarterly* 16, no. 1: 47–58.

López Levy, M. 2004. *We Are Millions: Neo-Liberalism and New Forms of Political Action in Argentina*. London: Latin America Bureau.

Marx, K. 1852/1974. *Anti-Duhring*. London: New Left Review.

———. 1867/1976. *Capital Volume One*. London: New Left Review/ Pelican.

Maurer, B. 2003. "Uncanny Exchange: The Possibilities and Failures of 'Making Change' with Alternative Money Forms." *Environment and Planning D: Society and Space* 21, no. 3: 317–40.

———. 2005. *Mutual Life, Limited: Islamic Banking, Alternative Currencies, Lateral Reason*. Princeton, N.J.: Princeton University Press.

McKay, G. 1996. *Senseless Acts of Beauty: Cultures of Resistance since the Sixties.* London: Verso.

McMillan, J. 2002. *Reinventing the Bazaar: A Natural History of Markets.* London: Norton.

McNally, D. 1992. *Against the Market: Political Economy, Market Socialism, and the Marxist Critique.* London: Verso.

Molineux, J. 1994. Lifestyle — Is It Enough? *Socialist Worker,* 30 July, 9.

Moreton, A. L. 1969. *The Life and Ideas of Robert Owen.* London: Lawrence and Wishart.

Morris, W. 1890/1993. *News from Nowhere.* London: Penguin.

Norman, K. 2002. "Barter Nation." *Buenos Aires Herald Magazine,* 6 April, 14–19.

North, P. 1995. "LETS and Communes." In *Diggers and Dreamers 96/97,* ed. A. Wood, 42–48. Winslow: Diggers and Dreamers.

———. 1996. "LETS: A Tool for Empowerment in the Inner City?" *Local Economy* 11, no. 3: 284–93.

———. 1998a. "Exploring the Politics of Social Movements through 'Sociological Intervention': A Case Study of Local Exchange Trading Schemes." *Sociological Review* 46, no. 3: 564–82.

———. 1998b. "LETS, Hours, and the Swiss Business Link: Local Currencies and Business Development Programmes." *Local Economy* 13, no. 2: 114–32.

———. 1999a. "Explorations in Heterotopia: LETS and the Micropolitics of Money and Livelihood." *Environment and Planning D: Society and Space* 17, no. 1: 69–86.

———. 1999b. "LETS Get Down to Business! Problems and Possibilities of Involving the Small Business Sector in CED Using Local Currencies." In *Community Economic Development,* ed. G. Haughton, 139–48. London: Stationary Office/Regional Studies Association.

———. 2005. "Scaling Alternative Economic Practices? Some Lessons from Alternative Currencies." *Transactions of the Institute of British Geographers* 30, no. 2, 221–33.

———. 2006. *Alternative Currencies as a Challenge to Globalisation? A Case Study of Manchester's Local Money Networks.* Aldershot, England: Ashgate.

North, P., and U. Huber. 2004. "Alternative Spaces of the 'Argentinazo.'" *Antipode* 36, no. 5: 963–84.

Notes-from-Nowhere, ed. 2003. *We Are Everywhere: The Irresistible Rise of Global Anticapitalism.* London: Verso.

Offe, C., and R. Heinz. 1992. *Beyond Employment.* Cambridge, England: Polity.

Ohmae, K. 1994. *The Borderless World: Power and Strategy in the Global Marketplace.* London: HarperCollins.

Olivaria, O. 2004. *¡Cochabamba! Water War in Bolivia.* Boston: South End Press.

O'Neil, P. 1998. *Revolution from Within: The Hungarian Socialist Workers Party and the Collapse of Communism.* Cheltenham, England: Edward Elgar.

Öniş, Z., and F. Şenses. 2005. "Rethinking the Emerging Post-Washington Consensus." *Development and Change* 36, no. 2: 263–90.

Osborne, S. P., and A. Kaposvari. 1997. "Towards a Civil Society? Exploring Its Meanings in the Context of Post-Communist Hungary." *Journal of European Social Policy* 7, no. 3: 209–22.

Owen, R. 1816. "A New View of Society; or, Essays on the Principle of the Formation of the Human Character, and the Application of the Principle to Practice." http://socserv2.socsci.mcmaster.ca/-econ/ugcm/3ll3/owen/newview.txt.

Pacione, M. 1997. "Local Exchange Trading Systems as a Response to the Globalisation of Capitalism." *Urban Studies* 34, no. 8: 1179–99.

Pearson, R. 2003. "Argentina's Barter Network: New Currency for New Times." *Bulletin of Latin American Research* 22, no. 2: 214–30.

Petras, J. 2002. "The Unemployed Workers Movement in Argentina." *Monthly Review* 53, no. 8, 32–45.

Pickvance, K. 1997. "Social Movements in Hungary and Russia: The Case of Environmental Movements." *European Sociological Review* 13, no. 1: 35–54.

———. 1998a. *Democracy and Environmental Movements in Eastern Europe: A Comparative Study of Hungary and Russia.* Boulder, Colo.: Westview.

———. 1998b. "Democracy and Grassroots Opposition in Eastern Europe: Hungary and Russia Compared." *Sociological Review* 46, no. 2: 187–207.

Pilling, J. 1996. "Funny Money Fills Argentine Pockets." *Financial Times* (London), 13 February, 17.

Podmore, F. 1903/1966. *Robert Owen: A Biography.* London: Allen and Unwin.

Polanyi, K. 1944/1980. *The Great Transformation.* New York: Octagon.

Powell, J. 2002. "Petty Capitalism, Perfecting Capitalism or Post-Capitalism? Lessons from the Argentinean Barter Experiments." *Review of International Political Economy* 9, no. 4: 619–49.

Poznanski, K. Z., ed. 1992. *Constructing Capitalism: The Re-emergence of Civil Society and Liberal Economy in the Post-Communist World.* Boulder, Colo.: Westview.

Primavera, H., C. De Sanzo, and H. Covas. 1998. "Reshuffling for a New

Social Order: The Experience of the Global Barter Network in Argentina." Paper presented at the conference Enhancing People's Space in a Globalising Economy, Espoo, Finland.

Putnam, R. 1993. *Making Democracy Work: Civic Traditions in Modern Italy.* Princeton, N.J.: Princeton University Press.

———. 2001. *Bowling Alone.* London: Simon and Schuster.

Rabinow, P. 1984a. "An Interview with Michel Foucault." In *The Foucault Reader,* ed. P. Rabinow, 381–90. Harmondsworth, England: Penguin.

———, ed. 1984b. *The Foucault Reader.* Harmondsworth, England: Penguin.

Ramada, C. 2001. "User Created Currencies in Latin America." Paper presented at the conference International Network of Engineers and Scientists for Global Responsibility, Stockholm.

Roberts, P. 2004. *The End of Oil.* London: Bloomsbury.

Rock, D. 2002. "Racking Argentina." *New Left Review* 2, no. 17: 55–86.

Samers, M. 2005. "The Myopia of 'Diverse Economies'; or, A Critique of the Informal Economy." *Antipode* 37, no. 5: 875–86.

Sassen, S. 1991. *The Global City: New York, London, Tokyo.* Princeton, N.J.: Princeton University Press.

———. 1996. "The Global City." In *Readings in Urban Theory,* ed. S. Fainstein and S. Campbell, 61–71. Oxford: Blackwell.

Schumacher, E. F. 1973: *Small Is Beautiful: A Study of Economics As If People Mattered.* London: Blond and Briggs.

Scott, J. C. 1985. *Weapons of the Weak—Everyday Forms of Peasant Resistance.* New Haven, Conn.: Yale University Press.

———. 1990. *Domination and the Arts of Resistance.* New Haven, Conn.: Yale University Press.

Sheppard, M. 1981. *Social Credit Inside and Out.* Dunedin, New Zealand: Caveman.

Sheppard, S. 1999. *Broken Circle: The Decline and Fall of the Fourth Labour Government.* Wellington, New Zealand: Public Solutions Limited Press.

Sik, E., and B. Wellman. 1999. "Network Capital in Capitalist, Communist, and Post-Communist Countries." In *Networks in the Global Village,* ed. B. Wellman, 225–55. Boulder, Colo.: Westview.

Simmel, G. 1908/1978. *The Philosophy of Money.* London: Routledge.

Sinclair, U. 1963. *The Autobiography of Upton Sinclair.* London: Allen.

Smiles, S. 1866/1996. *Self-Help.* London: Institute of Economic Affairs.

Smith, A. 1776/1981. *The Wealth of Nations.* London: Pelican.

Smith, A., and A. Swain. 1998. "Regulating and Institutionalising Capitalisms." In *Theorising Transition: The Political Economy of Post-Communist Transformations*, ed. J. Pickles and A. Smith, 25–53. London: Routledge.

Smith, D. 1987. *The Rise and Fall of Monetarism*. London: Pelican.

Solomon, L. 1996. *Rethinking Our Centralised Money System: The Case for a System of Local Currencies*. London: Praeger.

Spiro, M. 1970. *Kibbutz: Venture in Utopia*. Cambridge, Mass.: Harvard University Press.

St. John, S., and D. Craig. 2004. *Cut Price Kids: Does the 2004 "Working for Families" Budget Work for Children?* Auckland: Child Poverty Action Group New Zealand, 80.

Stephens, R. 1999. "Poverty, Family Finances, and Social Security." In *Redesigning the Welfare State in New Zealand*, ed. J. Boston,; P. Dalziel, and S. St. John. Auckland, New Zealand: Oxford University Press, 238–59.

Stiglitz, J. 2002. *Globalisation and Its Discontents*. London: Allen Lane.

——. 2003. *The Roaring Nineties*. London: Penguin.

Surette, L. 1999. *Pound in Purgatory. From Economic Radicalism to Anti-Semitism*. Urbana: University of Illinois Press.

Swain, N. 1992. *Hungary: The Rise and Fall of Feasible Socialism*. London: Verso.

Szendrö, S. J. 1999. *Kör Kézikönyv*. Budapest: Hungarian Non-Profit Human Services Agency.

Szirmai, V. 1997. "Protection of the Environment and the Position of Green Movements in Hungary." In *Environmental and Housing Movements: Grassroots Experience in Hungary, Russia, and Estonia*, ed. K. Láng-Pickvance, N. Manning, and C. Pickvance, 57–88. Aldershot, England: Avebury.

Thompson, E. P. 1963/1980. *The Making of the English Working Class*. London: Penguin.

Thorne, L. 1996. "Local Exchange Trading Systems in the UK—A Case of Re-embedding?" *Environment and Planning A* 28, no. 8: 1361–76.

Wade, R. H. 2002. "U.S. Hegemony and the World Bank: The Fight over People and Ideas." *Review of Political Economy* 9, no. 2: 215–43.

——. 2003. "What Strategies Are Viable for Developing Countries Today? The World Trade Organization and the Shrinking of 'Development Space.'" *Review of International Political Economy* 10, no. 4: 621–44.

——. 2004. "Is Globalization Reducing Poverty and Inequality?" *World Development* 4: 567–89.

Wall, D. 1990. *Getting There: Steps to a Green Society*. Totnes, England: Greenprint.

——. 2003. "Social Credit: The Ecosocialism of Fools." *Capital Nature Socialism* 14, no. 3: 99–122.

Ward, C. 1988. *Anarchy in Action*. London: Freedom Press.

Weston, D. 1992. "Delinking Green Pounds from the Big System." *New Economics*.

Williams, C., and J. Windebank. 2000. "Self-Help and Mutual Aid in Deprived Urban Neighbourhoods: Some Lessons from Southampton." *Urban Studies* 37, no. 1: 127–47.

Williams, C. C. 1996a. "Local Currencies and Community Development: An Evaluation of Green Dollar Exchanges in New Zealand." *Community Development Journal* 31, no. 4: 319–29.

———. 1996b. "Local Exchange Trading Systems: A New Source of Work and Employment?" *Environment and Planning A* 28, no. 8: 1395–1415.

———. 2005. *A Commodified World? Mapping the Limits of Capitalism*. London: Zed.

Williams, C. C., T. Aldridge, R. Lee, A. Leyshon, N. Thrift, and J. Tooke. 2001. *Bridges into Work? An Evaluation of Local Exchange Trading Schemes*. Bristol, England: Policy Press.

Wolf, M. 2005. *Why Globalization Works*. New Haven, Conn.: Yale Nota Bene.

Woodcock, G. 1963. *Anarchism*. Harmondsworth, England: Penguin.

Zavos, S. 1981. *Crusade: Social Credit's Drive for Power*. Wellington, New Zealand: INL.

Zelizer, V. 1997. *The Social Meaning of Money*. Princeton, N.J.: Princeton University Press.

———. 2005. *The Purchase of Intimacy*. Princeton, N.J.: Princeton University Press.

INDEX

Peter North is senior lecturer in geography at the University of Liverpool with an interest in understanding alternatives to capitalism.